Negro Slave Songs

IN THE UNITED STATES

NEGRO SLAVE SONGS

IN THE UNITED STATES

By MILES MARK FISHER

With a Foreword
BY RAY ALLEN BILLINGTON
William Smith Mason Professor of History
Northwestern University

THE CITADEL PRESS · SECAUCUS, N.J.

Third paperbound printing, 1978
Published by Citadel Press
A division of Lyle Stuart, Inc.
120 Enterprise Ave., Secaucus, N.J. 07094
In Canada: George J. McLeod Limited, Toronto
Manufactured in the United States of America
ISBN 0-8065-0090-5

The original edition of this book was published from a fund contributed to the American Historical Association by the Carnegie Corporation of New York.

CORNELL UNIVERSITY PRESS
LONDON: GEOFFREY CUMBERLEGE
OXFORD UNIVERSITY PRESS
FIRST PUBLISHED 1953

IN REMEMBRANCE OF

Dr. and Mrs. Solomon Whittier Smith

AT WHOSE HOME IN CHICAGO

THIS WORK WAS FIRST WRITTEN

FOREWORD

FOR many years musicologists have recognized the importance of Negro slave songs in the evolution of American music. The haunting strains of spirituals have inspired countless composers of our own generation, just as in the past they served as a basis for dozens of backwoods folk songs or fired the imagination of originators of hot jazz. Yet little has been known of the origins of these melodies, of what they meant to those who first sang them, and of the role that they played in the lives of the slaves.

The exciting possibility of investigating this subject first occurred to Miles Mark Fisher when, as a student at the University of Chicago, he was introduced by Professor J. M. P. Smith to the historical development of the Psalms. "The idea that spirituals might be more than folk music," he wrote some time later, "haunted me." With this inspiration, he persuaded his graduate instructors at Chicago to allow him to investigate Negro songs for his doctoral dissertation, which was submitted in 1945. The following book represents a complete rewriting of that thesis, based on greatly extended studies.

The result is a work that will fascinate the historian as well as the musicologist. For Dr. Fisher has written not a cold analysis of a musical form, but a warm appraisal of the mind of a people.

He accomplished this important result by approaching the subject from a completely fresh point of view. In Africa, he knew, where the

Negroes were illiterate, songs were a means of appraising contemporary happenings, preserving the story of the past, promoting religion, and commenting upon the everyday events of life. Why not assume that music played the same role in the lives of the slaves who reached America? Why not view their music as a record of their thoughts and actions in the grim world of bondage, rather than simply an expression of a desire to escape to a better world? Why not seek in their songs a hidden record of their thoughts, their emotions, and their desires?

This quest not only led Dr. Fisher over unexplored paths into the past, but allowed him to challenge and refute those students who have found in spirituals only an otherworldly quality bearing little relationship to reality. Instead he was able to demonstrate that they revealed the innermost thoughts of the slaves on religion, slavery, relations with their masters, aspirations for the future, and all the multitudinous problems faced by a people held in bondage. Under his expert analysis, the spiritual has been revealed as a master index to the mind of the slave.

This book, then, is of the utmost importance to the historian who would understand the pre-Civil War South. The Negroes pictured on its pages bear little relationship to the stereotypes found in most histories, even those written by the masters of their craft. Two or three instances will illustrate the revolutionary nature of Dr. Fisher's findings.

One constantly recurring theme in all slave songs was the longing for escape. Past students have pictured this as an unworldly desire; the horrors of slavery, they said, made death welcome. This view Dr. Fisher shows to be false. The desire to escape was there, of course, but the "heab'n" of the slave lay in Africa, not on some celestial shore. His all-consuming ambition was to be sent to Liberia by the American Colonization Society. The Negro's veneration for this society will shock many a modern historian who has succumbed to the popular fad of scorning "colonizers" as bigoted racists standing in the way of the equalitarian ideas of Theodore Dwight Weld and William Lloyd Garrison. Perhaps they were, but Dr. Fisher proves that the slaves worshiped the colonizers while ignoring the abolitionists; there is no mention of the latter in their songs. Historians may well revise their estimates of the Colonization Society as a result of these findings.

Equally startling is Dr. Fisher's discovery, through the medium of songs, that the slaves were dutiful, obedient, and well adjusted to their lot. For here again we have taken our cue from the abolitionists and their descendants among New England historians and have pictured the Negroes as surly, resentful, and constantly on the verge of rebellion. This view is flatly contradicted by the spirituals, which reveal in the bondsmen a strong sense of duty, a desire to please their masters—the "Lawd" in the vocabulary of their songs—and an eagerness to conform no matter how unpleasant their tasks might be. Apparently the slave must be pictured in the pattern of Uncle Tom rather than of Nat Turner.

Finally, Dr. Fisher is able to show that the Negroes, through their songs, were able to develop a vocabulary and means of expression that was entirely their own. This was done by sprinkling their melodies with symbols, images, and concepts borrowed from their African past and completely unknown to the whites. By developing this symbolism as a universal language among themselves, they were able to harbor and express thoughts that were not understandable to others. Their masters never realized this; instead they poked fun at the Negroes for using a jargon which apparently made little sense. The Negroes gladly endured this ridicule, knowing that by doing so they helped preserve a degree of intellectual freedom. Little did the whites realize, as they ridiculed the slaves for their "ignorance," that those slaves were enjoying the satisfaction which goes with a sense of superiority. Here, indeed, is a lesson in tolerance.

These revelations are typical of the many that dot Dr. Fisher's fine study. Startling as they are, they are dwarfed by another that emerges in his final chapters: the eagerness of the slaves for self-improvement. For in all the history of migration, few peoples have shown an ability to adapt to a strange civilization so completely as the Negroes. This was manifest—and reflected in their songs—from the time they were first introduced to the mysteries of the Caucasian world. During the Civil War, for example, they sang joyfully of the pride exhibited by colored troops when they learned the difference between right and left. After the war was over their eager absorption of book learning was reflected in the speed with which adverbs and adjectives invaded their hymns to supplement the simple nouns and verbs of the past. Anyone reading Dr. Fisher's sympathetic appraisal of these developments will be better able to understand the phenomenal progress of the colored people toward the goal that is rightfully theirs: a place of equality among the peoples of this nation and of the world.

This, then, is Dr. Fisher's story. Few other works have revealed with such sympathy and understanding the life and thought of the pre-Civil War Negro. As he himself has written: "Had every spiritual been preserved, a complete story of every emotion of American Negroes would be available."

RAY ALLEN BILLINGTON

Northwestern University

PREFACE

THE so-called "slave songs" of the United States are best understood when they are considered as expressions of individual Negroes which can be dated and assigned to a geographical locale. They are, in brief, historical documents. As such they reflect Negro behavior, which, as Frederick Law Olmsted concluded in 1860, emphasized African background patterns rather than the Christianity of the nineteenth century.[1]

During a historical study of the Psalms fully a quarter of a century ago in the Divinity School of the University of Chicago it occurred to me that slave songs might illumine the lives of Negroes. In 1945 the Department of Church History permitted me to investigate this theory as a research project. The results of this study were embodied in a doctoral dissertation, "The Evolution of Slave Songs of the United States." The present work is a revision of the dissertation. It condenses the discussion of Negro folk songs as folk music and as proof of various theories about the Negro but adds analyses of a number of well-known antebellum spirituals. (An explanation of my editorial use of brackets, italics, and parentheses in the songs printed in the text is given on page 26, footnote 97.)

[1] *A Journey in the Back Country* (New York, 1860), p. 71; cf. this observation with his earlier conclusion (*A Journey in the Seaboard Slave States with Remarks on Their Economy* [New York, 1856], p. 133).

Space will not allow acknowledgment to all to whom I am indebted. Mention must be made, however, of the great help given me by William Warren Sweet, formerly Professor of the history of American Christianity, and to Professors Sidney E. Mead, Amos N. Wilder, and Joachim Wach, all of the Federated Theological Faculty of the University of Chicago, who consented to act as advisers during my work on the dissertation. I wish to thank also a host of librarians from Durham to Boston to California, especially the librarians of Duke University; a colleague formerly at Shaw University, Caulbert A. Jones, head of the Department of History, who had arrived at similar conclusions independently; churches and schools that have employed me only to release me with pay to complete this study; Mrs. Maude E. Logan, who provided money to have the first manuscript typed; Mrs. Louise T. McCrea, typist from first to last; and my wife, Ada Virginia, my most constructive critic.

Mrs. Fisher, Mr. Jones, and Mrs. Frances Schooler, local teacher of English, merit my thanks for their assistance with the proofs. My gratitude is given to Hampton Institute for the use of the song, "Lord, I Want to Be a Christian," in *Religious Folk Songs of the Negro*, copyright 1909; to Dodd, Mead and Company, New York City, for permission to cite Francis (Milton) Trollope, *Domestic Manners of the Americans*, copyright 1911; to Penn Community Services, Incorporated, Saint Helena Island, South Carolina, for the use of the songs, "Let Us Break Bread Togedder" and "Look What a Wonder Jedus Done" in Nicholas George Julius Ballanta, *Saint Helena Island Spirituals*, copyright 1924; to the Associated Publishers, Inc., Washington, D.C., for the reference to Maurice Delafosse, *The Negroes of Africa*, copyright 1931; and to Theodore Presser Company, Bryn Mawr, Pennsylvania, for the privilege to quote "Sinner, Please," "You'd Better Min'," and from "O Mary, Don't You Weep, Don't You Mourn" from John W. Work, *American Negro Songs*, copyright 1940, and a song in *Etude, the Music Magazine*, copyright 1950; to Harvard University Press, Cambridge, Massachusetts, for the use of extracts from Dorothy Scarborough, *On the Trail of Negro Folk-Songs*, copyright 1925; and to Miss Eunice St. Clair Murphy for permission to use her mother's arrangement of "I Done Done" in Mrs. Jeannette Robinson Murphy, *Southern Thots for Northern Thinkers*, copyright 1906.

I wanted a reminder that the Carnegie Revolving Fund of the American Historical Association published this study, and so I insisted that the chairman of the committee, Professor Ray Allen Billington of Northwestern University, write the Foreword. I, of course, assume all responsibility for interpretations and errors.

MILES MARK FISHER

Durham's White Rock Church House

CONTENTS

HISTORY IN THE
MUSIC OF NEGROES

THE chief concern of African music was to recite the history of the people.[1] In the Sudan this task was assumed by professional musicians who formed associations to make money out of the people.[2] Among the Wolofs, a Sudanese tribe, bands of singers recited family and national history to the accompaniment of musical instruments. They might be men or they might be women, but they were all professional storytellers, magicians, gossipmongers, and musicians.[3] Among the Dahomeans, these ancient troubadours preserved the records of the kingdom. Their lucrative hereditary function was "the only form of education known to the Dahomeans." [4] One member

[1] Maud Cuney Hare, "Africa in Song," *Metronome,* XXXVIII (December, 1922), 61; [Francis] Nwia-Kofi Nkrumah, "The Significance of African Art" (unpublished term paper, Lincoln University, Chester, Pennsylvania, 1940), p. 5.

[2] Stéphen Chauvet, *Musique Nègre* (Paris, 1929), pp. 24 n. 2, 24 f.; cf. Richard Wallaschek, *Primitive Music: An Inquiry into the Origin and Development of Music, Songs, Instruments, Dances, and Pantomimes of Savage Races* (London, 1893), p. 66.

[3] Hutton Webster, *Primitive Secret Societies* (New York, 1908), p. 58; F. W. Butt-Thompson, *West African Secret Societies, Their Organizations, Officials and Teaching* (London, 1929), p. 16; Geoffrey Gorer, *Africa Dances: A Book about West African Negroes* (New York, 1925), pp. 52 f.

[4] Melville J. Herskovits, *Dahomey: An Ancient West African Kingdom* (New York, 1938), II, 321.

of the Nazima tribe of coastal West Africa wrote that its laws, customs, and history were handed down by these folk historians and musicians by word of mouth.[5] These "living encyclopedias," these mimes, poets, dancers, and mountebanks, were trained in secret meetings. They are not credited with producing perfect oral literature, for memory is not always reliable, but

in any case, it is great good fortune for science that, in the countries generally devoid of the aid of writing, there exists such an institution, thanks to which the important facts of history, the origins of tribes, the details of customs and beliefs have been preserved in the memory of man. And it is curious to note that peoples reputed to be ignorant and barbarous have found a means to take the place of libraries by supporting amongst themselves successive generations of living books, each one of which adds to the heritage it has received from the precedent. These so-called savages have at their call, historical compendiums and codes just as we have, only it is in the cerebral convolutions of their traditionalist griots, and not on paper, that their annals and their laws are imprinted.[6]

These singing people were found in every town. Men accompanied soldiers to the battlefields where they sang of "the great actions of their ancestors to awaken in them [soldiers] a spirit of glorious emulation." [7] They settled matters of tribal dispute and also had the final word concerning history, law, and liturgy. Their recitative and historical appearances were not impromptu performances but were only attainable after "long periods of rehearsals." Nevertheless, extempore songs were sung in honor of their chief men, or of any other persons who were willing to give "solid pudding for empty praise."

Rhythmic action was arranged to accompany these songs. Rhythm was so deeply a part of African life that the singer would click the fingernails of his thumbs, and onlookers would pat their feet and

---

[5] [Francis] Nwia-Kofi Nkrumah, "The History of Religion in a Critique of West African Fetichism" (unpublished term paper, Lincoln University, Chester, Pennsylvania, 1940), p. 9.

[6] Maurice Delafosse, *The Negroes of Africa*, trans. F. Fligleman (Washington, D.C. [c. 1931]), pp. 269–271.

[7] Mungo Park, *Travels* (New York, 1800), p. 276; also in John Pinkerton, *A General Collection of the Best and Most Interesting Voyages and Travels in All Parts of the World* (London, 1814), XVI, 878.

clap their hands while bodies swayed to syncopated time.[8] Dancing was the universal rhythmic accompaniment to singing. Africans danced for joy, and they danced for grief; they danced for love, and they danced for hate; they danced to bring prosperity, and they danced to avert calamity; they danced for religion, and they danced to pass the time.[9] In Dahomey each deity was worshiped with special dances. This dancing and singing or shouting, as Capuchin monks described it in the seventeenth century, "might be heard half a league off." [10] Dancing was a special branch of African education and was always performed to the sound of drums.

The West African drums were by far the oldest original rhythmic instruments. They were usually made of hollowed logs, with heads of animal skins tightened by pegs driven into the wood. They varied in size from the hand type about fourteen inches in diameter to the large varieties that were played with one stick and hand or with two sticks.[11] The *ntumpane,* or talking drums, made preferably from the skin of a female elephant's ear, were found in Ashanti and in other parts of Negro Africa.[12] After ceremonial consecration, they were ready to imitate the sound of the human voice.[13] These drums were played with the female one on the left and the male on the right. They might call a chief by name, or they might give notice of danger, of the approach of an enemy or a stranger, or of fire, death, or a summons to arms. In the Adae ceremony of Ashanti, where ancestral spirits were worshiped, these drums recited the entire history of a particular clan. A traveler in Guinea in the early eighteenth century

[8] A. B. Ellis, *The Tshi-speaking Peoples of the Gold Coast of West Africa* (London, 1887), p. 327.

[9] Also, Catherine Miller Balm, *Fun and Festival from Africa* (New York, 1935), p. 1.

[10] R. R. F. F. Michael Angelo and Dennis De Carli, "A Curious and Exact Account of a Voyage to Congo in the Years 1666 and 1667," in Pinkerton, *op. cit.,* XIV, 160.

[11] A. B. Ellis, *op. cit.,* p. 326; R. S. Rattray, *Ashanti* (Oxford, 1923), p. 242; Jewel Huelster Shwab, *In the African Bush* (New York, c. 1928), pp. 6 f.; Herskovits, *Dahomey,* II, 318.

[12] Chauvet, *op. cit.,* p. 51; cf. Nicholas George Julius Ballanta, "Gathering Folk Tunes in the African Country," *Musical America,* XLIV (September 25, 1926), 3.

[13] Rattray, *Ashanti,* pp. 243, 260–263, and *Ashanti Proverbs* (Oxford, 1916), p. 134.

3

observed ten or more varieties of drums that accompanied the blowing of horns. He said that their sound afforded "the most charming asses' music that can be imagined; to help out this they always set a little boy to strike upon a hollow piece of iron, with a piece of wood which makes a noise more detestable than the drums and the horns together." [14] Drums were found throughout Africa, though there were, of course, local modifications in both the drums and their uses.

A distinction must be made between African instruments of rhythm and those of music. Drums and other percussion instruments were in the former class, as were the rattles or calabashes—gourds filled with shells, beans, or stones. [15] Congo men were once reported as having been seen carrying two gongs in their hands and striking them with a stick. [16] The xylophonelike marimba was a most elaborate instrument. Sometimes called the little portable piano, it consisted of fifteen gourds hung about the neck so that it might be played with two sticks. Its tones resembled an organ's and made "a pretty agreeable harmony, especially when three or four of them play[ed] together." [17]

Wind instruments also were used for rhythm. These included trumpets of horn, of wood, and of reed. In the seventeenth century a priest noticed a trumpet of ivory and hand drums that were used in the army. These instruments were played in concert and were "grateful at a distance, but harsh and ungrateful near at hand." Natives of Sierra Leone were said to be able to communicate at great distances on horns.

Of the instruments played for musical effect, one that had five or six strings similar to a small harp was agreeable in sound to non-

[14] [William Bosman], "A New and Accurate Description of the Coast of Guinea, Divided into the Gold, the Slave, and Ivory Coasts" (London, 1705), in Pinkerton, *op. cit.,* XVI, 394.

[15] Frederick August Ramseyer, *Four Years in Ashantee* (London, 1875), pp. 119 f.; A. B. Ellis, *op. cit.,* p. 326.

[16] Especially [Girolamo Merolla], "A Voyage to Congo, and Several Other Countries, Chiefly in Southern Africa," in Pinkerton, *op. cit.,* XVI, 245; Herskovits, *Dahomey,* II, 319 f.

[17] Herskovits, *Dahomey,* II, 316; Wilber C. Harr, "A Christian Approach to a Pagan People in the Wurhum Hills of Northern Nigeria" (unpublished S.T.M. thesis, Union Theological Seminary, 1940), p. 170.

Africans. There were many kinds of these stringed instruments as well as flutes in Africa.

Whenever African Negroes assembled, they accompanied their songs and dances [18] with percussion, wind, and stringed instruments.[19] They used their voices and their bodies as well as instruments in making music. Groups of instruments formed "orchestras," and vocal, rhythmic, and instrumental expression was employed to celebrate all the various life situations, both ritualistic and festival. For example, African music was employed during love-making, at marriage, at the birth of a child, at the child's initiation into the tribal cult; [20] in farming, fishing, and hunting; in the educational process, including counting games with fruit and seeds or magical designs; for recreation such as telling tales, proverbs, riddles, and enigmas; and for promoting the military spirit. There were songs at feasts for the dead, at wakes, and at funerals.[21]

The vocal scores of Negro music reveal that songs at the secret meetings were about group morality or were prayers, maxims, hero tales, and the like. These were unchanged from generation to generation. On public occasions a majority of the transmitted airs were fixed, but their words were variable. A refrain would be repeated by different singers, sometimes challenging and answering one another, and finally the chief of an "orchestra" would improvise an impromptu song, generally in a minor key. Thus, though an individual would begin a chant at public ceremonials, he or she would soon be joined by men, women, and children with varying voices.[22] A song often consisted of a recitative and a short chorus, one individual tak-

[18] R. S. Rattray, *Religion & Art in Ashanti* (Oxford, 1927), p. 184.

[19] Mungo Park, *op. cit.*, p. 275; Elizabeth Donnan, *Documents Illustrative of the History of the Slave Trade to America* (Washington, 1930–1935), II, 288.

[20] William Moister, *Memorials of Missionary Labours in Western Africa, the West Indies, and at the Cape of Good Hope* (3rd ed., London, 1866), p. 132; Chauvet, *op. cit.*, p. 3.

[21] [Andrew Battell], *The Strange Adventures of Andrew Battell of Leigh, in Essex. Sent by the Portuguese Prisoner to Angola* . . . (London, 1901), p. 78; also in Pinkerton, *op. cit.*, XVI, 317–336; A. B. Ellis, *op. cit.*, pp. 237–243.

[22] Chauvet, *op. cit.*, p. 23. Ruth H. Gillum, "The Negro Folksong in American Culture," *Journal of Negro Education*, XII (Spring, 1943), 173–180,

ing up when another was tired. In this way a passer-by might be praised or ridiculed. The rendition of these songs differed widely because they were secretive, "weird," joyful, syncopated, or even meaningless. The songs are classified into different types only for convenience, since African life was not partitioned.[23] All of it was religious, and thus the music was also. Secret meetings that trained Negroes for all of life provided models of songs for every occasion.

Everyday experiences were the subjects of Negro songs in Africa. Such a common thing as a Dahomean child's loss of his first tooth was the occasion for an original song. The child gathered his playmates together for a dance. He threw the tooth upon the roof of his mother's hut. The children danced in a circle, clapping their hands, and sang that he who had lost a tooth could not eat salt. When a girl reached puberty in Ashanti, the news was flashed to all villages, particularly if she was of the royal family. The old women came out and sang *bara* (menstruation) songs. As the girl sat in the street, others of her sex paraded and sang *bara* songs of congratulation. The girl was taken to a river and immersed.[24] As she was sponged in the water, three old women rubbed limes over her head and sang about it. Next the girl was taken to her home, where the women danced around her with their special drums called *Dono* drums.

---

seemed to have an understanding of the characteristics of African music, which Natalie Curtis Burlin, *Songs and Tales from the Dark Continent* (New York, [c. 1930]), p. xii, summed up by saying that "music is not only an individual expression accompanying daily tasks and reflecting experiences; more than that it is the voice of tribal, and even of racial prayer, the moulding, in art-form, of communal group sentiment, and the living fluent utterance of the people's inspiration; particularly is this true of African songs."

[23] Melville J. Herskovits and Frances S. Herskovits, *An Outline of Dahomean Religious Beliefs* [Menasha, 1933], p. 9; Herskovits, *Dahomey,* I, 105; II, 308, 312, 317.

[24] The bodies of African Negroes are ceremonially washed on many occasions (G. R. Crone [ed. and tr.], *The Voyages of Cadamosto* [London, 1937], p. 32; A. B. Ellis, *op. cit.,* pp. 223, 225; George W. Ellis, *Negro Culture in West Africa* [New York, 1914], p. 69; Edwin W. Smith, *The Secret of the African* [2nd ed., London, 1930], p. 140; Nkrumah, "The History of Religion in a Critique of West African Fetichism," p. 29). In *The Myth of the African Past* (New York, [c. 1941]), p. 153, Herskovits suggests that West African water rites account for the fact that Baptists are so numerous among American Negroes.

News went the rounds in Nigeria that a native, Nbwola, had stolen something from one of the missionaries, and other natives immediately made a song of the incident telling the rogue that thieving was bad. Another experience of a native African was contained in a traditional Swahili song in which a wife found reason to weep and to wail. The African language of this song did not hide its moving action and repeated repetition [25] from its non-African recorder.

Public exhibitions of the pursuit of creature desires by African Negroes might be witnessed by outsiders after the skills and techniques had been sufficiently mastered in secret meetings. Onlookers generally reported these public festivities as ceremonials, dances, and parades.

The Ashanti made the greatest stir about annually banishing the devil from all the towns. This ancient festival of eight days' duration was called the Apo ceremony. In it a priest was heard singing, to the accompaniment of his gong, the praises of the river god, Tano. In this and other ceremonies the participants wore masks, so that they could not be recognized. The ordinary villager was held in high esteem, but natives felt free to abuse outsiders in song, including the typist of Captain Rattray, who was making anthropological studies of Ashanti culture. Besides burlesque, Apo songs reviewed exact historical situations. King Prempeh was banished by the British in 1896 because it was alleged that, by stirring up tribal wars,[26] he stood in the way of civilization, of trade, and of the interests of the people themselves. Over fifty years afterward the Ashanti sang that Prempeh's banishment was possible because the Ashanti knew nothing about guns.[27]

Ceremonials about food getting were most important. In Ashanti the Yam ceremony glorified that staple crop. While the walls of the shrine rooms were being whitewashed under the supervision of the chief priestess, the laborers kept singing. The Afahye ceremony observed the eating of the first fruits with appropriate songs, instruments, and dances. The natives interspersed songs with talking drums for fully four hours.

[25] C. Court Treatt, "Swahili Lament," MS, Library of Congress.
[26] Major R. S. S. Baden-Powell, *The Downfall of Prempeh, A Diary of Life with the Native Levy in Ashanti, 1895–1896* (London, 1896), pp. 17, 18.
[27] Rattray, *Ashanti*, p. 156.

Their environment was both kindly and harsh to African Negroes. After they planned their economy, it was often destroyed by forces that they did not control.[28] The Swahili sang a traditional song about their pursuit of lions that destroyed their cattle. They swore woe to them and defiantly sang over and over again that they were in pursuit. This chant was rendered as the hand or the spear clanged on the shield.[29] The Swahili had another song about a lion running like a frightened jackal.[30]

The Swahili worked to the rhythm of a traditional song about the great amount of labor expected for little money.[31] All Negro experiences were appraised in such songs. After Africans had hollowed out a log for a boat, twelve stout Mandingoes rowed a Christian missionary to his station in 1833. En route he noticed that the rowers paddled to the time of a song which repeatedly referred to the white minister. He learned that the natives were singing for his success on the maiden voyage.[32]

Africans often talked in ambiguous terms about situations and received adverse criticism for this characteristic. Once in Ashanti seventy-six priests were executed for not saying unequivocally that a certain king had died. At last a seventy-seventh priest was called in to give his version of the matter. He was wise enough to save himself from death by singing that the king was dead.

Africans frequently had funerals in which natives tried to outdo each other in burial extravagance.[33] Music enlivened these funerals among Negroes. Dahomeans as well as other Africans sang about every detail of the funeral ritual and of the family relationships. The

[28] Ralph Randolph Gurley, *Life of Jehudi Ashmun, Late Colonial Agent in Liberia* (Washington, 1835), p. 131.

[29] C. Court Treatt, "Swahili Lion Hunt Chant," MS, Library of Congress.

[30] C. Court Treatt, "Swahili Hunt Song," MS, Library of Congress.

[31] C. Court Treatt, "Swahili Laboring Song," MS, Library of Congress.

[32] Moister, *op. cit.,* p. 185. Maud Cuney Hare wrote of these common boating songs in Negro Africa. Negroes there customarily fashioned boats from logs (Muhammed ibn abd Allah, called Ibn Batutah, *Travels in Asia and Africa 1325–1354,* trans. and selected by H. A. R. Gibb [London, 1929], p. 333; Richard Hakluyt, *The Principal Navigations, Voyages, Traffiques & Discoveries of the English Nation* [Glasgow, 1904], X, 18).

[33] Mary H. Kingsley, *Travels in West Africa* (London, 1897), p. 491; Herskovits, *Dahomey,* I, 74, 97, 304, 305, 401.

best friend of a Dahomean deceased person dressed him in the loin cloth, the *gudo,* while singing about it. Singing *dopwe* were the secret society which took charge of the preliminary and definitive funerals of a native. Funeral rites in Ashanti were repeated on the fifteenth, the fortieth, and the eightieth day of demise, and again on the first anniversary. Laughter, dancing, mourning, drinking, carrying the body to the grave on a run, and stamping down the grave dirt were elements of the funeral ritual which were enlivened by music. The Adae ceremony in Ashanti preserved similar funeral customs.

In addition to the songs about life situations that were taught in the secret meetings, there were storytelling songs. These, like the others, abounded in repetitions. The storytelling art, which was partly recitative, was only permitted in Ashanti after dark. Then these "realistic and clever" tales were dramatized.[34] Such tales provided safety valves for the people in addition to two other Ashanti customs. The annual Apo ceremony of tribal purification and restoration was one of them. The *bo akutia* custom was the other. In it an aggrieved native took a friend to the house of his adversary. The offended person then vilified his friend in the presence of the adversary for whom the abuse was really intended.[35] Like other songs, those telling stories were not on lofty and elevated subjects but carried over themes of daily experiences with much repetition, subtle attacks, and accompanying action or demonstration. Fictitious names were substituted in these tales for those of real persons. Alliteration or the fitting of words to the objects described was a successful literary device of Negro Africa.

The "golden rule" of African culture, passed on to each generation of Negroes in secret meetings, is contained in a tale about an eagle. Once an eagle magically healed an old woman of grievous sores and peopled a town over which the woman was placed as mistress upon her vow that the eagle would never be harmed. In return the eagle desired only the liberty of a silk-cotton tree in which she built a nest, hatched two eggs, and then flew off for food for her eaglets. Presently, the old woman's grandchild whimpered, "Ehe!

[34] Rattray, *Ashanti,* p. 162; *Among the Arabs: Adventures in the Desert, and Sketches of Life and Character in Tent and Town* (London, 1875), *passim.*

[35] Rattray, *Akan-Ashanti Folk-Tales* (Oxford, 1930), pp. xii f.

Ehe!" because he wanted to chew "an Eagle's children." He repeated this saying, "If I don't get some to chew, I shall die."

The old woman did not want her grandchild to die, and so she sent to the townspeople to chop down the eagle's silk-cotton tree in order to take her young. The axes were hewing "Pinpin! Pinpin!" and the tree was about to fall when one eaglet stood on the edge of the nest and sang for her mother. The mother eagle heard. She flew back with wings sounding "Fa!" and said to the tree, "Sanguri."

The tree was restored. Food was then given the eaglets with the advice to submit to the old woman if she again tried to have them taken. Then the mother flew away. Shortly thereafter the axes of the cutters were again resounding at the foot of the silk-cotton tree. One frightened eaglet sang to her mother as formerly, but the mother did not come. The tree fell "Brim!" One eaglet was taken, but the other one escaped to tell her mother. Immediately the eagle set off for the old woman's house. On finding the grandchild eating her eaglet, which had been roasted, the eagle said, "Old woman, I congratulate you."

Then the eagle turned to the town and pronounced her "Sanguri." Every person disappeared. Another "Sanguri" made every house vanish. Again "Sanguri" made the town into a forest, and a fourth "Sanguri" restored the old woman's sores. Then the eagle said: "Old woman, you have seen, that is why the elders say, if some does good to you thank him by doing good to him and do not take evil to thank him."

Songs that were taught to each generation of African boys and girls separately in secret meetings were vehicles for instilling the morality of the African cult. When African Negroes were brought to the Americas, they carried with them their music of bodily rhythm, voice, and instrumentation. They possessed fixed songs for all life situations and had the ability to create impromptu ones.

Unfortunately, the colonial records of the Western Hemisphere rarely have much to say about the secret meetings of Negroes. They attempted to supply the worship with which transplanted Africans had been accustomed at home, although they were legally prohibited for their insurrectionary possibilities. A brief description of one meeting occurs in a report of Jemmy's revolt in South Carolina in 1739, which alarmed everybody. Twenty Angola Negroes "assembled" en route to St. Augustine, Florida, to take advantage of the freedom promised by the Spaniards. The African cult "plundered," "burnt," and "killed," then "halted in a field and set to dancing, Singing and beating Drums. . . ." This casual notice of transplanted African music includes bodily rhythm, voice, and instrumentation. It is also significant that Jemmy's gang would not harm Mr. Wallace, a tavern keeper, because "he was a good man and kind to his slaves." [36] Tacky's revolters in Jamaica in 1760 killed upwards of forty people, but they did not molest Abraham Fletcher whom Negroes respected. A historian tried to account for this by saying that

the rebels, though strangers, had heard his character; and from gratitude, a principle which is strongly impressed upon the minds of the most ferocious and unjust, and from that respect to a virtuous conduct, which is implanted in the breasts of all men, spared his life;—at a time, too, when they considered the destruction of the whites, as essential to their own safety.[37]

Perhaps a song tale such as that of the Ashanti eagle had taught the slaves not to harm those who treated Negroes well.

On Sunday, May 29, 1774, a British traveler was present at the worship of Africans at Nanjemoy, Maryland, where there was no church. He called their convocation a Negro "ball" and wrote:

They [Negroes] generally meet together and amuse themselves with Dancing to the Banjo. This musical instrument (if it may be so called) is made of a Gourd something in the imitation of a Guitar, with only four strings and played with the fingers in the same manner. Some of them sing to it, which is very droll music indeed. In their songs they generally relate the usage they have received from their Masters or Mistresses in a very satirical manner. Their poetry is like the Music—Rude and uncultivated. Their Dancing is most violent exercise, but so irregular and grotesque I am not able to describe it. They all appear to be exceedingly happy at these merry-makings and seem if they had forgot or were not sensible of their miserable condition.[38]

[36] Allen D. Candler, *The Colonial Records of the State of Georgia* (Atlanta, 1904–1916), XXII, Part 2, 231–234; B. R. Carroll, *Historical Collections of South Carolina* (New York, 1836), I, 359; cf. J. S. Buckingham, *The Slave States of America* (London, [1842]), I, 105.

[37] Robert Renny, *An History of Jamaica* (London, 1807), p. 66.

[38] [Nicholas Cresswell], *Journal, 1774–1777* (New York, 1924), pp. 18 f.

This view of Negro spirituals was not supported until August, 1862, when J. McKim, agent of the Port Royal Relief Society, stated that slave songs were related to contemporary occurrences. His daughter Lucy accompanied him to the Sea Islands of South Carolina and arranged a "No. I" collection of "Songs of the Freedmen of Port Royal." From Philadelphia she sent a copy to Editor John S. Dwight of the *Journal of Music,* who published the collection in November. Like her father, Lucy McKim was convinced that the songs contained the historical background of the Negro people although they were described as otherworldly.[39] Help in making a forthcoming volume of such songs highly representative was asked of readers of the *Nation* on May 30, 1867.

Issues of the *Nation* in November, 1867, announced the publication of the first book of Negro songs as:

SLAVE SONGS OF THE UNITED STATES

One Hundred and Thirty-Six Songs from all parts of the South,
never before published or brought together;
historically of the greatest possible value.

WITH AN INTRODUCTION AND ILLUSTRATIVE
NOTES

Ready November 15
Price $1.50

Early orders solicited from the trade. Address
A. Simpson & Co., Publishers
69 Duane Street, New York

In the third week the editor announced that conditions in the South were reflected in the Negroes' songs: "This book, of which we had the pleasure of first announcing the inception, is a remarkable proof of the stringent separation of North and South, in consequence of slavery, before the war." He explained that one would be mistaken should he presume that these songs

evince the easiness of the yoke of bondage. They are, rather, the embodiment of the mental and physical anguish of a bruised race—the safety

---

[39] "Negro Songs," *Dwight's Journal of Music,* XXI (August 9, 1862), 148; "Letter of Lucy McKim, Philadelphia, November 1, 1862," *ibid.,* XXI (November 8, 1862), 254 f.

valve of their complaining and revolt against oppression. "Heaven" is to the slave not merely nor principally the reward of virtue, but a refuge from the lash. "Heab'n shall-a be my home" is the solace of "Poor Rosy, poor Gal," and it is no moral conflict, no striving of conscience, alluded to in

> "Nobody knows the trouble I've had,
> Nobody knows but Jesus."—

It was trouble with "maussa," trouble with the driver, trouble with the Government halting in its policy of Confiscation. But in these considerations we must not indulge. . . .

Before the year had passed, commendation had come from the New York *Independent,* the New York *Citizen,* the Brooklyn *Standard,* the New York *Tribune,* the New York *World,* and *Le Messager Franco-Americain.* These notices were bound with a new edition of this popular book which shortly appeared. The *Living Age* reprinted verbatim the Introduction of *Slave Songs.*[40]

Notwithstanding the fact that music which told of the strivings and aspirations of African Negroes was brought to the Western Hemisphere by slaves and that the first extended collection of slave songs was advertised as historical documents from Negroes, slave songs found difficulty in maintaining their primary significance. Their texts were altered. Christian hymns and songs were substituted for spirituals. Negroes accepted acculturation. They were learning other than oral means of keeping records.

The great majority of the original texts of slave songs are not available, for the earliest language which Negroes used was the African, and only a few African songs have been preserved. The greater number of them circulated in the language of the dominant peoples of the West Indies, South America, Central America, and North America. When Negro singing was understood in Virginia, it was in a mixture of African and English. Around Louisiana slaves sang in a dialect that was a jargon of African and French, such as was used in South Carolina and in Haiti. Negro singing retained this linguistic synthesis throughout slavery.[41] Contentions for a pure dia-

---

[40] "Slave Songs of the United States," *Living Age,* XCVI (January 25, 1868), 230 ff.

[41] Sidney Andrews, *The South since the War* (Boston, 1866), p. 227.

lect of slave songs are negatived when the locality of their origins and the literacy of their antebellum authors are considered. Moreover, when these linguistic approximations of the black masses are translated or transliterated into Portuguese, Spanish, French, and other tongues, the possibilities of textual errors are numerous.

The English words show both accidental and intentional errors of transmission. Sometimes collectors were uninformed about Negroes, as were the editors of *Slave Songs of the United States*. They could obtain no explanation for the line "Rain fall and wet Becca Lawton" and the word "Wappo," even though they made an effort to win the confidence of Negroes. A collector may have been sleepy and exhausted, and his informant careless or deceptive. No uniform or consistent spelling would be possible when the songs were heard from Negroes on different levels of culture. There were corrections in the orthography, grammar, and style of the spirituals. Effort was made to present Negro folk in the most favorable light. Unchaste and questionable language was generally eliminated, although "Titty," an adjective used to distinguish a female by her breast, was preserved in the earliest collection in spite of the statement that Negro songs did not employ "coarse expressions." [42] Doctrinal meanings descriptive of the world above were read into the word "heaven."

In order to fit the tones of Negroes to words, "many orthographical experiments" were performed. A collector of slave songs before the Civil War found that the rich, unctuous, and guttural tones of Negroes could not be written.[43] Slave songs went to school under Civil War missionary teachers, and many collections were published.[44] Diverse persons took liberties with Negro songs but did

[42] Lily Young Cohen, *Lost Spirituals* (New York, 1928), p. x.

[43] J. J. Trux, "Negro Minstrelsy—Ancient and Modern," *Putnam's Monthly Magazine*, V (January, 1855), 79.

[44] Richard F. Fuller, *Chaplain Fuller: Being a Life Sketch of a New England Clergyman and Army Chaplain* (Boston, 1863), p. 180; I. W. Brinckerhoff, *Advice to Freedmen* (New York, 1864, 1867), *passim;* J. E. Hilary Skinner, *After the Storm* (London, 1866), I, 53; Thomas Wentworth Higginson, *Army Life in a Black Regiment* (Boston, 1870), p. 24; [Theodore F. Seward], *Jubilee Songs: Complete with an Introduction by E. M. Cravath* (New York, 1872), p. 3; Thomas P. Fenner [arr.], "Fifty Cabin and Plantation Songs," in M. F. Armstrong and Helen W. Ludlow, *Hampton and Its Students* (New York, 1874), p. 192; Theodore F. Seward and George W.

not reveal that fact. One of the few exceptions to this unacknowl-
edged editing is a collection of the songs of Georgia Negroes whose
editor said:

I have used the pruning knife freely, removing ineffective stanzas, and
trimming back most of the ever-present repetition. Whatever beauty,
whatever strange effectiveness may appear in these songs, was already
there. I have added nothing to it. My task has been to preserve it and
to make it stand out a little more sharply on the printed page.[45]

Through the years the American people have discovered that
Negro music was the omnibus which carried forward the entire
African cult. Some leaders from colonial days had advocated the
Christianization of Negroes in order that Negro slaves might be
taught to be peace-loving and tractable. As a result of feverish activity on behalf of slaves, Negroes were confused [46] and said, in song,
that they did not know what to do.[47]

Negro slaves reacted in at least three ways to what they called the
miracle of emancipation that went on before their very eyes. Some
Negroes wanted to show that they were worthy of freedom and sang
songs that were taught them because these represented the changed
status of black folk. Other Negroes had no way of knowing that their
distinctive music was declining in proportion as they united it with
songs of their environment,[48] and they expressed freedom by combining a bit of an old spiritual with verses of a new song, say a hymn
of Watts. Such an old spiritual as "Remember Me" combined the

White, *Jubilee Songs; As Sung by the Jubilee Singers* (New York, 1884), p. 3;
I. W. Brinckerhoff, "Mission Work among the Freed Negroes," *passim,* MS,
American Baptist Historical Society; Walter F. Fleming, *Documentary His-
tory of Reconstruction, Political, Military, Social, Religious, Educational &
Industrial 1865 to the Present Time* (Cleveland, 1906–1907), II, 175.

[45] Robert W. Gordon, "Palmettos, Folksongs of Georgia Negroes," *Golden
Book Magazine,* IX (May, 1929), 76; also, William Knapp, "An Interview
with H. T. Burleigh," *Baton,* V (March, 1926), 2.

[46] Elizabeth Huce Botume, *First Days amongst the Contrabands* (Boston,
1893), p. 272; [H. Dobbins], *Life and Labors of Rev. Frank Dobbins, Pastor
of Zion Baptist Church, Columbia, S.C.* (Columbia, 1878), p. 6.

[47] See p. 163.

[48] William Francis Allen, Charles Pickard Ware, and Lucy McKim Garrison (comp.), *Slave Songs of the United States* (New York, 1867), p. xx;
hereafter referred to as *Slave Songs.*

ancient plea of a slave for his master, or a prayer to God to have
mercy upon him, with stanzas of a hymn in common meter:

> Chorus:
> Remember me, remember me,
> O Lord, remember me.
>
> Am I a soldier of the cross,
> A foll'wer of the Lamb,
> And shall I fear to own His cause
> Or blush to speak His name?

A Civil War missionary appended the words of twelve songs to both
editions of his *Advice to Freedmen*,[49] and present-day hymnals of
Negro Baptists, African Methodists, and African Zion Methodists
omit few of these songs.

A minority of Negroes paid little attention to Lincoln's proclamation of emancipation but continued to live their lives as before.[50]
Living almost wholly in the past but without attaching any historical
significance to it, conservative Negroes combined various snatches
of antebellum lore. Hall Johnson's arrangement of "Honor! Honor!"
is such a modern song. Perhaps the original singer was glorifying
secret meetings down by the riverside in a freedom medley which
showed that its author knew the difference between day and night:

> King Jesus lit de candle by de waterside,
> To see de little chillun when dey truly baptize.
> Honor! Honor! unto de dying Lamb.
>
> Oh, run along chillun, an be baptize
> Might pretty meetin' by de waterside.
> Honor! Honor! unto de dying Lamb.

[49] Brinckerhoff, *Advice to Freedmen, passim.*

[50] [J. W. Brockenbrough McGuire], *Diary of a Southern Refugee, during
the War* (2nd ed., New York, 1868), p. 19; Susan Dabney Smedes, *A Southern Planter* (4th ed., New York, 1890), p. 195; Victoria V. Clayton, *White
and Black under the Old Regime* (Milwaukee, [1899]), pp. 99, 113, 147, 156,
194; Mary A. H. Gay, *Life in Dixie during the War, 1861–1862–1863–
1864–1865* (4th ed., Atlanta, c. 1897), p. 159; Sarah Morgan Dawson, *A
Confederate Girl's Diary* (Boston, 1913), p. 221; Mary Boykin Chesnut, *A
Diary from Dixie,* ed. Isabella D. Martin and Myrta Lockett Avary (New
York, 1929), pp. 85, 92, 345, 364, 381, 388; Kate Virginia Morrill, *My Confederate Girlhood* (Richmond, 1932), p. 30.

I prayed all day, I prayed all night
My head got sprinkled wid de mid-night dew,
Honor! Honor! unto [de] dying Lamb.[51]

The combination of many elements in such a medley made it extremely difficult to understand that Negro songs possessed historical value. The very air was filled with questions, uncertainties, and contradictions concerning the nature of Negro songs. As Negroes mastered various ways of keeping records, several interpretations of Negro singing were given.

Negro songs were said to be true musical expression, but this view of Negro spirituals leaves unanswered the question why musicians worked so carefully to rearrange the songs. More than one person expressed doubt that Negro spirituals were primarily music.[52] At Leipzig, musicologists did not publicize the singing of Negro spirituals by Roland Hayes as music "at all." [53] To Negroes, their music was even more important as a carrier of burdens. It is suggestive that Negro peddlers offered coal, ice, or vegetables for sale by singing of their value [54] and that preachers of the larger racial churches regularly displayed their gospel to crowded audiences when they "moaned" it. The tunes were not nearly so important as the commodities.

Another interpretation of Negro songs said that they proved this or that about Negro people. In so doing, contradictory opinion was evident, particularly when spirituals were traced to the Western Hemisphere through African Negroes and, at the same time, were called Christian products. More generally, Negro spirituals were said to have received their Christianization from the American environment of the nineteenth century. It was claimed that in antebellum

[51] *Marian Anderson* [*Program*] (New York, 1947–1948), p. 18.

[52] D. C. P., "Nathaniel Dett," *Musical Standard*, XV (January 1, 1920), 38 f.; "The Blight of Jazz and the Spirituals," *Literary Digest*, CV (April 12, 1930), 20; Eva Mary Grew, "The Colour Bar," *British Musician and Musical News*, VII (November, 1931), 229.

[53] MacKinley Helm, *Angel Mo' and Her Son, Roland Hayes* (Boston, 1942), p. 216.

[54] Harriette Kershaw Leiding, *Street Cries of an Old Southern City* (Charleston, 1910), *passim;* [Samuel Wood], *The Cries of New York* (New York, 1822; reprinted, Chicago, 1936), *passim.*

days Negroes turned to the Old Testament and to the New for sources of spirituals. People were told that preachers gave the incentive for the Negro's turning to the Bible.[55] "What faith!" was exclaimed more than once about authors of Negro songs.[56] Those who thought that Christianity had wrought miraculous changes in Negroes through spirituals [57] did not explain how it happened that Christianity left much to be desired in contemporary society.

At the organizational meeting of the American Folklore Society at Harvard University on January 4, 1888, the wish was expressed "that thorough studies . . . [be] made of Negro music and songs." It was thought that such inquiries would be difficult to make and would be impossible in a few years. The Society at once became so popular because of its endorsement by Professors Francis J. Child, Franz Boas, and George Kittredge, as well as others from great universities, that Negro songs were ever afterwards called folk music.[58] Early

[55] Cf. Howard Thurman, *Deep River: An Interpretation of Negro Spirituals* (Mills College, Calif., 1945), p. 1, with Willard L. Sperry, *Religion in America* (Cambridge, 1946), p. 186; Howard Thurman, *The Negro Spiritual Speaks of Life and Death* (New York, 1947), p. 2.

[56] John W. Work, *Folk Songs of the American Negro* (Nashville, 1915), pp. 22, 37; also, William Owens, "Folklore of the Southern Negro," *Lippincott's Magazine*, XX (December, 1877), 748–755; Newman I. White, "Racial Feeling in Negro Poetry," *South Atlantic Quarterly*, XXI (January, 1922), 17, 28.

[57] Newman I. White, *American Negro Folk Songs* (Cambridge, 1928), pp. 33–44; also, Roy F. Nichols, "The Progress of the American Negro in Slavery," *Annals of the American Academy*, CXL (November, 1928), 119; Mason Crum, *Gullah* (Durham, 1940), p. 156.

[58] *Journal of American Folk-Lore*, I (April, 1888), I, 5; Lee J. Vance, "Folk-Lore Study in America," *Popular Science Monthly*, XLIII (September, 1893), 586. See also, Howard W. Odum, "Folk-Song and Folk Poetry as Found in the Secular Songs of the Southern Negroes," *Journal of American Folk-Lore*, XXIV (July–October, 1911), 255–294, 351–396; Mellinger Edward Henry, *A Bibliography for the Study of American Folk-Songs with Many Titles of Folk-Songs (and Titles That Have to Do with Folk-Songs) from Other Lands* (London, 1937), *passim;* R. W. Gordon, *Folk Songs of America* (New York, 1939), *passim; 75 Years of Freedom, Commemoration of the 75th Anniversary of the Proclamation of the 13th Amendment to the Constitution of the United States* (Library of Congress, December 18, 1940), *passim;* L. H. Correa de Ozevedo, "Folk-Lore in the Music Curriculum in

opinion held, indeed, that Negro music was the only American folk music.[59]

According to these early folklorists, slave songs had to do with traditional beliefs, customs, and legends. This definition included superstition and magic along with anonymity and "human fantasy" as distinct from literature and cultural anthropology.[60] When a Negro was heard singing about a railroad train, a folklorist imagined that words about the engine, "breathing out fiery smoke," related to a mythological dragon.[61] Indeed, because the southern Negro used a sign and meaning for everything,[62] folklorists attached great significance to the expressions of Negroes while the words of Negro songs were generally minimized.[63] Although Negro language was such as

---

Brazil," *Proceedings of the Music Teachers' National Association,* 36th series (1914), pp. 66 f.; W. T. Couch (ed.), *Culture in the South* (Chapel Hill, 1934), p. 570.

[59] Harry Edward Krehbiel, *Afro-American Folksongs* (New York, [c. 1914]), *passim;* "Negro Folk Song Acclaimed as America's Musical Treasure," *Musical America,* XXVIII (August 3, 1918), 20; "Negro Folk Song," *Music Student,* XI (September, 1919), 518; Cleveland O. Allen, "The Negro's Contribution to American Music," *Current History,* XXVI (May, 1927), 245; Alaine Locke, "The Negro's Contribution to American Art and Literature," *Annals of the American Academy,* CXL (November, 1928), 245; Cleveland G. Allen, "The Negro and His Songs," *Musical Courier,* CIII (October 3, 1931), 7.

[60] "Folk-Music," *New Century Dictionary,* I, 596; "Folk-Music," *Oxford English Dictionary,* IV, 390; "Folk-Music," *Webster New International Dictionary,* p. 980; Martha Warren Beckwith, *Folklore in America* (Poughkeepsie, 1941), pp. 1, 35.

[61] Dorothy Scarborough, *On the Trail of Folk-Songs* (Cambridge, 1925), p. 238.

[62] Sara M. Handy, "Negro Superstition," *Lippincott's Magazine,* XLVIII (December, 1891), 738.

[63] Fenner, "Fifty Cabin and Plantation Songs," Armstrong and Ludlow, *op. cit.,* p. 172; J[ames] W[entworth] Leigh, *Other Days* (London, [1921]). pp. 155 f.; J. Rosamond Johnson, *Utica Jubilee Singers Spirituals* (Boston, 1930), p. 5; Clarence Cameron White, "Negro Music Contribution to the National Music of America," *Musical Observer,* XIX (March, 1920), 13; Reed Smith, *Gullah* (Bulletin of the University of South Carolina, Columbia, no. 190, November 1, 1926), p. 30; James Weldon Johnson, "Negro Folk Songs and Spirituals," *Mentor,* XVII (February, 1929), 51.

uneducated white people used,[64] the beliefs of a Negro were not even mildly ridiculous. His philosophy was "virile and indicative of a higher order of invention." [65]

By such confusing and confused opinions scholars confessed their inability to give meaningful definition to what Negroes said and how they acted.

At about the turn of the twentieth century, a Negro doctor of philosophy, a Harvard graduate, applied critical study to Negro music. He affirmed that spirituals "stirred the nation" back in the 1830's, although they were "siftings of the centuries." He classified them as first African songs, next Afro-American, then mixtures with white songs; finally they became an influence upon songs like "Swanee River" and "Old Black Joe." [66] Immediately, in contrast with these findings of W. E. Burghardt Du Bois, a static source of spirituals was advocated by Booker T. Washington when he pronounced their origins as "in the camp meetings, the revivals, and in other religious exercises." In 1905 these views were published in his Preface to *Twenty-Four Negro Melodies Transcribed for the Piano* by Samuel Coleridge-Taylor. Here Washington made the statement that Negro music told of the rock from which Negroes were hewn.[67] A definite evolutionary hypothesis for spirituals which appeared about thirty years later set seven periods for their beginnings, the earliest being "Before 1830–1. *The Age of Plantation Shout and 'Breakdown.'* " [68]

During the Reconstruction period, in her Preface to the songs of Music Director Fenner of Hampton Institute, Miss Helen G. Ludlow had written that "no one exactly knows" the origin of spirituals. In 1909 Howard W. Odum's dissertation for the Doctor of Philosophy degree viewed the pursuit of the origin of spirituals as "always . . . an interesting theme, proving full of fascination for him who finds it,

[64] William Cecil Elam, "Lingo in Literature?" *Lippincott's Magazine,* LV (February, 1895), 286.

[65] "Black Voices," *Nation,* XCIX (September 17, 1924), 278.

[66] W. E. Burghardt Du Bois, *The Souls of Black Folk* (Chicago, 1903), pp. 251, 256.

[67] Undoubtedly original with William E. Barton, *Old Plantation Hymns; A Collection of Hitherto Unpublished Melodies of the Slave and the Freedman, with Historical and Critical Notes* (New York, 1899), pp. 224 f.

[68] Alaine Locke, *The Negro and His Music* (Washington, 1936), p. 11.

nymphlike, vanishing from his grasp. Still the songs of a people are ever present and appear, almost like myths, to have sprung into life in some way and at some time which no one can exactly tell." [69]

Anonymity was no characteristic of Negro spirituals. Odum later collaborated with Guy B. Johnson in classifying Negro makers and disseminators of songs in North America as "songsters," who regularly sang songs and originated them; "musicianers," who were proficient with instruments like banjos, guitars, and fiddles; and "music physicianers," itinerant combiners of both of these functions. Indeed, these last-named persons were "professional" people. In slavery days songsters were paid to increase the work upon southern plantations by inducing the laborers to sing. These "singing bosses," who had a variety of designations, were usually women; they were also heard in Haiti. [70]

Others besides Thomas R. Carlton and R. Emmet Kennedy observed that preachers originated songs for their congregations. Black mammies fashioned them as they nursed white children. [71] "Sister Bumaugh" was not the only songster upon whom William E. Barton relied for the songs published in *Old Plantation Hymns* (New York, 1899). The authorship of specific songs was so plain to one collector that he named presumable authors. [72] The originators of spirituals were so well known that the title of James Weldon Johnson's poem, "O Black and Unknown Bards," was not completely accurate. Johnson did know some of the "bards," such as "Ma" White and "Singing" Johnson. [73] Folklorists contradicted themselves by claiming

[69] Howard W. Odum, *Religious Folk-Songs of Southern Negroes.* Reprinted from the *Journal of Religious Psychology and Education,* III (July, 1909), 17.

[70] H. G. Osgood, "Sperichils," *Musical Courier,* XCIII (August 12, 1926), 14; Harold Courlander, *Haiti Singing* (Chapel Hill, 1939), p. 183.

[71] Martha S. Gielow, *Mammy's Recollections and Other Sketches* (New York, 1898), *passim;* "Mammy Song: A Negro Melody As Taken Down by Mrs. Julia Neely Finch," *Music,* XII (March, 1899), 604–605; Jeannette Robinson Murphy, "The Survival of African Music in America," *Popular Science Monthly,* IV (September, 1899), 670; Odum, *Religious Folk-Songs of the Southern Negro,* p. 17.

[72] Work, *Folk Songs of the American Negro,* pp. 77 ff., 82–86, 88.

[73] James Weldon Johnson, "Negro Folk Songs and Spirituals," *Mentor,* XVII (February, 1929), 51.

anonymity for the authorship of spirituals while at the same time they knew the originators of certain songs.

Folklorists also attempted the "impossible": they assigned a time when spirituals originated.[74] Negro songs were said by some to have begun during "the first half of the nineteenth century." [75] Others set the *terminus ad quem* of the origination of spirituals in 1863,[76] while certain experts have stated that more spirituals are being made today than during the days of slavery.[77]

The theory of the static origin of spirituals gave support to the hypothesis that Negro spirituals were copied from white revival songs. A popular history of church music called Negroes "simply imitators who pathetically cried in their captivity." [78] Five years later, in 1928, laymen had a spokesman for this white-to-Negro theory in the late Newman I. White of Duke University. In 1930 a professor of sociology at the University of North Carolina found that of eighty-two songs of Negroes on St. Helena Island ten were similar to white-folk songs.[79] After the books of George Pullen Jackson of Vanderbilt University began to appear in 1933, Guy B. Johnson of the University of North Carolina felt certain that Negro spirituals were the "revival and rural church" songs of the southern white people. At first 20 such songs, then 60, and finally 116 were said to have been copied outright by the Negroes. Thus had the Negroes' great power of receptivity and assimilation of art [80] reached its cul-

[74] Reed Smith, *op. cit.,* p. 42.

[75] Newman I. White, *American Negro Folk Songs,* p. 57; George Pullen Jackson, *White Spirituals in the Southern Uplands* (Chapel Hill, 1933), p. 244; George Pullen Jackson, *White and Negro Spirituals, Their Life Span and Kinship* (New York, [1943]), p. 92.

[76] Hiram Kelly Moderwell believed that "when freedom was at last gained there were no more songs about it. There are few preserved from slavery days" ("The Epic of the Black Man," *New Republic,* XII [September 8, 1917], 155; also, Cleveland G. Allen, "The Negroes' Contribution to American Music," *op. cit.,* pp. 248–249).

[77] Howard Odum and Guy B. Johnson, *Negro Workaday Songs* (Chapel Hill, 1926), p. 188.

[78] Edmund S. Lorenz, *Church Music: What a Minister Should Know about It* (New York, [c. 1923]), p. 377.

[79] Guy B. Johnson, *Folk Culture on St. Helena Island* (Chapel Hill, 1930), p. 127.

[80] Diedrich Westermann, *The African To-day and Tomorrow* (London, 1939), p. 94.

mination.[81] It was "fair to say" that the "stream of Negro music in America starts and finishes with white men." [82]

Because only subjective, and not objective, standards existed at that time for the estimate of the musicality of a people, phonophotography was developed to define music.[83] For years the phonograph had been used to record songs, but only after about 1922 did Carl E. Seashore of the Department of Psychology of the University of Iowa employ European methods of preserving and measuring songs and singers. Of the more than twoscore instruments of song measurement, those designed to measure the senses of pitch, intensity, consonance, tonal memory, and rhythm are most important. The songs collected by Odum and Johnson furnished source material.[84] A chief purpose of the phonophotographers was scientific testing of the presumable superiority of the musical abilities of Negroes over Caucasians. No superiority was found. Said Guy B. Johnson: "I have no doubt that on the average the Negro voice is superior to the white voice, but this is due to an emotional difference between the races in the organs of vocalization, and does not reflect a superior musicality." [85]

A list of the advocates of an antievolutionary hypothesis for the origin of spirituals would include travelers, men of the army, missionaries, statesmen, music teachers, critics, educators, both laymen and clergymen, and professors of anthropology, chemistry, English, Latin, psychology, and sociology. Members of all these groups have spoken authoritatively, but inconsistently, about song materials

[81] Timothy Flint, *Recollections of the Last Ten Years* (Boston, 1826), p. 345; Caroline Gilman, *Recollections of a Southern Matron* (New York, 1838), p. 76; W. F. Allen [Marcel], "The Negro Dialect," *Nation*, I (December 14, 1865), 745; *Slave Songs*, p. vii.

[82] Sigmund Spaeth, "Dixie, Harlem, and Tin Pan Alley: Who Writes Negro Music and How?" *Scribner's Magazine*, XCIX (January, 1936), 24.

[83] Milton Metfessel, *Phonophotography in Folk Music: American Negro Songs in New Notation* (Chapel Hill, 1928), p. 178; Eva May Grew, "The Sense of Pitch," *British Musician and Musical News*, VII (May, 1931), 112 f.

[84] Carl E. Seashore, "Three New Approaches to the Study of Negro Music," *Annals of the American Academy*, CXL (November, 1928), 190 ff.; Metfessel, *op. cit.*, pp. vii, x, 16, 17, 19.

[85] Guy B. Johnson, "The Negro and Musical Talent," *Southern Workman*, LVI (October, 1927), 443 f.; Yale S. Nathanson, "The Musical Ability of the Negro," *Annals of the American Academy*, CXL (November, 1929), 186–190.

which the first collectors had advertised as historical documents from Negroes themselves. Evidently these persons were speaking outside their own fields of specialization.

Nevertheless, the Lorenz-White-Johnson-Jackson white-to-Negro song trends proved that spirituals have been influenced by their authors' environment. One man said that the science of folklore would yield historical facts; [86] and before this view was pronounced of "no utility," [87] a most provocative statement "that every folksong must have once been the utterance of an individual" was made by Harry Edward Krehbiel. In other words, a certain individual lived at some time and place and composed a particular message.

Specialists in primitive music were now told to look for the historical viewpoint,[88] and it was pointed out that, though American Indians had no written history, some records of their past are preserved in song.[89] Robert Russa Moton aroused historical interest in Negro songs when in the Preface to the 1909 edition of *Religious Folk Songs of the Negro,* compiled by Musical Director Fenner of Hampton Institute, he wrote:

Though the words are sometimes rude and the strains often wild yet they are the outpourings of an ignorant and poverty-stricken people whose religious language and ideals struggled for expression and found it through limited vocabularies and primitive harmonies. They are not merely poetry. They are life itself in the life of the human soul manifesting itself in rude words, wild stories, and curious tho beautiful harmonies.[90]

In the 1920's at least two authorities asserted that Negro songs tell racial history.[91] By the next decade another expert had reached the

[86] George Lawrence Gomme, *Folklore as an Historical Science* (London, [1908]), p. 8.

[87] Alexander Haggarty Krappe, *The Science of Folk-Lore* (London, [1930]), p. xx n. 2.

[88] George Herzog, "Research in Primitive and Folk Music in the United States," *American Council of Learned Societies, Bulletin no. 25* (April, 1936), p. 50 [610].

[89] Frances Densmore, "Traces of Foreign Influences in the Music of the American Indians," *American Anthropologist,* new ser., XLVI (January–March, 1944), 152.

[90] Quoted in R. Nathaniel Dett (ed.), *Religious Folk-Songs of the Negro as Sung at Hampton Institute* (Hampton, 1927), p. lx.

[91] "The Soul of a Race," *Music and Youth,* II (January, 1927), 105; Al-

same conclusion.[92] Even racial chauvinists had not arrived at the opinion of a writer of that decade who went so far as to say that, if Negro music is the American folksong, "then the history of America" is "the history of the slave." [93]

A member of the younger generation of Negroes indicated in 1939 that he was discussing the historical material of spirituals when he wrote that the slave "took a good look at this world and told what he saw." His "true interpretation" of spirituals held that they were evidences of the Negroes' obsession with freedom and justice and that they included plans of strategy by which these could be achieved. After such a suggestive beginning the writer proceeded to interpret the allegory by dubbing anyone who mistreated a slave as "Satan." King Jesus was the slave's benefactor, Babylon and winter were slavery, hell was being sold farther south, and Jordan was the first step toward freedom. Thus the familiar concepts of Negroes were concrete things which fitted into the scheme at one time or another.[94] Such allegorizing ran back at least fifty years to one who asserted that the slaves believed themselves to be oppressed Israelites, that slaveholders were cruel Egyptians, and that Canaan was the land of freedom. Bondage, of course, was slavery.[95]

The historical burden of Negro spirituals was settled upon by another who wrote that "there is more, far more than the ordinary Christian zeal embedded in Negro spirituals. They are not mere religious hymns written or recited to sweeten the service or improve the ritual. They are the aching, poignant cry of an entire people." [96]

That Negro spirituals are historical documents from the Negro people may be postulated in five statements. The primary function

---

berta Williams, "A Race History Told in Songs," *World Review*, IV (February 14, 1927), 30.

[92] P. F. Laubenstein, "Race Values in Aframerican Music," *Musical Quarterly*, XVI (July, 1930), 378–403; Albert Sidney Beckham, "The Psychology of the Negro Spirituals," *Southern Workman*, LX (September, 1931), 391–394.

[93] Sidney Grew, "Random Notes on the Spirituals," *Music and Letters*, XVI (April, 1933), 105 f.

[94] John Lovell, "The Social Implication of the Negro Spiritual," *Journal of Negro Education*, VIII (October, 1939), 636–643.

[95] Murphy, "The Survival of African Music in America," *op. cit.*, p. 662.

[96] V. F. Calverton, "The Negro and American Culture," *Saturday Review of Literature*, XXII (September 21, 1940), pp. 17 f.

of African music was to give the history of a people. African Negroes were transplanted to the Americas along with their gifts of song. The first extended collection of slave songs was advertised as historical documents from the Negro people. Such an evolution of slave songs was perceived by divers people. Negro spirituals are best understood in harmony with this historical interpretation.

The following chapters summarize the evidence for the evolution of slave songs. The usual questions regarding their texts, their authors, their dates, their places of origin, and their messages are discussed.[97] The European, the Oriental, the African, and the American environments will be shown to throw light upon the lives of the authors, to clarify the nature of Negro singing, and to explain the genesis of the so-called "secret strain" theory, that Negro music "was a sort of secret password" into the lives of slaves.[98]

[97] The texts of slave songs are given as reported by collectors. In the following pages brackets [ ] enclose words added by the present writer, rejected words are in *italics,* and alternative readings are given in parentheses with the word "or." Words in parentheses without "or" are so given in the original and were presumably intended for a second voice.

[98] John W. Work quoted in Paul F. Labenstein, "An Apocalyptic Reincarnation," *Journal of Biblical Literature,* LI (December, 1932), 247.

"SINNER, PLEASE"

Sinner, please don't let this harvest pass;
Sinner, please don't let this harvest pass, harvest pass;
Sinner, please don't let this harvest pass,
And die and lose your soul at last.[1]

GREAT harvests of souls were gathered in revival assemblies in North America. During the late eighteenth and early nineteenth centuries protracted meetings for the purpose of confessing religion were held in the woods on the frontier.[2] These camp meetings were similar to the secret tribal assemblies of Negro Africa. At this time when the religious experiences of white and black people were similar, one Negro songster urged his fellows, in the words given above, not to forsake the meetings as opportunities to protest against the injustices of slavery.[3] His song added that Negroes might lose their

---

[1] John W. Work, *American Negro Songs: A Comprehensive Collection of 230 Folk Songs, Religious and Secular* (New York, [1940]), p. 191. Used by permission of Theodore Presser Company, Bryn Mawr, Pa., from *American Negro Songs.*

[2] B. W. Gorham, *Camp Meeting Manual* (Boston, 1854), p. 14; S. C. Swallow, *Camp-Meetings: Their Origin, History, and Utility* (New York, 1879), pp. 7–8.

[3] Robert Park, "The Conflict and Fusion of Culture," *Journal of Negro History,* IV (April, 1917), 118, stated that Negroes brought only their color and temperaments to the Americas. E. Franklin Frazier, one of his disciples, was in South America in 1940 where he was reported as having told the Free School of Sociology and Politics at São Paulo, Brazil, that American

lives by such militant gatherings, but otherwise they might lose their souls. On the frontier the popular denominations of Presbyterians, Baptists, and Methodists provided accommodations for Negroes at these meetings,[4] as if Christian evangelism would make militant Negroes pacific. Some colonial Negroes had paid no attention to the Christian religion.[5]

Group protests against captive conditions had been made ever since African Negroes were first forced to go on the middle passage to the Americas. Hardly arrived in the Western Hemisphere, Negroes revolted in Haiti as early as the sixteenth century. Murderous insurrections in Venezuela and attempted escapes to the Indians from servitude in what is now South Carolina were well known. Negro secret meetings occurred during the seventeenth century in the West Indies, in South America, and in Central America, but they were said not to have existed in North America.[6]

Nevertheless Negro insurrections occurred in North America periodically from 1526 through the legal duration of slavery.[7] They differed only environmentally from other Negro demonstrations in the Western Hemisphere. At first, an individual Negro might con-

---

Negroes had completely lost their culture (*Afro-American*, November 23, 1940). Some experts affirmed an African background for certain Negro characteristics (W. E. Burghardt Du Bois, *The Negro Church* [Atlanta, 1903], pp. 5 f.; Frederick Morgan Davenport, *Primitive Traits in Religious Revivals* [New York, 1908], p. 45; Carter G. Woodson, *The African Background Outlined* [Washington, 1936], *passim;* Herskovits, *The Myth of the Negro Past*, pp. 90 f.).

[4] P. Stanbury, *A Pedestrian Tour of Two Thousand Three Hundred Miles in North America* (New York, 1822), p. 18; Richard McNemar, *The Kentucky Revival* (New York, 1846), p. 24; Francis Lieber, *The Stranger in America* (London, [n.d.]), II, 259; William May Wightman, *Life of William Capers, D.D.* (Nashville, [1858]), p. 430; Catharine C. Cleveland, *The Great Awakening in the West, 1797–1805* (Chicago, [1916]), p. 77.

[5] Marcus W. Jernegan, "Slavery and Conversion in the American Colonies," *American Historical Review,* XXI (April, 1916), 504–527.

[6] E. Franklin Frazier, *The Negro Family in the United States* (Chicago, 1939), p. 163, and "The Negro Family in Bahia, Brazil," *American Sociological Review,* VII (August, 1942), 455.

[7] Joseph Cephas Carroll, *Slave Insurrections in the United States, 1800–1865* (Boston, [c. 1938]), *passim;* Herbert Aptheker, *American Negro Slave Revolts* (New York, 1943), *passim.*

vene his secret meeting by means of a drum or a horn, as in Africa.
After the Colony of Virginia took the lead in 1676 in prohibiting the
assemblage of Negroes by drum beat, a non-Christian slave there
might have sung this spiritual for a gathering of his fellows:

> *Let us* [Ah] praise Gawd *togedder* on *our* [mah] knees.
> *Let us* [Ah] praise Gawd *togedder* on *our* [mah] knees.
> *Let us* [Ah] praise Gawd *togedder* on *our* [mah] knees.
> *When* Ah falls on mah knees
> Wid mah face to de risin' sun;
> Oh, Lawd, hab mercy on me.[8]

If this spiritual sung as a communion hymn after the Civil War were
amended by substituting words such as a beginner in a language
would use, a song to convene a secret meeting of Negroes would be
suggested. It relates hardly at all to holy communion, which does not
necessarily require early morning administration or a devotee who
faces east. Here it seems was a signal song of Virginia Negroes of the
eighteenth century who used it and similar ones to convene their
secret meetings.

By the time of the colonial revivals the Negroes' song gifts were
recognized and used.[9] Samuel Davies, who in 1748 went from Pennsylvania to the Scotch-Irish Presbyterians of Virginia, was determined to avoid the handicaps which had embarrassed slave evangelism. He saw that "the pacific religion of Jesus" was necessary for
Negroes. The behavior of slaves made him apprehensive of insurrections against white people and massacres of them at the time that the
French and Indians were invading the country. He soon had the help
of three other Presbyterian ministers when the Hanover Presbytery
was organized in December, 1755. Davies utilized music to encour-
age Negroes to cheerfulness and to counteract their militancy. In the
spring he sent thanks to the London Society for Promoting Christian
Knowledge for sending the Negroes song books. After Davies gave
the books out, he felt that he had not had a similar experience in all
of his life "that met with such gratitude from the receiver." He wrote

[8] Nicholas George Julius Ballanta, *Saint Helena Island Spirituals* (New
York, [c. 1925]), p. 47.

[9] Frederika Bremer, *The Homes of the New World,* trans. Mary Howitt
(New York, 1854), I, 307 f., 312.

for more of "Watt's Psalms and Hymns and Bibles," saying that "the Negroes above all the human species I ever knew, have an ear for music, and a kind of ecstatic delight in Psalmody; and there are no books they learn so soon, or take so much pleasure in, as these used in that heavenly part of divine worship." [10]

Negro slave traders also found that music charmed savage feelings. One traveler described banjo music accentuated by bodily rhythms and the voices of Negroes on a North American ship which had arrived at Savannah, Georgia, from Guinea:

We saw them dance, and heard them sing. In dancing they scarcely moved their feet, but threw about their arms, and twisted and writhed their bodies into a multitude of disgusting and indecent attitudes. Their song was a wild yell devoid of all softness and harmony, and loudly chanted in harsh harmony.

He also observed the singing of Negroes upon a slave ship in the West Indies. "They have a great amusement," he wrote, "in collecting together in groups and singing their favorite African songs; the energy of their action is more remarkable than the harmony of their music." [11]

Disadvantaged Negroes responded to this encouragement. They felt free to go to their Presbyterian friends in Virginia and unbosom themselves. In 1756 one of the slaves went to Davies with a request "in broken English": "I come to you, sir, that you may tell me some good things concerning Jesus Christ and my duty to God, for I am resolved not to live any more as I have done." [12]

In other words, a slave in Virginia told Samuel Davies in 1756 that he wanted to become a Christian. This slave like many other Negroes could now appreciate Christianity which walked upon the earth. There is a spiritual in which its author says over and over again that he wants to become a Christian:

> Lord, I want to be *a Christian* [Christun] In-a my heart,
> *in-a my heart,*

[10] William Henry Foote, *Sketches of Virginia: Historical and Biographical* (Philadelphia, 1850–1855), pp. 286–292.

[11] George Pinckard, *Notes on the West Indies* (London, 1816), I, 103; II, 455.

[12] Foote, *Sketches of Virginia*, p. 291.

Lord, I want to be *a Christian* [Christun] In-a my heart.
In-a my heart, in-a my heart,
Lord, I want to be *a Christian* [Christun] In-a my heart.

The author was Oriental enough to use the word *Lord* in the sense of the possessor or master. With him it meant no more than a polite *sir*.[13] In freedom this spiritual contained verses which compared adjectives. Then it was written down saying:

> *Lord, I want to be more loving In-a my heart, etc.*
> *Lord, I want to be more holy In-a my heart, etc.*
> *I don't want to be like Judas In-a my heart, etc.*
> *Lord, I want to be like Jesus In-a my heart, etc.*[14]

The quiet dignity of the tune of this song, devoid of the wild abandon of some other Negro songs, and the fact that a person had to seek membership in the Christian community commend this song as a spiritual from a Presbyterian environment. It fits the Virginia ministry of Davies between 1748 and 1759 and is specifically in accord with the slave's request at Hanover in 1756, the probable place and date of origin.

Colonial churches made efforts to instruct Negroes with a view to enrolling them as members. Before baptism Presbyterian slaves had to remain catechumens for some time. Negroes were ready for baptism when they understood something about Christian doctrine as found in the *Mother's Catechism* and in the New Testament and after they exhibited a change of behavior. In song, they settled upon praise to God as being their chief instruction for Christianization. James Weldon Johnson's derivative song says Negroes were "glad" that they had done what they were told to do. Perhaps the original spiritual of that thought was lost. Everything except the joy that slaves experienced when they accepted Christianity is incorporated in a freedom nursery medley whose chorus a black mammy sang "with rollicking abandon":

[13] W. Faux, *Memorable Days in America* (London, 1823), p. 99, remarked that in the South a white person "was a god for Negroes to worship."

[14] [Thomas P. Fenner] (arr.), *Religious Folk Songs of the Negro* (Hampton, 1924), p. 156. Both these verses and the original "Lord, I want to be a Christian" above are used by permission of Hampton Institute, Hampton, Va.

[Chorus:]
I done, done, I done, done, I done, done;
I done, done, I done, done, I done, done
What yer tole me ter do.

Hush leetle baby, don't yer cry,
I done, done, what yer tole me ter do.
Yo' mudder and fadder born ter die,
I done, done, what yer tole me ter do.

Yer tole me to sing,
        shout,

          pray,

           talk,

Leetle white honey lef her throne,
I done, done, what yer tole me ter do.
Gwine ter Zion hill ter mourn,
I done, done, what yer tole me ter do.[15]

The "done" of Virginia was quite a different verb from the "been" of South Carolina.[16] In the second verse of the song the nursemaid remembered four elements of praise to God in monosyllabic words. Probably each item of the praise ritual was sung about like this:

> Lawd tell me to sing;
> Lawd tell me to sing.
> Lawd tell me to sing.
> I done, done-a what you tell me to do.

Native African secret meetings had brought Christianization to American Negroes. So secret meetings of Negroes had been convened for positive usefulness as well as for negative protests against slavery. They supplied all of the sacred ministries to which Negroes had been accustomed at home when they were sick, when they "married," and when they died.[17] Negroes needed the comfort of group

[15] Jeannette Robinson Murphy, *Southern Thoughts for Northern Thinkers and African Music in America* (New York, [1904]), p. 34.

[16] Higginson, *Army Life in a Black Regiment*, p. 202.

[17] Morgan Godwyn, see Morgan Godwin, *The Negroe's & Indian's Advocate Suing for Their Admission into the Church* (London, 1680), pp. 97 f., 136; David Humphreys, *An Historical Account of the Incorporated Society for the Propagation of the Gospel in Foreign Parts* (London, 1730), p. 238; [John Woolman], *The Journal of John Woolman* (Boston, 1871), p. 109.

fellowship in order to condition themselves to slave situations. Camp meetings were definite rivals of the African cult.

The African cult had trained Negroes to dress their finest for worship. In Africa they wore cotton, silk, and velvet beautifully ornamented with embroidery and jewelry of gold and silver.[18] In the West Indies a law of 1540 prohibited Negro women from wearing jewelry, pearls, or silks unless they were married to Spaniards; [19] and in South Carolina in 1735 another law had to be renewed to confiscate the "finer" clothes which slaves wore. Indeed, Negroes often dressed more elaborately than Caucasians in the United States [20] or working people in England.[21] Travelers commented upon characteristic Negro finery in the nineteenth century in the West Indies, South America, Central America, and North America. At a camp meeting in Indiana in 1829,

one tent was occupied exclusively by Negroes. They were all full-dressed, and looked exactly as if they were performing a scene on the stage. One woman wore a dress of pink gauze trimmed with silver lace; another was dressed in pale yellow silk; one or two had splendid turbans; and all wore a profusion of ornaments. The men, in snow white pantaloons, with gay coloured linen jackets. One of these, a youth of coal-black comeliness, was preaching with the most violent gesticulations, frequently springing high from the ground, and clapping his hands over his head. Could our missionary societies have heard the trash he uttered, by way of an address to the Deity, they might perhaps have doubted whether his conversion had much enlightened his mind.[22]

A song heard in Charleston, South Carolina, told that a character representing Moses was known at camp meetings by his clothes. Though Negroes generally were prohibited from holding meetings of their own at night, a spiritual made it known that no such regulation applied to interracial camp meetings, and there, according to

[18] Delafosse, *op. cit.,* p. 155; Batutah, *op. cit.,* p. 329.

[19] Hubert Howe Bancroft, *History of Central America* (New York, [n.d.]), II, 389 n. 5.

[20] Henry Bradshaw Fearon, *Sketches of America* (London, 1819), p. 9; Buckingham, *The Slave States of America,* II, 427, 480.

[21] J. S. Buckingham, *The Eastern and Western States of America* (London, [1842]), I, 11.

[22] Frances Trollope, *Domestic Manners of the Americans* (New York, [1901]), I, 237 f.

African custom, pseudonymous Moses was indispensable. No doubt his songs carried native African tunes; Negroes remembered that some tunes of their songs came directly from Africa.[23] At a camp meeting Moses looked so different from his workaday appearance that a singer was not at all certain that he was the same person. The "yonder" of his spiritual places it among the contemporaneous Negro "yonder" hymns of 1801: [24]

> I see brudder Moses yonder,
> And I think I *ought to* know him,
> *For* I know him by [he clothes] *his garment,*
> *He's a blessing* [Dere's a meeting] here to-night.
> *He's a blessing* [Dere's a meeting] here to-night,
> And I think I *ought to* know him
> *He's a blessing* [Dere's a meeting] here to-night.[25]

This song was characteristic of the religion of Negroes. It incorporated other ideas through the years but never ceased saying that the dress of Negroes determined their preparation for religious devotion. A crew of South Carolina slaves sang such a song over and over as they rowed toward their destination.[26] When the editors of *Slave Songs of the United States* recorded this piece at the close of the Civil War, it had gathered additional words. A new verse sung at each person's name made it seem almost endless.[27] A collector of

[23] Murphy, "The Survival of African Music in America," *op. cit.,* pp. 552, 666.

[24] Richard Allen, *A Collection of Hymns & Spiritual Songs from Various Authors* (Philadelphia, 1801), p. 25.

[25] *Slave Songs,* p. 9; William Francis Allen, Charles Pickard Ware, and Lucy McKim Garrison (comp.), *Slave Songs of the United States* (New York, 1929), p. xxxix. This edition will hereafter be referred to as Allen (comp.), *op. cit.*

[26] Laurence Oliphant, *Patriots and Filibusters* (London, 1860), p. 141, recorded:
> "Oh, I take my text in Matthew,
> And some in Revelation;
> Oh, I know you by your garment,
> There's a meeting here to-night."

[27] A longer and hence a later variant of *Slave Songs,* p. 9, was:
> "I take my text in Matthew,
> And by de Revelation,

Negro songs for the Jubilee Singers of Fisk University believed that conduct rather than clothes should characterize a religious person. So he revised this traditional spiritual to say: "I know you by your daily walk, etc." [28]

Settlers in the older colonies of the East would usually not tolerate the emotional expressions of Negroes as frontiersmen did, although churches in Virginia sometimes invited the Negroes to remain on the outside of the buildings after they had chosen convenient seats.[29] Often Negroes were not permitted to enter Methodist church buildings at all,[30] since they disturbed quiet and dignified worship by beating out the rhythm of songs with feet patting and hands clapping, in the place of African instruments. Moreover, Negroes shouted in religious services, exercising their bodies until their odors were quite repulsive.[31]

I know you by your garment,
Dere's a meeting here to-night.

"Chorus:
"Dere's a meeting here to-night,
Oh! (or Brudder Tony,) Dere's a meeting here to-night,
Oh! (or Sister Rina,) Dere's a meeting here to-night,
I hope to meet again.

"Brudder John was a writer,
He write de laws of God;
Sister Mary say to brudder John,
'Brudder John, don't write no more.'

"Chorus:
"Dere's a meeting here to-night, Oh! (or Brudder Sandy,) (*bis*)
Dere's a meeting here to-night,
I hope to meet again."

[28] J. B. T. Marsh, *The Story of the Jubilee Singers: with Their Songs* (rev. ed., Boston, 1880), pp. 182 f.

[29] Foote, *Sketches of Virginia*, p. 369.

[30] [Francis Asbury], *The Journal of the Rev. Francis Asbury, Bishop of the Methodist Episcopal Church* (New York, 1821), I, 228; II, 412; III, 52, 177, 297.

[31] *A Short Journey in the West Indies* (London, 1790), I, 133; Thomas Jefferson, *Notes on the State of Virginia* (1st Am. ed., Philadelphia, 1788), p. 148; Lieber, *op. cit.*, II, 200 f.; C. H. Wilson, *The Wanderer in America, or Truth at Home* (Thirsk, [Eng.], 1822), p. 193; P. Campbell Scarlett, *South*

The reaction of Negroes to their exclusion from church was preserved in a spiritual about weeping Mary. Strong men comforted her, in song, by stating that Pharaoh once got drowned and that the dominant race was again trying to stop the spiritual progress of Negroes. Negroes decided to flee to free territory where there was no such exclusion. This is their verse which described a real historical situation:

> When I get to Heaven goin' to sing and shout,
> Nobody there for turn me out.[32]

Slave Songs of the United States included a late variant of this spiritual with exact Biblical information about another Mary who was weeping at the tomb of Jesus. The earliest collection justified and apologized for the slaves' desire to flee in the common meter hymn, "Hinder Me Not," which Negroes sang with the meaning that their singing and shouting should not be prevented. An appropriate time for Negroes to use such a hymn would have been the first quarter of the nineteenth century. Yet slaves undoubtedly thought "de world da gwine" for them immediately after cotton gins were operated upon southern plantations at the turn of the century. Worship or prayer in the woods was deemed necessary; so

> You'*d better* pray, de world da gwine
> No man can hinder me!
> De Lord have mercy on my soul,
> No man can hinder me! [33]

"Walk in, kind Saviour, No man can hinder me!" were opening words of a freedom spiritual which expanded this simple theme to nine verses.[34]

The South was now "hell" to a slave from the Port Royal Islands, South Carolina. This heaven-home concept would be catalogued as

---

America and the Pacific (London, 1838), I, 35; William Howard Russell, *My Diary North and South* (Boston, 1863), p. 143; Henry Latham, *Black and White: A Journal of a Three Months' Tour in the United States* (London, 1867), p. 12.

[32] Work, *American Negro Songs*, p. 176. Used by permission of Theodore Presser Company, Bryn Mawr, Pa., from *American Negro Songs*.

[33] *Slave Songs*, p. 11.   [34] *Ibid.*, pp. 10 f.

part of the Liberian colonization trend of about 1824 had a Negro the determining voice in his residence. An original singer of spirituals decided upon location in the North. In his worship service of singing and praying the decision was to flee to free territory:

> Before I stay in hell *one day,*
> Heaven *shall-a* be my home;
> I sing and pray my soul away,
> Heaven *shall-a* be my home.[35]

The first census of the United States in 1790 estimated that there were 48,887 Negroes in the North. By 1810 there were 102,137 such Negroes, inclusive of 3,454 in the Northwest Territory, whose sixth article forbade slavery and involuntary servitude. In all of the North only 10,851 persons were listed as slaves.[36] This presence of Negroes in the North was attributable more to the habit of southern Negroes of running away than to direct importation of slaves [legally prohibited in 1807] or to the institution of slavery in the North. Negro churches were founded in the northern states: the Baptists in 1805 at Boston and the Presbyterian in 1807 at Philadelphia. Bishop Asbury indicated that Negro Methodists had reasons to go North. Bethel African Methodist Episcopal Church was dedicated in Philadelphia in 1794; Mother Zion was the nucleus of the African Methodist Episcopal Zion denomination in New York City in 1796. Union American Methodist Episcopal Church was an outgrowth of Peter Spencer's Ezion Church at Wilmington, Delaware, in 1805.[37] The Negro migrants expected aid from Negro preachers and received it. Richard Allen, founder of the African Methodist Episcopal Church, kept his house open for fugitive Negroes.[38] At the turn of the century it was significant and important that he collected familiar hymns and spiritual songs into a book that gave evidence of what fugitive Negroes were singing about. "Free grace" was expected. "Weary trav-

---

[35] *Ibid.,* p. 7; Allen (comp.), *op. cit.,* p. xxxix.

[36] See United States Bureau of Census, *Third Census, 1810* (microfilmed from the National Archives at Washington by Duke University, June 29, 1944).

[37] Carter G. Woodson, *The History of the Negro Church* (Washington, [1921]), *passim.*

[38] Daniel A. Payne, *History of the African Methodist Episcopal Church* (Nashville, 1891), p. 84.

elers," "Canaan," "farewell," and "yonder" were words of Negro songs of the period.[39]

Annanias Davisson, ruling elder of the Presbyterian Church,[40] expressed disapproval because his denomination in his native Virginia sought out Negro songsters to improve the worship of Presbyterian churches after it had become apparent that the spiritual singing of Negroes was according to the ideals of the African cult and, as he wrote, did "not constitute that worship which God requires." In the very year that Davisson was born, the Hanover Presbytery of Virginia entered in its journal on October 26, 1780, that it had a memorial upon the subject of improving psalm singing within the presbytery. Proposals for "purchasing Slaves and having infant Slaves baptized" for choir duties were referred to the afternoon session. There was not time to consider the matter in the afternoon, and so it was deferred until the next meeting of the presbytery. Perchance the will of Presbyterian slaveholders prevailed, for the minutes of the next meeting of the Hanover Presbytery were "lost." [41]

Davisson was nurtured in resentment. In 1815 at Harrisonburg, Virginia, he printed and sold a so-called *Kentucky Harmony*. In the second edition of 1817 Davisson included "A Few Observations on Sacred Music," which showed disappointment with his denomination. He quoted verbatim the commendation of Negro singing by Samuel Davies in 1755 but observed that it was shamefully abused to promote vice. He pointed out the importance of white people's learning how to perform sacred music with taste and regularity.[42] There was to be no "shouting" or other emotional demonstration with this singing, for "a Choir of Singers" should court "that pleasing solemnity that should attend the sacred worship of the Deity." In rehearsals "all whispering, laughing, talking, or strutting about the floor is ridiculous in the time of school, and should not be suffered." [43]

[39] Richard Allen, *op. cit., passim.*

[40] Jackson, *White Spirituals in the Southern Uplands,* p. 26.

[41] "Minutes of the Hanover Presbytery," II, 114 f., 141, MS (photostat), Presbyterian Historical Society."

[42] Annanias Davisson, *Kentucky Harmony or a Choice Collection of Psalm Tunes, Hymns, and Anthems; in Three Parts* . . . (2nd ed., Harrisonburg, 1817), pp. 154 ff.

[43] *Ibid.* (1817, 1821, 1826), p. 12.

It was impossible for white people to remain uninfluenced by the behavior and singing of black folk. In the Great Awakening in Virginia a contemporary observed that Negroes were commonly more noisy during preaching than the whites, were more subject to bodily exercise, and, if they met any encouragement in these things, they often grew extravagant.[44] The ejection of slaves from white churches, the splitting of denominations, and the foundation of small colleges had the result of causing white people to control such emotionalism as Negroes demonstrated in North America. Truly, a Negro confessed Christianity in keeping with his unlettered state and outdid white people in a way that "baffles description." [45]

Years later white people figuratively sang out of the *Original Sacred Harp* without embarrassment:

> And I'll sing hallelujah,
> And you'll sing hallelujah,
> And we'll all sing hallelujah,
> When we arrive at home.[46]

After Negroes shouted, white people shouted as much as they pleased. William Hauser of Georgia went to the defense of shouting in two songs of the *Hesperian Harp* (1848).[47]

The African cult saw to it that transplanted Negroes continued to promote their own culture by music. It did not occur to the whites that their neglect of the advancement of Negroes would make the continuance of the African cult in the Americas a necessity. Overlords were defended for promoting slavery even though apology was made for class distinctions in society by saying that God had predestined some folks for advantaged positions and others for places of disadvantage. Black folks were still thought of as nonhuman animals who were called "black cattle."

Arminianism, which believed in the possibilities for salvation of every person, reorganized itself in North America in 1784 under the name of the Methodist Episcopal Church. At the reorganizational

[44] John Leland, *The Virginia Chronicle* (Fredericksburg, Va., 1790), p. 13.
[45] William Henry Foote, *Sketches of North Carolina, Historical and Biographical, Illustrative of the Principles of a Portion of Her Settlers* (New York, 1846), pp. 402 f.
[46] Jackson, *White Spirituals in the Southern Uplands*, p. 225.
[47] *Ibid.*, pp. 183 f.

conference in Baltimore, Maryland, that church seemingly repented for acts of unbrotherliness of Methodists by stating more than once that "we are deeply conscious of the Impropriety of making new Terms of Communion for a religious society already established excepting on the most pressing Occasion and such we esteem the Practise of holding our Fellow-Creature in slavery." [48] The antislavery rulings of Methodism had to be rescinded within six months. Methodism was sneered at as "nigger religion," [49] but Bishop Francis Asbury treated Negroes as worth-while people. Negroes had no tangible way to tell him that they were thankful, but they promptly immortalized him in a great spiritual. He was their Moses. The Bishop did not resent the encomiums which Negroes lavished upon him but wrote in his journal on September 18, 1797: "O, it was going down into the Egypt of South Carolina after these poor souls of Africans I have lost my health, if not my life in the end. The will of God be done." Surely, at that time, if not before, Negroes of Maryland were understood to sing the simplest form of their traditional song about their patron saint, saying:

> Go down, Moses,
> Way down in Egypt land,
> Tell ole Pharoh
> Let my people go. [50]

Notwithstanding that the aspirations of the African cult were thus well known, the people of the United States settled upon an alternative for liberty for Negroes.

[48] Peter G. Mode, *Source Book and Bibliographical Guide for American Church History* (Menasha, [c. 1921]), pp. 325, 326; Charles Baumer Swaney, *Episcopal Methodism and Slavery with Sidelights on Ecclesiastical Politics* (New York, [c. 1926]), p. 3.

[49] Guion Griffis Johnson, *Ante-Bellum North Carolina: A Social History* (Chapel Hill, 1937), p. 345.

[50] Seward, *op. cit.*, pp. 22 f.

"DEEP RIVER"

Deep River, my home is over Jordan, Deep River,
Lord, I want to cross over into camp ground;
Lord, I want to cross over into camp ground;
Lord, I want to cross over into camp ground;
Lord, I want to cross over into camp ground.[1]

QUAKERS in North Carolina bought numerous slaves and, through their Manumission Society, which was established on July 19, 1816, sent them to other countries. The North Carolina Yearly Meeting, co-operating in this work, reported on June 9, 1825, that their agents endeavored "collectively to confer with the people of color under Friends' care respecting their willingness to go to other governments." [2] Africa was one of the places to which American Negroes desired to go.[3] In a song called "Deep River" that originated in Guilford County, North Carolina (where it was the name both of a body of water and of a meetinghouse of Quakers), a conservative slave told his Quaker benefactor that he wanted to "cross over" to Africa, the home of camp meetings. He said this more than the usual three times because the Quakers, as they said, had difficulty in placing confidence in the ambiguous speech of Negroes.[4]

[1] Marsh, *op. cit.*, pp. 196 f.

[2] "Minutes of the North Carolina Yearly Meeting," 1825, p. 230, MS, Guilford College, North Carolina.

[3] *African Repository*, II, 122 f.

[4] "Minutes of the Manumission Society of North Carolina," *passim*, MS, Guilford College.

41

Negroes loved Africa. Sometimes captives on slave ships jumped overboard and tried to swim back home.[5] Even the kind attentions of London royalty, including Her Majesty, Queen Caroline, did not prevent Job ben Solomon, a Maryland slave whom Oglethorpe had thought might be of service to the newly founded British Museum, from wanting to go home to Africa, where he was sent in 1734. Interest in African missions was aroused during the Great Awakening when it was proposed in 1755 to send three or four Africans in North America to the College of New Jersey (Princeton) to be educated for service in Africa. Nearly twelve hundred former slaves, sympathizers with the British cause during the American Revolution, left cold Canada for Sierra Leone, West Africa, in January, 1792.[6] Most of their places were shortly filled by Twelawny maroons from Jamaica, who had vexed the white population there for centuries by making disturbances at their secret meetings. To many of these maroons Canada was so unpleasant that hundreds of them went to Sierra Leone in 1800, arriving in October.[7] Haitian Negroes also sang that they wanted to be at home in Africa.[8] African colonization became part of an international plan of race relations for the benefit of Negroes, and among the latter it was a tenet held with the religious zeal of revivalism.[9]

[5] Donnan, *op. cit.*, II, 232 n. 3; III, 321; also, J. S. Buckingham, *America, Historical, Statistic, and Descriptive* (London, [1841]), I, 434, 435 f.; [Nancy Prince], *A Narrative of the Life and Travels of Mrs. Nancy Prince* (2nd ed., Boston, 1853), p. 7.

[6] Sierra Leone Company, *Substance of the Report Delivered by the Court of Directors of the Sierra Leone Company, to the General Court of Proprietors, on Thursday, March 27th, 1794* (Philadelphia, 1795), p. 7; J. J. Crooks, *A History of the Colony of Sierra Leone, West Africa* (Dublin, 1903), *passim*. Sierra Leone had been established as an asylum for Negro British subjects in 1787 (Andrew Hull Foote, *Africa and the American Flag* [New York, 1854], p. 77).

[7] Bryan Edwards, *The History, Civil and Commercial of the British Colonies in the West Indies* (3rd ed., London, 1793–1801), I, 522–576; II, 106–113; R. C. Dallas, *The History of the Maroons, from Their Origin to the Establishment of Their Chief Tribes at Sierra Leone* (London, 1803), II, 284.

[8] Laura Bowman and Le Roy Antonin, *The Voice of Haiti: An Unusual Collection of Original Native Ceremonial Songs, Invocations, Voodoo Chants, Drum Beats and Rhythms, Stories of Traditions, etc. of the Haitian People* (New York, [n.d.]), p. 3.

[9] See [Isaac Candler], *A Summary View of America* (London, 1824), p.

Samuel Hopkins and Thomas Jefferson were among those who advocated colonization elsewhere of the Negroes of the United States. The latter's view of emancipating all Negro slaves and then expatriating them was criticized on the ground that Negroes were making contributions to the American nation, but by December, 1816, a Society for Colonizing Free People of Colour of the United States, with their consent, was organized by Robert Finley, a Presbyterian minister.[10] Bushrod Washington, one of the judges of the Supreme Court, was elected president. At least some humanitarian and Christian people were convinced that Negroes loved Africa.[11]

The American Colonization Society continued to call attention to the need for a gradual emancipation of Negroes and an ultimate removal of slavery. The practicality of such a program was assured by Paul Cuffee, a Negro Quaker sea captain of New Bedford, Massachusetts, who made two trips to Africa, taking out thirty-eight Negro colonists in 1815.[12] To make certain that other Negroes would not lose hope in their eventual return to Africa, three letters from Cuffee's emigrants at Sierra Leone, West Africa, dated May 18, 1818, were published in the *Report of the American Colonization Society* and reprinted in denominational periodicals. In one letter, Samuel Wilson asked Richard Allen and other free Negro opposers of the Society: "Do you not know that the land where you are is not your own? Your fathers were carried into that to increase strangers' treasure, but God has turned it all to good, that you may bring the gospel into your country." He added that Negro ministers were not doing the will of God by remaining in the United States. Another emigrant, Perry Locke, wrote, "Your mother country . . . is like the land of

---

304; William Warren Sweet, *Revivalism in America, Its Origin, Growth and Decline* (New York, 1945), p. 159.

[10] [Robert Finley], *Thoughts on the Colonizing of Free Blacks* [Washington, 1816], *passim*.

[11] John Bristed, *America and Her Resources* (London, 1818), p. 149; John M. Duncan, *Travels through Part of the United States and Canada in 1818 and 1819* (New York, 1823), II, 261; *Report of the American Colonization Society* (1825), VIII, 26; James L. Sibley and D. Westermann, *Liberia— Old and New* (New York, 1928), p. 5.

[12] *Report of the American Colonization Society,* I (1818), 5, 7; II (1819), 151; H. N. Sherwood, "Paul Cuffee," *Journal of Negro History,* VIII (April, 1923), 184 ff., 193–202.

Canaan." His closing words were these: "Dear Friends, let this be printed, if you please." An open letter from these colonists and nine others went to the "Dear Friends and Brethren" of America, commending Samuel J. Mills and Ebenezer Burgess, the two "missionaries" sent to find an eligible colonial site on the West Coast of Africa, as witnesses that expatriated Negroes were in the "Land of Canaan." It was asserted that Cuffee's colonists were on their way to make fortunes in Africa.[13] These letters were undoubtedly edited by colonizationists, but it is nevertheless clear that their authors were in favor of the experiment.

Such letters as these influenced the recruiting of colonists for Africa and kindled hopes for emancipation in the breasts of slaves. The first shipload of eighty Negro colonists, under three white colonial agents of the American Colonization Society, sailed from New York in the winter of 1820.[14] The sudden death from fever of the agents and of fully a fourth of the emigrants checked colonizationists at first. They were, however, determined to succeed, and they sent replacements of agents and colonists in February, 1821. Cape Montserado was bought from the natives that year for $300, mostly in trinkets, and the surviving colonists were moved from the environs of Sierra Leone to their home, called Liberia, in 1822.[15] Colonizationists made a considerable stir about their achievements, naming the Liberian settlement Monrovia, in honor of the President of the United States. In 1823 fully 156 American Negroes were sent to Africa in three ships.

In song, Negroes followed closely what the American Colonization Society was saying and doing. When they knew that Liberia had been established, the slaves burst forth in a spiritual about this African home. The last words of the song, "at last," indicate that it was a late contemporary of "Sinner, Please," which also ended with the words "at last." On the Port Royal Islands, South Carolina, during

[13] *Latter Day Luminary,* I, 297–300; *Report of the American Colonization Society,* II (1819), 150–155.

[14] "Emigrant Register, 1820–1835," pp. 1 f., MS, Library of Congress; *African Repository,* I (1825), 3.

[15] *Report of the American Colonization Society,* VI (1823), 17; *African Repository,* II (1826), 114–119; *Report of the American Colonization Society,* VII (1824), 9–14.

the Civil War Negroes sang a simply conceived song about their African home which their forefathers knew about in 1823.

> I *am huntin'* [see] *for a city,* [home] *to stay awhile,*
> I *am huntin'* [see] *for a city,* [home] *to stay awhile,*
> I *am huntin'* [see] *for a city,* [home] *to stay awhile,*
> O Believer [Po' sinner] got a home at las['.] [16]

So many months passed before the third colonization ship sailed in June, 1822, taking out only twenty-five emigrants from Maryland and twelve from Pennsylvania, that Negroes in regions farther south felt that they might never get a chance to go. It was not, indeed, until 1827 that a few Negroes as far south as Georgia went to Africa. Yet, with great faith, Negroes of Florida said ambiguously, in song, that they were patiently waiting for their masters to manumit them for emigration, or that they were waiting for Jesus or his representative to "land them on Canaan's shore."

> O brothers, don't get weary,
> O brothers, don't get weary,
> O brothers, don't get weary,
> [Us] *We're* waiting for the Lord.
> [Us] *We'll* land on Canaan's shore,
> [Us] *We'll* land on Canaan's shore,
> *When we* [us] land on Canaan's shore,
> [Us] *We'll* meet *forever more.*[17]

Negroes in the United States were not easily discouraged; they intended to follow earlier colonists and traditionally expressed their intentions in words like "efn I live and nothing happens." [18] About 1824 a song which Negroes sang on the Port Royal Islands echoed

---

[16] *Slave Songs,* p. 18; Allen (comp.), *op. cit.,* p. xxxix. "Huntin' " for this residence to dwell in was deleted from the song because Negroes were forbidden to hunt in antebellum days, for example in the Carolinas (Walter Clark, *The State Records of North Carolina* [Goldsboro, 1895–1907], XXIII, 918; John Spencer Bassett, *Slavery and Servitude in the Colony of North Carolina* [Baltimore, 1899], p. 15) and in the West Indies (Edwards, *op. cit.,* II, 202, 224).

[17] *Slave Songs,* p. 95; Allen (comp.), *op. cit.,* p. xli.

[18] Roark Bradford, "Swing Low, Sweet Chariot," *Colliers,* XCVI (September 21, 1935), 16.

the colonization propaganda that emigrants were doing their Father's will by expatriating themselves to Liberia. This spiritual was made almost endless by repeating the same verse for each person present, like "Titty Mary" and "Brudder William."

Titty Mary, you know I gwine follow,
[Titty Mary, you know] I gwine follow,
[Titty Mary, you know I] gwine follow,
Brudder William, you know I gwine to follow,
For to do my Fader will.

'Tis well and good I'm a-comin' here tonight,
I'm a-comin' here to-night, I'm a-comin' here to-night,
'Tis well and good, I'm a-comin' here tonight,
For to do my Fader will.[19]

Notwithstanding these evidences of intention, so few Negroes sailed to Africa that even the warmest sympathizers with African colonization came to view the plan as impractical. Negroes, however, attributed their delays in being manumitted for African colonization to their inherited belief in the devil,[20] who was known in the Americas as Satan. African devil worship was taught in secret meetings and was associated with serpent symbolism.[21] On April 21, 1864, several Negro slave children were heard seriously "shouting" their ancient beliefs about the devil.[22] A song which suits the 1824 period told of the hindering work of Satan.

What make ole Satan da follow me *so?*
Satan hain*'t* nottin' *at all* [tall] *for* to do wid (*or Long o'*) me. (*Run seeker.*)

Hold your light, (Sister Mary,) (or All de member, Turn seeker).
Hold your light, (Seeker turn back?)
Hold your light on Canaan shore.[23]

[19] *Slave Songs,* p. 18; Allen (comp.), *op. cit.,* p. xxxix.
[20] Hakluyt, *op. cit.,* X, 20; "Letter from Mrs. Sarah Williamson Shields Coleman," ex-missionary to Liberia, New Orleans, Louisiana, February 13, 1940, in agreement with George W. Ellis, *op. cit.,* pp. 49 f.; Sibley and Westermann, *op. cit.,* p. 176.
[21] See Wilfrid D. Hambly, *Serpent Worship in Africa* (Chicago, 1933), pp. 55, 73.
[22] Mary Potter [Thacker] Higginson, *Thomas Wentworth Higginson* (Boston, 1914), p. 219.
[23] *Slave Songs,* p. 10; Allen (comp.), *op. cit.,* p. xxxix.

Yet a Negro in Augusta, Georgia, sang his great faith that his mother, who had been trying to get over the hill to Africa for a long time, would succeed. She had the requirements for manumission. She was a religious person and, according to Negro ideology, was one of the chosen people.

> O yonder's my ole mother,
> Been a-waggin' at de hill so long;
> I really do believe she's a child of God,
> She'll git home to heav'n bime-bye.[24]

A contemporary singer from the same Georgia city knew of additional work of Satan. He also sang, about 1824, of his belief that he was religiously fit for African colonization, and he repeated colonization talk that the friendly Jesus had brought African Negroes to the American shores in order that they might return home with gospel light. Jesus had been prevented from doing this perfect work by a "busy ole" Satan who rolled stones in the way:

> 1. Ole Satan is a busy ole man,
>   He roll stones in my way;

[24] *Slave Songs,* p. 72. A variant song is mentioned as "My Lord Called Daniel." It was heard in Nashville, Tennessee, but its text was not quoted.

In Caroline County, Virginia, Negroes sang a variant song which had gathered ideas through the years. The original concepts of a mother who had waited long for something to change her status plus the faith of a singer were there. Verses about the thunder and the lightning of "Steal Away" and concepts from other spirituals had been incorporated to make it a freedom medley.

"1. Bendin' knees a-achin', Body racked wid pain,
   I wish I was a child of God, I'd git home bime-by.

   [Chorus:]
   "Keep prayin', I do believe We're a long time waggin' o' de crossin';
   Keep prayin', I do believe We'll git home to heaven bime-by.

"2. O yonder's my ole mudder, Been a waggin' at de hill so long;
   It's about time she cross over, Git home bime-by.
   "Keep prayin', I do believe, etc.

"3. O hear dat lumberin' thunder, A-roll from do' to do'.
   A-callin' de people home to God; Dey'll git home bime-by.
   "Little chil'n, I do believe, etc.

"4. O see dat forked lightnin' A-jump from cloud to cloud,
   A-pickin' up God's chil'n; Dey'll git home bime-by.
   "Pray mourner, I do believe, etc."

Mass' Jesus *is* my bosom friend,
He roll 'em out o' my way.

[Chorus:]
O come-e go wid me,
O come-e go wid me,
O come-e go wid me,
A-walkin' in de heaven I *roam* [go].

2. I did not come here myself, my Lord,
   It was my Lord *who brought* [bring] me here;
   And I really do believe *I'm a* child of God
   A-walkin' in de heaven I *roam* [go].[25]

Since 1822 two brigs and a schooner had sailed to Liberia—in March and June, 1823, and in January, 1824. This encouragement excited slaves, who were propagandized to believe that they should be attracted to their African "home" to do God's will, to carry the gospel, and to follow Jesus.

About 1824 Caesar, a Negro singer of the Port Royal Islands, South Carolina, was more realistic. He wanted to go to Africa because he had been jilted in love by his "Rosy." His "poor heart" had been broken, and his life was now in hell, recalling the identical words of a fugitive slave. Caesar knew that he was a good religious fellow such as the American Colonization Society had a reputation for selecting for emigration. Yet his master had not seen fit to manumit him for colonization. Neighboring slaves knew of the love affair between Rosy and Caesar. They might have been both amused and sorrowful that Caesar could not live as he once had. He "had left children in Africa when stolen away." This aged Negro was undoubtedly one hundred years old when he was seen at Port Royal in 1863.[26]

1. Poor Rosy, poor gal (or Poor Caesar, poor boy);
   Poor Rosy, poor gal;
   Rosy break my poor heart,
   Heav'n *shall-a* be my home.

[25] *Slave Songs*, pp. 57 f.
[26] Edward L. Pierce, "The Freedmen at Port Royal," *Atlantic Monthly*, XXI (September, 1863), 301.

[Chorus:]
I cannot stay in hell one day,
Heav'n shall-a be my home;
I'll sing and pray my soul away,
Heav'n shall-a be my home.

2. *Got hard trial in my way, (ter)*
Heav'n shall-a be my home.
O when I talk (or Walk), I talk (or Walk) wid God, (bis)
Heav'n shall-a be my home.

3. I dunno *what* de people (or Massa) want of me, (*ter*)
Heav'n *shall-a* be my home.[27]

There was a lingering tradition with Negro soldiers of Col. Thomas Wentworth Higginson's regiment in the Civil War that when a Negro called by them "Moses" got an opportunity to go to Africa, he readily accepted. Negro thinking about Moses reached its height between 1824 and 1827. Up to that time only two boys by that name had sailed to Africa; one, four years old, from Maryland, and the other, fifteen years old, from Virginia. The soldiers were simply elated that "Brudder Moses," whom they did not like, had gone to Africa:

Brudder Moses gone to de promised land,
Hallelu, hallelujah.[28]

It was inspiring to other Negroes that slaves whom they familiarly knew as Stephen and George knew in advance that they were going to Africa. They sang:

Brudder George *is* a-gwine to glory,
Take car' *de sinsick* [o' he] soul
Brudder George *is* a-gwine to glory,
Take car' *de sinsick* [o' he] soul
Brudder *Stephen's* [George] gwine to glory,
Take car' *de sinsick* [o' he] soul.

[Brudder Stephen's gwine to glory, etc.] [29]

[27] *Slave Songs,* p. 7.   [28] *Ibid.,* p. 49.   [29] *Ibid.*

49

No matter how roseate slave life had become under a very few beneficent masters, slaves in Virginia at the same time of the "hallelu, hallelujah" rejoicing of the song about "Brudder Moses" knew that they wanted to go to Africa because they were forced to work in the rain and in the burning sun for long hours at a time. Families were broken up by the slave system, and Negroes seeking preferment tattled on one another. Slaves imagined that in Liberia "every day *shall* be Sunday," the day they were legally forbidden to work.[30]

1. No *more* rain *fall for* wet you,
   Hallelu, hallelu,
   No *more* rain *fall for* wet you,
   Hallelujah.

2. No *more* sun *shine for* burn you.

3. No *more* parting in *de kingdom* [heav'n].

4. No *more* backbiting in *de kingdom* [heav'n].

5. Every day *shall* be Sunday.[31]

Colonization interpretation is also possible for a song about poor Rebecca Lawton, who knew in advance that she would never enjoy the benefits of African colonization. A song leader poked fun at her for counting upon African colonization so strongly. Other Negroes joined in the fun, as if to say, that "Becca Lawton" now ought to be convinced that relief from slavery would have to come by some other means. She was obliged to remain a slave on the Port Royal Islands and to let the "rain *fall and* wet" her continually, even though Jesus

[30] The collectors arranged this spiritual among the ones of the southeastern slave states of South Carolina, Georgia, and the Sea Islands. Emigrants did not go to Africa from that section until in the late 1820's. Thus this song was assigned to Virginia, which from 1820 through 1824 had sent 164 Negroes to Africa. For slaves forbidden to work on Sunday, see "Extracts of the Journals of Mr. Commissary Von Reck," in Peter Force, *Tracts and Other Papers . . . to the Year 1776* (Washington, 1836–1846), IV, 9; in 1712 slaves were prohibited by law from working in South Carolina (Thomas Cooper [ed.], *The Statutes at Large in South Carolina* [Columbia, 1840], II, 397); in 1715 Negroes were similarly restricted in North Carolina (Walter Clark, *op. cit.,* XXIII, 4); the custom prevailed in Georgia also (Candler, *op. cit.,* XXIII, 190).

[31] *Slave Songs,* p. 46.

was over in Liberia, saying, "Come unto me, all ye that labour and are heavy laden, and I will give you rest." This was the verse of the spiritual which read: *"Do, Becca Lawton, come to me yonder, etc."* The "yonder" of this song places it with the other "yonder" spirituals of the first quarter of the nineteenth century. The chorus and verses were repeated to suit the whim of the singer.

> [Chorus:]
> Rain *fall and* wet Becca Lawton (or All de member, etc.),
> Oh! [32]
> Rain *fall and* wet Becca Lawton,
> Oh!
> Brudder (or *We* [Us] all, Believer, etc.) cry holy!

> 1. Been (or Beat, Bent, Rack) back holy,
>   I *must* come slow*ly;*
>   Oh!
>   Brudder cry holy!

> 2. *Do,* Becca Lawton, come to me yonder.

> 3. *Say, brudder Tony, what shall I do now?*

> 4. *Beat back holy, and rock salvation.*

Later the song lost its primary significance. Its rhythm was used by rowers, and its chorus had such words as

> *Sun come and dry all de member.*[33]

After 1823 most of the Liberian colonists sailed from southern ports.[34] The departures of colonization ships, bearing mostly southern Negroes, were very dramatic. Some of the farewell songs of the emigrants have been preserved in Negro churches as parting spirituals. One song from the southeastern slave states was as follows:

> *O* fare you well, my brudder,
> [F]are you well by de grace of God,

[32] This "Oh" is held for two measures of 2/4 time, as many beats as are allotted to the preceding line. These notes seem like poking fun.

[33] *Slave Songs,* p. 21.

[34] *Report of the American Colonization Society,* IX (1826), 2 f.; X (1827), 33; XI (1828), 34; Archibald Alexander, *A History of Colonization on the Western Coast of Africa* (Philadelphia, 1846), pp. 224, 227.

For I'*se* gwinen home;
I'*se* gwinen home, my Lord,
I'*se* gwinen home.

Massa Jesus gib me a little broom,
For to sweep my heart clean;
Sweep 'em clean by de grace of God,
An' glory in my soul.[35]

The parting songs of Negroes who sailed to Africa conditioned the remaining slaves for colonization. These people compared the difficulty of securing manumissions for expatriation to the deliverance of Daniel from the den of lions. This early concept about Daniel was heard in a Negro song in Florida during Civil War days:

You call yourself church-member,
You hold your head so high,
You praise God with your glitt'ring tongue,
But you leave all your heart behind.
O my Lord *delivered* [saved] Daniel,
O [my Lord saved] Daniel, *O Daniel,*
O my Lord *delivered* [saved] Daniel,
O *why not* [Lord] *deliver* [save] me *too.*[36]

During the Civil War Negroes on the Port Royal Islands were understood to sing that Daniel locked the lion's jaw, though the thought was not clearly expressed. Their song, however, was saying that Negroes could afford to wait until opportunity came for them to go home.

1. Wai', poor Daniel,
   He *lean* on de Lord'*s* side;
   (*Say*) Daniel rock de lion joy,
   Lean on de Lord'*s* side.

In this song of "poor Daniel," which is contemporary with spirituals about "poor sinner," "poor Rosy," and "poor Becca Lawton," Daniel was given the place which belonged to Samson. The freedom version of this, "Who Is on the Lord's Side?" was sung two verses at a time.

[35] *Slave Songs,* pp. 47 f.
[36] *Ibid.,* p. 94; Allen (comp.), *op. cit.,* p. xli.

2. (*Say*) *De golden chain* (*or Band*) *to ease him down.*

3. *De silver spade to dig his grave;*
   He lean, etc.[37]

By late 1824 the interest of Negroes was waning in African colonization. A transport ship had sailed for Africa in January, 1824; the next one did not arrive there until more than twelve months later. Some slaves imagined that they were to blame for not being transported home. They used their farewell songs for parting hymns at their religious gatherings. One of the Negroes of Charleston, South Carolina, asked the Lord, meaning, perhaps, both God and his earthly master, to make him willing to wait like "poor Daniel."

> Lord, make me *more patient* (*or holy, loving, peaceful, etc.*) [wait],
> Lord, make me *more patient* [wait],
> Lord, make me *more patient* [wait],
> *Un*til *we* [us] meet again;
> *Patient, patient, patient,*
> *Until we meet again.*[38]

Such a spiritual may have been the genesis of the familiar hymn, "God Be with You 'Til We Meet Again." [39]

In such an emergency Negroes began about 1824 to implore Moses to come over from Africa to the North American shores and to work another one of his miracles by delivering Negroes from slavery. Now,

[37] *Slave Songs,* p. 100; Allen (comp.), *op. cit.,* p. xlii.

[38] *Slave Songs,* p. 52; Allen (comp.), *op. cit.,* p. xl.

[39] According to *The Methodist Hymnal* (New York, 1905), p. 553, Jeremiah Eaves Rankin (1828–1904) wrote the words of this hymn. Yet he was not born when the genesis of the above spiritual was sung by Negroes. George Pullen Jackson, *Spiritual Folk Songs of Early America* (New York, [1937]), p. 207, credited a song, entitled "O Brother Be Faithful," appearing in the *Wesleyan Psalmist* (1842) but quoted from the *Revivalist* (1868, 1872), with being the inspiration of this hymn both in "tune and words." In 1842 Rankin was only fourteen years of age. Yet he was sixty-one years old when "God Be with You 'Til We Meet Again" was published among his *Hymns Pro Patria and Other Hymns, Christian and Humanitarian* (New York, 1889), pp. 131 ff. In that very year that distinguished Congregational minister became the president of Howard University, the federal school in Washington, D.C., which trained Negroes (Dwight O. W. Holmes, "Fifty Years of Howard University," *Journal of Negro History,* III [October, 1918], 374 ff.).

"don't get lost," Moses, they sang over and over again. To this primary thought more than one Negro added that he, too, was a child of God who knew that Negro emancipation was just. God was pleading that cause for Negroes by sitting down in Africa, answering black people's prayers. So "come across," Moses, and "Stretch out your rod." This evolution of ideas which had come with the years eventually lost its significance, and Judy, Aaron, or the name of any other Negro who was present was substituted for "Moses" in the song. Its singing was so popular that minstrels circulated a copy, entitled "Git Along, John." [40]

> [Chorus:]
> Come along, Moses (or Judy, Aaron), don't get lost,
> [Come along, Moses,] don't get lost, *don't get lost,*
> Come along, Moses, don't get lost,
> *We are* [Us be] the people (or Children) of God.

> 1. *We have a just God to plead-a our cause, to plead-a our cause, to plead-a our cause.*
>   *We have a just God to plead-a our cause,*
>   *We are the people of God.*

> 2. *He sits in the Heaven and he answers prayer.*

> 3. *Stretch out your rod and come across.*[41]

For the immediate present slaves were spared speculation as to why bitter slavery had been fastened upon them. Instead they gossiped about what they overheard was happening in Liberia. Although the American Colonization Society had attempted to select only deeply religious (and thus pacific) Negro emigrants, a colonizing missionary preacher in Liberia, Lott Cary, led his fellows in mutiny in 1823 and 1824 because the colonists were denied their expected home rule, for which they had often petitioned the Society's slave-holding Board of Managers.[42] The Board got the government of the

---

[40] *The New Negro Forget-Me-Not Songster . . . as Sung by Sable Harmonists* (Cincinnati, [n.d.]), pp. 67 f.

[41] *Slave Songs,* p. 104; Allen (comp.), *op. cit.,* p. xliii.

[42] Miles Mark Fisher, "Lott Cary, the Colonizing Missionary," *Journal of Negro History,* VII (October, 1922), 397–401; "Proceedings of the Board of Managers, American Colonization Society," I, 173 f., 176, 179 f., 180 ff., MS, Library of Congress; *African Repository,* I (1825), 24 f.; III (1827), 78.

United States to send the warship *Porpoise* to Liberia. Happily, Ralph Randolph Gurley, secretary of the Society, was on board. Disembarking in August, 1824, he soon comprehended the situation. When he left after eight days, the Liberian colonists had their first constitution, which provided for elective officers, the highest being vice-agent. Everybody was happy; no guns were fired.[43]

In the latter months of 1824 or early in 1825 when slaves in the southeastern states heard distant rumblings of what had happened in Liberia, many of them wished that they had been there. It was necessary for their safety that the songs of that "wish" should be veiled. Years afterward, during the Civil War, Negroes were still singing the *"too* pretty" spiritual, wishing they had been there:

> O my sister light de lamp, and de lamp light de road;
> I wish I been dere for to hearde Jordan roll.[44]

It was not long before this song, "The White Marble Stone," recorded verses about every person who was present:

1. Sister Dolly (or Believer, Patty, etc.) light the lamp,
      and the lamp light the road,
   And I wish I been there for to yedde Jordan roll.

2. O the city light the lamp, the white man he will sold,
   And I wish I been there, etc.

3. O the white marble stone, and the white marble stone.[45]

When the primary concept of the "wish" had lost its historic meaning entirely, a Negro around Port Royal lay sick with fever and headache. These maladies were enough to make him "wish" that he was in the heavenly kingdom instead of in Africa, sitting by the side of his Lord.

> O my body*'s racked* wid de fever,
> My head *rack'd* wid de pain I hab,

[43] *Constitution, Government and Digest of the Laws of Liberia, As Confirmed and Established by the Board of Managers of the American Colonization Society, May 23, 1825* (Washington, 1825); Gurley, *op. cit.,* p. 215; *Report of the American Colonization Society,* VIII (1825), II, 12, 13; *American Missionary Register,* VI (1825), 142, 199.

[44] *Slave Songs,* p. 42.   [45] *Ibid.,* p. 42.

> I wish I was in de kingdom,
> A-settin' on de side ob de Lord.[46]

At first slaves wished that they had been in Liberia during the mutiny because they would gladly have laid down their lives in what they believed a righteous war. Fighting to make that country right for its people would have been progress, that is, climbing Jacob's ladder, and, being engaged in this holy war, they would have merited "de starry Crown." This is expressed in the song which follows:

> [1.] My mudder, you follow Jesus,
> My *sister* [mudder], you follow Jesus,
> My *brudder* [mudder], you follow Jesus,
> To fight *un*til I die

> [Chorus:]
> I wish I been dere (yonder),
> To climb Jacob's ladder,
> I wish I been dere (yonder),
> To wear de starry crown.

> [2. My sister, you follow Jesus, etc.]

> [3. My brudder, you follow Jesus, etc.] [47]

These "wish" songs heard on the Port Royal Islands, South Carolina, must have provoked a number of broad smiles. Some were on the faces of the singers who were saying something which their masters or overseers did not understand. Others were those of white persons who saw slaves dancing around to something seemingly unintelligent. It was funny, as one traveler said, because "there is nothing more futile, more completely stupid, than a negro's ideas. He will talk for two hours about a musquito, about the buttons on his coat, or the length of his nails." [48]

So about 1824 and 1825 the Jacob's ladder theme was heard in Negro spirituals. After 1865 Jacob's ladder was combined with the

[46] *Ibid.*, p. 33.

[47] *Ibid.*, p. 29; Allen (comp.), *op. cit.*, p. xl. The stanza which the collectors printed with "mudder," "sister," and "brudder" was three separate stanzas according to the way in which the song was sung later.

[48] M. de Grandfort, *The New World*, trans. Edward C. Wharton (New Orleans, 1855), p. 56.

antebellum door-to-door theme, with exact Biblical information about the mote and the beam, to make a medley. Collectors said that the tune appeared to be borrowed from "And Are Ye Sure the News Is True?" but they retained the song because the tune was "so much changed," and the words were "so characteristic":

1. *I saw de beam in my sister's (or Titty Peggy, Brudder Mosey, etc.) eye,*
   Can't saw de beam in mine;
   You'd better lef' your sister door,
   Go keep your own door clean.

2. *And I had a mighty battle like-a Jacob and de angel,*
   Jacob, time of old;
   I didn't 'tend to lef' 'em go
   Till Jesus bless my soul.

3. *And blessèd me, and blessèd my,*
   And blessèd all my soul;
   I didn't 'tend to lef' 'em go
   Till Jesus bless my soul.[49]

For two years, beginning in 1823, not a word was heard directly from the Liberian colonists. Then, in 1825, the censorship on African news was removed.[50] The recipients of mail from Africa called the Negroes together, probably to decipher the letters. Negroes on the Port Royal Islands were still singing in freedom that they had heard directly "from heaven" in 1825:

[Chorus:]
Hurry (or Travel) on, my weary soul,
And I yearde from heaven to-day,
Hurry on, my weary (or My brudder, Brudder Jacob, Sister Mary) soul,
And I yearde from heaven to-day.

1. *My sin is forgiven and my soul set free,*
   And I yearde from heaven to-day,
   My sin is forgiven, and my soul set free,
   And I yearde from heaven to-day.

2. *A baby born in Bethlehem,*
   And I yearde, etc.

[49] *Slave Songs,* pp. 17 f.; Allen (comp.), *op. cit.,* p. xxxix.
[50] *Latter Day Luminary,* VI, 115 f., 312.

3. *De trumpet sound in de oder bright land (or World).*

4. *My name is called and I must go.*

5. De bell *is a-ringin'* [rings] in de oder bright *world* [land].[51]

This song is extremely important even though each verse except the last is a late addition. The first verse preserved the conversion formula of Negro secret meetings,[52] but its conclusion about the "free" soul suggests emancipation. Likewise, the exact Biblical information that Jesus was born at Bethlehem bespeaks Civil War missionary teachings.[53] The trumpet idea and African colonization reached their climaxes about 1831 in the aftermath of Nat Turner's rebellion. The "oder bright land" is a characteristic Negro expression of the first quarter of the nineteenth century.

That actual letters had at last been received from Liberia was too much for some slaves to believe. They had doubted that any message would ever come directly from Africa. A spiritual dealing with this situation came from Negroes on the Port Royal Islands in 1867. In it an original singer argued with the faithless that he had heard from heaven and concluded that only the devil would dispute his testimony. He sang that in Liberia all a Negro had to do was to sit down. He knew a Negro who was doing just that. A religious revival broke out in Liberia after the new constitution was ratified,[54] but the song may have referred to a later revival which was contemporary with the Civil War. The verse mentioning the home of a Mr. Hawley in Paradise undoubtedly complimented the kind James R. Hawley, colonel of the Seventh Connecticut Volunteers, who was stationed at St. Augustine, Florida, during the Civil War.[55]

> [Chorus:]
> *Good news, member, good news, member,*
> *Don't you mind what Satan say;*
> *Good news, member, good news,*
> *And I hearde from heav'n to-day.*

[51] *Slave Songs,* p. 2; Allen (comp.), *op. cit.,* p. xxxix.

[52] I. W. Brinckerhoff, *The Freedman's Book of Christian Doctrine* (Philadelphia, 1864), p. 13.

[53] *Ibid.*   [54] Gurley, *op. cit.,* p. 53.

[55] Brinckerhoff, *op. cit.,* pp. 80, 85.

1. *My brudder have a seat and I so glad,*
   Good news, member, good news;
   My brudder have a seat and I so glad,
   And I hearde from heav'n to-day.

2. *Mr. Hawley have a home in Paradise.*

3. *Archangel bring baptizing down.*[56]

Beginning about 1825, the American Colonization Society enjoyed its greatest success. Numerous individuals including state legislators endorsed the Society, along with local and national bodies of Presbyterians, Episcopalians, Congregationalists, Baptists, Dutch Reformed members, and Methodists. More than ever before thanks were extended to "the Rev. Clergy throughout the United States for their active benevolence in advancing the views of the Society." [57] No one could misunderstand its expressed views, namely, "to the people of the North it has endeavored to exhibit itself as most humane and disinterested and to those of the South as utterly opposed to any measure which might infringe upon the rights of property or disturb the peace." [58]

Slaves knew that the Society was not removing a large number of Negroes to Africa. From 1823 to 1827 only one ship a year took colonists to Liberia, except in 1826 when two ships sailed, one of these vessels going from Boston with Rhode Island Negroes. Southern Negroes felt a severe spiritual strain. They had begged Moses to "come across" and perform another one of his miracles, but it had been all to no avail. In sheer desperation they added Jesus to their already full pantheon of worthies. Him they pathetically entreated to "come *along* [across]" and lead Negroes back to Africa. As in the "Hurry (or Travel) on" spiritual, also of 1825, they imagined that they heard the church bell ringing in Liberia as it rang for convocation in the United States. They later likened themselves to those who knew which road to take to get "home." A singer from the Port Royal

[56] *Slave Songs,* pp. 97 f.; Allen (comp.), *op. cit.,* p. xli.

[57] *African Repository,* I (1825), 5–7; cf. *Christian Spectator,* VII (August 1, 1825), 405–408; *Report of the American Colonization Society,* V (1822), 8; X (1827), 4.

[58] *African Repository,* I (1825), 225; *Report of the American Colonization Society,* IX (1826), 126 f.

Islands said that in spite of their Christian worship Jesus just sat "on de water*side"* and paid them no attention:

> Heaven bell a-ring, *I know de road,*
> Heaven bell a-ring, *I know de road,*
> Heaven bell a-ring, *I know de road,*
> Jesus sittin' on de water*side.*
>
> *Do* come *along* [across], *do let us go,*
> *Do* come *along* [across], *do let us go,*
> *Do* come *along* [across], *do let us go,*
> Jesus sittin' on de water*side.*[59]

A singer from the neighboring state of North Carolina resented this slander upon his deity. He sang out that the angels were defeating African colonization. Hence the term "bright" as applied to "angels" is omitted, although the adjective was a descriptive colonization word. Other terms in the spirituals about the first quarter of the nineteenth century are "poor sinner" and "Mary." The singer desired Mary to accompany him to Africa, where they both would join "the social band," which meeting was peaceful. Perhaps "Aunty" was a pseudo kinsperson and was a contribution of this spiritual. In this connection Mungo Park noticed that eighteenth-century Africans frequently spoke of one another as blood relatives.

> *Bright* [De] angels on the water,
> *Hovering* [Sittin'] by the light;
> Poor sinner stand in the dark*ness,*
> *And* [Him] can['] *not* see the light.
> I want Aunty Mary (or Brother David) for to go with me,
> I want Aunty Mary for to go with me,
> I want Aunty Mary for to go with me,
> To join the social band.[60]

So another Negro from the Port Royal Islands included the name "Jehovah" in his song. Maybe the trouble was that deity had not been called by the right name. Genesis 22:8 said "God will provide." Including words in contemporary use such as "hallelujah," "dunno," and "weary," he rang out:

[59] *Slave Songs,* pp. 28 f.; Allen (comp.), *op. cit.,* p. xl.
[60] *Slave Songs,* p. 105; Allen (comp.), *op. cit.,* p. xliii.

Jehoviah, Hallelujah,
De Lord *is* perwide,
Jehoviah, Hallelujah,
De Lord *is* perwide.

De foxes have-a hole, An' de birdies have-a nest,
De Son of Man he dunno (or hanno)
    where to lay de weary head.[61]

In an early "Ship of Zion" spiritual, a slave singer from North Carolina wondered whether he should ever be freed to go sailing over to Africa:

1. *Don't you* see that ship a-sailin'
   [See that ship] a-sailin', *a sailin',*
   Don't you see that ship a-sailin',
   Gwine over to the Promised Land?

   [Chorus:]
   I asked my Lord, *shall* I *ever* be *the one,*
   [I asked my Lord] *shall* I *ever* be *the one,*
       shall I ever be the one,
   [I asked my Lord I be,]
   To go sailin', *sailin', sailin', sailin',*
   Gwine over to the Promised Land? [.]

2. *She sails like she is heavy loaded.*

3. *King Jesus is the Captain.*

4. *The Holy Ghost is the Pilot.*[62]

Such an elaborate song presupposes a simple original, which is probably this spiritual of the nineteenth-century "yonder" days:

    Sail, O believer, sail,
    Sail over yonder;

    Sail, O my brudder, sail,
    Sail over yonder.[63]

Colonizationists were everywhere alert to the problems of slavery. William Cullen Bryant and other editors of leading North American

---

[61] *Slave Songs,* p. 2; Allen (comp.), *op. cit.,* p. xxxix.
[62] *Slave Songs,* pp. 102 f.; Allen (comp.), *op. cit.,* p. xliii.
[63] *Slave Songs,* p. 24.

periodicals helped to make a case for African colonization.[64] American authors likewise defended it, as for example, in "The Negro's Dream," apparently the work of a white: [65]

> 'Twas then, from around and above,
>   Rich harmony fell on my ear,
> And a voice sung of Freedom and Love:
>   It was happiness only to hear.
> And it sung of an African shore,
>   Where black men can also be free—
> When I heard that, I listened the more,
>   For I thought that the voice was to me.[66]

In Brazil the Portuguese canonized "the miraculous San Bento, Protector of Angola," for promoting an effectual scheme for "keeping slaves in subjection," [67] and in the United States literary persons wrote in defense of African colonization.

Proslavery people in North America tried their hands at making "spirituals." Even in dialect their songs were inferior to Negro creations. A typical one, preserved by Fisk University, was:

> My ship is on the ocean,
> My ship is on the ocean.
> My ship is on the ocean,
> Poor sinner, fare you well.

> 1. I'm going away to see the good, old Daniel;
>   I'm going away to see my Lord.

> 2. I'm going away to see the weeping Mary;
>   I'm going away to see my Lord.

> 3. Oh! don't you want to live in that bright glory?
>   Oh! don't you want to go to see my Lord? [68]

---

[64] *African Repository,* I (1825), 6; II (1826), 320 ff.

[65] "The African's Dream" was written by a Miss W. Clark and was sung to the tune of "Emigrants' Lament" (George W. Clark, *The Harp of Freedom* [New York, 1856], p. 238).

[66] *African Repository,* I, 96.

[67] Thomas Ewbank, *Life in Brazil* (New York, 1856), pp. 289, 292, 352.

[68] [Seward], *op. cit.,* p. 50; G. D. Pike, *The Jubilee Singers, and Their Campaign for Twenty Thousand Dollars* (Boston, 1873), p. 205; Marsh, *op. cit.,* p. 165; Seward and White, *op. cit.,* p. 50.

Strangely enough, this song called the Atlantic an "ocean." Previously, that body of water had been likened to the Red Sea, which Moses divided and which Negroes wanted to cross to Africa, to the Jordan River, or to just a hill which an old lady could climb, but it was never an "ocean."

This song pretended to know what those in a ship on an ocean were saying. For the first time colonizationists defined a "poor sinner": a free Negro who did not care to go to Africa. To the colonizationists it did not matter that Daniel had died centuries before, if, indeed, he had ever lived, and that weeping Mary was likewise symbolic of a people. Daniel was now in Africa, "good" and "old," too. Weeping Mary was also in the land of "that bright glory," where it was implied that she did not have to weep any more. Both of these characters actually were walking around in Africa. In addition, the Lord Himself walked the streets—in Africa. The song referred to the Lord three times. Free Negroes, "Oh! don't you want to go?"

This pseudo spiritual was, nevertheless, significant because at the height of African colonization, around 1825, it represented a song manufactured by colonizationists out of the familiar concepts and words of Negroes. Negroes actually were singing about colonization ships upon the Atlantic, "poor sinner," "Fare you well," "good," "old," and "bright glory," but not all in one song.

It must have evoked smiles from the colonizationists to have heard slaves, after being thus primed, sing with uncritical faith that their worthies were in Africa. Through the years Negroes added the question why African colonization worked in their behalf so slowly. Devotional freedom medleys combined this thought and parts of other antebellum spirituals with Scripture to say that persons of Holy Writ were in Africa. These songs differed environmentally. From the northern seaboard slave states came one example:

[Chorus:]
John sawr-O, John sawr-O,
John saw de holy number (member) settin' on de golden altar!

1. It's a little while longer yere below, yere below, yere below,
It's a little while longer yere below,
Before de Lamb of God!

2. And home to Jesus we will go, we will go, etc.;
   We are de people of de Lord.
   John sawr-O, etc.

3. Dere's a golden slipper in de heavens for you, etc.,
   Before de lamb of God.

4. I wish I'*d* been dere when prayer begun, etc.

5. To see my Jesus about my sins, etc.

6. Then home to glory we will go, etc.[69]

In North Carolina Negroes sang:

> Oh John, John, de holy member,
>   Sittin' on de golden ban'.
> O worldly, worldly, let him be,
>   Let him be, let him be;
> Worldly, worldly, let him be,
>   Sittin' on de golden ban'.[70]

A South Carolina version around the Port Royal Islands was:

> John, John, wid de holy order (or John, John, de holy Baptist),
> Sittin' on de golden order;
> John, John, wid de holy order,
> Sittin' on de golden order;
> John, John, wid de holy order,
> Sittin' on de golden order,
> To view de promised land.
> O Lord, I weep, I mourn,
> Why don't you move so slow?
> I'm a huntin' for some guardian angel
> Gone along before.
> Mary and Marta, feed my lamb (or Paul and Silas bound in jail),
>   feed my lamb, feed my lamb;
> Simon Peter, feed my lamb, a-sittin' on de golden order.[71]

The words of the variant heard at Hiltonhead Island were:

> I went down sing polka, and I ax him for my Saviour;
> I wonder de angel told me Jesus gone along before.

---

[69] *Slave Songs*, p. 77.   [70] *Ibid.*, p. 17.   [71] *Ibid.*, pp. 16 f.

I mourn, I pray, although you move so slow;
I wonder, etc.[72]

The task of the colonizationists was yet incomplete. They had to supply Negroes with actual ships on the ocean, and they did so. Nine transport ships went to Liberia under the auspices of the American Colonization Society between 1827 and 1830.[73]

Thus the Society took the necessary steps to demonstrate its claim to humanitarianism. Its first development had been along the lines of benevolence revived during the Great Awakening of religion. Economic, political, and social motives soon colored this conservative movement of race relations. Notwithstanding, its evolution was in conformity with what Negroes wanted, and its permanent organization to send Negroes outside the United States provided that it be "with their consent." Richard Allen and William Lloyd Garrison should not be considered interpreters of the aspirations of Negroes to the neglect of colonizationists like Lott Cary and Jehudi Ashmun. Nineteenth-century North Americans were persuaded that free Negroes could not become better than they were in the United States. Free Negroes as well as slaves were misrepresented. Yet only a few slaves were emancipated for colonization. All of the first emigrants to Liberia were denied expected home rule. Religion finally reasserted itself even though in the process colonizationists attempted to make Negro spirituals.

[72] *Ibid.,* p. 17.
[73] "Register of Emigrants, 1835–1853," inside cover, MS, Library of Congress.

65

1800 **4** 1831

"STEAL AWAY"

Steal away, steal away,
Steal away to Jesus,
Steal away, steal away home,
I hain't got long to stay here.[1]

SECRET meetings were convened by songs. Negroes stole away
from numerous plantations to African cult meetings just as Nat Turner of insurrectionary notoriety convened his companions by the
ironical singing of "Steal Away." [2] The external evidence of Turner's
revolt against slavery coincides with the internal evidence of this
song. He knew that should he be caught meeting with other Negroes
the oft-repeated burden of the song would be true: "I hain't got long
to stay here." Yet, he was in a quandary how else to act when his
personal Lord was calling him like a patrol officer with a trumpet by
"the thunder," "by the lightening," "by green trees" bending at will,
and by signs of the judgment. He who sang so sweetly stood
"*a*-tremblin' " as he understood full well that he was a "poor sinner,"
to say the least. The saddened melody of the song bespoke that its
author was melancholy about beginning his slave revolt at the house
of his kind master.[3] The circumstances all point to Nat Turner of

[1] [Seward], *op. cit.*, p. 28; Pike, *op. cit.*, p. 187.

[2] Thomas W. Talley, *Negro Folk Rhymes* (New York, 1923), pp. 30 f.

[3] Cf. [Thomas R. Gray], *The Confessions of Nat Turner, the Leader of the
Late Insurrection in Southampton, Va.* (Baltimore, 1831), *passim.*

Southampton County, Virginia, as the author of "Steal Away," about 1825, the time of his call to be a prophet.

The African cult had been legislated against since colonial times. Maryland joined Virginia in outlawing it in 1695, but neither outlawry nor soldiery prevented it from having hemispheric significance. In the mid-seventeenth century thousands of Negro slaves in Jamaica decided upon disobedience to Britain, fled to the mountains, and defied Cromwell and the Governor and Council of Jamaica.[4] Two centuries later Jamaican Negroes were heard singing of the cruelty of some masters, whom they opposed with militancy.[5] Today Negroes in Jamaica remember an African cult song which told about "One morning so soon." [6] Once in Dutch Guiana, South America, all but one of eight rendezvous for secret meetings were discovered after Negroes had murdered people and had plundered plantations. Soldiers hoped to make the captive slave leaders tell of the remaining secret place. They treated one of the leaders named Amsterdam in such a way that "humanity" shuddered, but he would tell nothing. He chose to die, as was said, "with a degree of fortitude and heroism worth a better cause." [7]

In Haiti secret meetings of Negroes flourished under the leadership of priests, who told Negro devotees that, should they be killed they would be revived on the other side of the Atlantic.[8] During the Haitian revolution under Toussaint L'Ouverture, the Negro who withstood Napoleon, Negroes marched with a band whose musicians played tambourines, shells, and trumpets, and they had sorcerers who sang that they were invulnerable. They carried bamboo and powder of dust for cannons and long strings of beef to turn the enemy

[4] [Edward Doyley], *A Narrative of the Great Success God Hath Pleased to Give His Highness Forces in Jamaica, against the King of Spain's Forces* . . . (London, 1658; photostat in the John Carter Brown Library); Dallas, *op. cit.,* I, *passim;* Thomas Wentworth Higginson, *Travellers and Outlaws: Episodes in American History* (Boston, 1889), *passim.*

[5] Matthew Gregory Lewis, *Journal of a West Indian Proprietor, Kept during a Residence in the Island of Jamaica* (London, 1834), pp. 228, 322 f.

[6] Martha Warren Beckwith, *Black Roadways: A Study of Jamaican Folk Life* (Chapel Hill, 1929), pp. 192, 196.

[7] Pinckard, *op. cit.,* I, 370–379.

[8] Thomas Madiou, *Historie d'Haiti: années 1492–1799* (2nd ed., Port-au-Prince, 1922), I, 41.

balls.[9] Toussaint was called L'Ouverture from the office of doorkeeper which he performed in his voodoo cult.

All of the ritual of this secret cult was composed of songs and fables learned by Negroes from infancy.[10] Only men were included in those convocations. Women and men held secret meetings separately as in Africa.

Firsthand information on this African cult in North America during the nineteenth century is preserved in *Slave Songs of the United States*. No song, however, was preserved from the Gabriel Prosser plotters against Richmond, Virginia, who at the turn of the century sang in jail as they had done in their frequent secret sessions in the woods.[11] The "Deep River" spiritual came from a slave of the nineteenth century who knew of the general racial disturbances of the United States.

In 1823 Denmark Vesey of Charleston, and thirty-four Negro men, all slaves except himself, were hanged. First nine and then three other Negroes were expatriated. Finally twenty-one more were sentenced by the Charleston City Council to be transported out of the United States. All of them were accused of plotting in secret meetings the annihilation of all the white people of the city.[12] A spiritual based on a well-known Methodist hymn, "Ain't I glad I got out of the wilderness" presented the arguments that may have been used by Vesey and his fellow plotters. It repeated as a chorus the view that by going into the wilderness the Lord would take away the sin of the world, which was slavery. While many persons were urging Negroes to wait for African colonization, Vesey was determined to wait on the Lord by militant protests from Negroes. The rumor that weeping Mary was in Africa where she no longer had to weep was not the truth. Weeping Mary was still at large within the United States. If she who symbolized the sufferings of Negroes wanted relief, then let her "go in de wilderness." Slaves who weep and mourn and who are grieved and disillusioned, join those whom you know, even

---

[9] *Ibid.*, pp. 246 f.

[10] *Ibid.*, p. 3.

[11] William Pitt Palmer, *Calendar of Virginia State Papers and Other Manuscripts, 1652–1781* (Richmond, 1875), IX, 144 f.; T. W. Higginson, "Gabriel's Defeat," *Atlantic Monthly*, X (September, 1862), 338.

[12] *Negro Plot* (Boston, 1822), pp. 31, 36, 47 f.

church members of the community, down at that secret place where "Jesus a waitin' to meet you," the song said.

[Chorus:]
I wait *upo*n de Lord,
I wait *upo*n de Lord,
I wait *upo*n de Lord, *my God, Who* take away de sin of the world.

1. *If* you want to find Jesus, go in the wilderness,
   [You want to find Jesus,] Go in the wilderness,
      go in the wilderness,
   Mournin' brudder, [You want to find Jesus,]
      go in the wilderness,
   I (or O), wait *upo*n de Lord.

   3. You want to be *a Christian* [Christun].

   4. You want to get religion.

   5. *If you spec' to be converted.*

   6. O weepin' Mary.

   7. *'Flicted sister.*

   8. *Say, ain't* you *a* member?

   9. *Half-done Christian.*

   10. *Come, backslider.*

   11. *Baptist member.*

   12. O seek, brudder Bristol.

   13. Jesus a waitin' to meet you in de wilderness.[13]

One reason for the condemnation of the secret meetings was that they were African rather than American. It is noteworthy that one of the leaders in the Vesey plot, Monday Gell, bore the name of a day of the week as do many Africans.[14]

Peter Poyas, a class leader of the local Methodist Church at Charleston, was an organizer of the plot. If in the song the name of Bristol is a pseudonym for Poyas, the spiritual continued an African custom of having a pseudonymous person for an actual one. The

[13] *Slave Songs,* p. 14; Allen (comp.), *op. cit.,* p. xxix.
[14] Mary H. Kingsley, *West African Studies* (2nd ed., London, 1901), p. 147.

Negroes in the plot found justification for their conduct by comparing themselves to the oppressed Israelites and by reading their Bibles at Zechariah 14:1-3 and Joshua 6:21. Said one slave to another: "Many have joined, and if you will go with me, I will show you the man who has the list of names, and who will take yours down." [15]

Negro cultists in many instances acted as though they were invulnerable. A picture of one of their banners in Africa, drawn by a slave trader of the eighteenth century, shows the cultist carrying a large grigri bag. In it were charms to preserve one from hurt or harm. If Negroes with these bags were hurt, they attributed it to a neglected sacrifice or to some other nonsensical cause.[16] One West African secret society carried its banner to its new home. Jemmy's insurrectionists in South Carolina in the eighteenth century and the Vesey plotters of that same area in the nineteenth century were reckless because of dependence upon their banners. Jack Pritchard, alias Gullah Jack, a native Angola conjurer and physician, told the Vesey cultists that a crab claw in their mouths would make them immune to wounds. His sentence of death on July 9, 1822, carried this rebuke: "Jack Pritchard, . . . you represented yourself as invulnerable; that you could neither be taken nor destroyed, and that all who fought under your banner would be invincible. . . . Your boasted charms have not preserved yourself and of course could not protect others."

Negro slaves sometimes accepted Christianity because Jesus was declared to be a guarantee against all hurt, harm, or danger. Since the heavenly Jesus had been to earth and had died in the place of man, insurrectionists reasoned, poor sinners would not have to die at all. This thought was preserved in a spiritual whose "done" indicates its Virginia origin.[17]

[15] T. W. Higginson, "Denmark Vesey," *Atlantic Monthly,* VII (June, 1861), 729, 731 f., 739; cf. William Wells Brown, *The Negro in the American Rebellion, His Heroism and His Fidelity* (Boston, 1867), p. 16.

[16] Nicholas Owen, *Journal of a Slave-Dealer:* "A View of Some Remarkable Axcedents in the Life of Nics. Owen on the Coast of Africa and America from the Year 1746 to the Year 1757," ed. Eveline Martin (London, 1930), Plate X, 50; also, Butt-Thompson, *op. cit.,* p. 65.

[17] Higginson, *Army Life in a Black Regiment,* p. 202.

[Chorus:]
O de Lamb done been down here an' died,
De Lamb done been down here an' died,
O de Lamb done been down here an' died,
Sinner won't die no mo'.

1. *I wonder what bright angels, angels, angels,*
   I wonder what bright angels,
   De robes all ready now.

2. *O see dem ships come a-sailing, sailing, sailing,*
   O see dem ships come a-sailing,
   De robes all ready now.[18]

More than one song preserved the Negro's belief in the divine protection of cultists. For instance, in a spiritual using words generally associated with "John Brown's Body" [19]—a spiritual which is known to have been sung at Augusta, Georgia, after the Civil War—Negro participants in secret meetings declared that they did not care if their shouting attracted the attention of their masters.

1. Shout on, chil'en, you never die;
   Glory hallelu!
   You in de Lord, an' de Lord in you;
   Glory hallelu!

2. *Shout an' pray both night an' day;*
   How can you die, you in de Lord?

3. *Come on, chil'en, let's go home;*
   O I'm so glad you're in de Lord.[20]

The spiritual return to earth of those who had died was retained in the religion of Negroes [21] even after they had come in contact with Christianity. It is not certain that the African Negro believed

[18] *Slave Songs,* p. 85; Allen (comp.), *op. cit.,* p. xli.
[19] Brinckerhoff MS, p. 221.
[20] *Slave Songs,* p. 60; Allen (comp.), *op. cit.,* p. xl.
[21] [Simon Berington], *The Life and Adventures of Sig. Guadentio di Lucca* (1st Am. ed., Norwich, 1796), p. 95; A. B. Ellis, *op. cit.,* p. 149; Edwin W. Smith, *African Belief and Christian Faith* (London, 1936), p. 46; Diedrich Westermann, *Africa and Christianity* (London, 1937), pp. 80, 94.

in future rewards and punishments. Mungo Park thought that Man-
dingo Negroes held to this, but William Bosman, Diedrich Westermann, and Edwin W. Smith maintained a contrary view. In America
Negroes preferred belief in African reincarnation to Christian im-
mortality. The Biblical account of Lazarus who lived again upon this
earth was particularly appealing to American slaves. Women around
the Port Royal Islands, South Carolina, enjoyed singing about the
ideal death of Lazarus:

> I want to (Titty 'Ritta) die like-a Lazarus die,
> [I want to] Die like-a Lazarus die;
> I want to die like-a Lazarus die,
> like-a Lazarus die, like-a Lazarus die.[22]

By the time of the Civil War the Negroes of the Islands had been
taught that the death of Jesus was the ideal and supreme one, although they still sang about Lazarus. In America as in Africa a de-
cent, even an elaborate, burial was the end of living. Since Jesus was
given burial by a friend, a singer from the Port Royal Islands asked
his overlord, in song, to arrange burial for him. He felt that his request was simple enough, for he was not seeking one of the iron
coffins of the day, but suggesting that no coffin at all would do, according to burial customs in some parts of Africa.[23] It would be
enough just to stretch his body and arms out in the grave. To an antebellum Negro, death was "er shades and er darkness; hit's like er
spider's web, 'cept 'ez hit's black." [24] According to this singer, death
was a little man who went from cabin door to cabin door taking
names. Not knowing that death was natural among those who had
fatal diseases, who were aged, who met with fatal accidents, or who
imposed it on themselves, the singer was simply certain that death
enrolled recruits from among those who were crippled up by the slave
system.[25] He was still alive for his divine destiny, namely, to hold
secret meetings, to "pray." Yet he felt that his end was near:

[22] *Slave Songs,* p. 98; Allen (comp.), *op. cit.,* p. xlii.

[23] Park, *Travels* (1810), pp. 859 ff.

[24] Eli Shepard, "Superstitions of the Negro," *Cosmopolitan,* V (March,
1888), 47.

[25] Higginson, *Army Life in a Black Regiment,* pp. 210 f., wrote that the
words "cripple up" were sung by Negroes during the Civil War; Faux, *op. cit.,*
pp. 69, 73–77, 102, 127, 406, gave circumstances of the wanton murder of a

1. *Oh* Deat' *he* [him] *is a* little man,
    And he [him] goes from do' to do',
    He [Him] kill *some souls* and *he* [him]
        wounded some [cripple up],
    And *he* [him] lef' *some souls* [me] to pray.

    [Chorus:]
    Oh (or *Do*) Lord, remember me,
    Do Lord, remember me;
    Remember me (or I pray (cry) to de Lord)
        as de year roll around,
    Lord, remember me.

2. *I want to die like-a Jesus die,*
    And he die wid a free good will,
    I lay out in de grave and I stretchee out e arms,
    Do, Lord, remember me.[26]

Secret meetings were in the ascendancy among American Negroes during the first half of the nineteenth century. In them Negroes sought the abundant life that the Christian churches associated with Jesus. Churches everywhere declared that they had found Him, but Negroes were not convinced. They sang:

> *Hunt* [Seek] till you find him, Hallelujah,
> *And a-huntin'* [a-seekin'] for de Lord;
> [Seek] Till you find him, Hallelujah,
> *And a-huntin'* [a-seekin'] for de Lord.[27]

While colonizationists were saying that Jesus could be found over in Africa, and Richard Allen was preaching that the good life for Negroes was within the United States [28] (possibly meaning within the African Methodist Episcopal Church), one singer was sure that Negroes could feel at home nowhere save "in de wilderness" where he was going. Now, this wilderness meant any woods in which Ne-

---

valuable slave. That story was used in a pamphlet by the Rev. John Wright, Unitarian minister of Georgetown, Maryland, and received wide publicity in the United States and in England; cf. Philo Tower, *Slavery Unmasked* (Rochester, 1856), pp. 203 ff.

[26] *Slave Songs,* p. 12; Allen (comp.), *op. cit.,* p. xxxix.

[27] *Slave Songs,* p. 13; Allen (comp.), *op. cit.,* p. xxxix.

[28] Charles H. Wesley, *Richard Allen; Apostle of Freedom* (Washington, [c. 1935]), pp. 219 f.

groes met secretly.[29] So well known was a convocation of Negroes in the Dismal Swamp of Virginia that Longfellow published a poem called "The Slave in Dismal Swamp." There was no need to wonder that Negro preachers had few churches in which to preach.[30] A singer of spirituals traveled a long way from the neighborhood and the familiar hymn of Wesley to say that he had found free grace in the woods. Why, his father had been preaching in the wilderness for years:

1. I *sought* [seek] my Lord in de wilderness,
   [I seek my Lord] in de wilderness, *in de wilderness;*
   I *sought* [seek] my Lord in de wilderness,
   For I'm a-going [I gwinen] home.

   [Chorus:]
   For I'm going home,
   For I'm going home;
   I'm just getting ready,
   For I'm going home.

2. I *found* [find] free grace in the wilderness.

3. My father preaches in the wilderness.[31]

Slaves on St. Helena Island had a tradition that the much-sought Jesus was born in their secret meetings in the woods of South Carolina. Partly because of this tradition, Negroes formed the habit of tiptoeing as quietly as possible in early morning secret meetings in order not to disturb the "Babe of Bethlehem." One song told that "Mary had de leetle baby." [32] In freedom Negroes of Louisiana sang about "Po Li'l Jesus." [33] Negroes, of course, knew that their secret

[29] Charles Darwin, *Journal of Researches into the Natural History and Geology of the Countries Visited during the Voyage of H. M. S. Beagle around the World* (New York, 1855), I, 19; Duncan, *op. cit.,* II, 71; George Lewis, *Impressions of America and the American Churches* (Edinburgh, 1845), p. 174; [Catherine Cooper Hopley], *Life in the South* (London, 1863), I, 261; Brinckerhoff MS, pp. 93 f.

[30] Richard Parkinson, *A Tour in America, in 1798, 1799, and 1800* (London, 1805), II, 459.

[31] *Slave Songs,* p. 84; Allen (comp.), *op. cit.,* p. xli.

[32] Ballanta, *Saint Helena Island Spirituals,* p. 5.

[33] R. Emmett Kennedy, *Black Cameos* (New York, 1924), pp. 75 f.; R. Emmett Kennedy, *Mellows* (New York, [c. 1925]), pp. 78 f.

meetings were prohibited by law, so the chief reason for being quiet was in order not to be caught.[34] When such a spiritual had lost its primary meaning, it was suited for greeting purposes at a church convocation:

1. *I meet little Rosa early in de mornin',*
   O Jerusalem, early in de mornin';
   An' I ax her, how you do my darter?
   O Jerusalem, early in de mornin'.

   [Chorus:]
   Walk 'em easy round de heaben,
   Walk 'em easy round de heaben,
   Walk 'em easy round de heaben,
   Till all living may join dat [Jine de] *band*
        (or *O shout glory till 'em join dat ban'*).

2. *I meet my mudder early in de mornin',*
   An' I ax her, how you do my mudder?
   Walk 'em easy, etc.

3. *I meet brudder Robert early in de mornin';*
   I ax brudder Robert, how you do, my sonny?

4. *I meet titta-Wisa (Sister Louisa) early in de mornin';*
   I ax titta-Wisa, how you do, my darter? [35]

Ever since colonial times Negroes had used holidays and Sundays for their secret meetings. As early as 1695 Maryland had attempted to prevent the "frequent assembling of Negroes" on Sundays by publishing quarterly in the several parish churches its legislation against such meetings,[36] but Methodists evangelized Negro slaves at inconvenient early morning meetings. Bishop Asbury said in his journal at Charleston, South Carolina, on January 22, 1797, that he had "to meet the African people every morning between five and six o'clock" at his lodging "with singing, reading, exhortation and prayer," [37] the precise ritual of secret meetings. This heritage of early

---

[34] Probably they did not often adopt the attitude of bravado expressed in the songs on pp. 71, 79.

[35] *Slave Songs,* p. 44; Allen (comp.), *op. cit.,* p. xl.

[36] *Archives of Maryland* (Baltimore, 1883–1938), XXXVII, 49.

[37] Asbury, *op. cit.,* II, 331.

morning praise services was possible in the Americas not only because American Negroes continued their African traditions but also because on Sunday mornings masters would most likely be sleeping late. When an original singer contemplated the work to be done in secret meetings, he had to exclaim, "Oh"!

> *On* Sunday mornin' I seek my Lord;
> Jine 'em, jine 'em oh!
> Oh jine 'em, believer, jine 'em *so;*
> Jine 'em, jine 'em oh! [38]

Americans marveled that Negroes met for prayer at midnight, knowing that slaves had to go to work "with the first dawn of morning." No matter if this was believed to constitute a difference between black and white folk,[39] with Negroes secret meetings were an African heritage. One variant of the above spiritual called the faithful at Hiltonhead Island, South Carolina, to meet at night:

> *Join, brethren, join us* [Jine, brethren, jine we] O,
> *Join us, join us* [Jine we, jine we] O.
> *We* [Us] meet to-night to sing and pray;
> In Jesus' name *we'll* [us] sing and pray.[40]

Dominant peoples in the Western Hemisphere viewed the assembling of Negroes with alarm,[41] but secret meeters were extremely

[38] *Slave Songs,* p. 21; Allen (comp.), *op. cit.,* p. xxxix.

[39] Jefferson, *op. cit.,* pp. 25 f.

[40] *Slave Songs,* p. 21; Allen (comp.), *op. cit.,* p. xxxix.

[41] Duke de la Rochefoucauld-Liancourt, *Travels through the United States of North America* (London, 1799), II, 291; Bristed, *op. cit.,* p. 389; Duke Karl Bernhard of Saxe-Weimer Eisenach, *Travels through North America* (Philadelphia, 1828), II, 5, 7; Robert Walsh, Jr., *An Appeal from the Judgment of Great Britain Respecting the United States of America* (2nd ed., Philadelphia, 1819), p. 405; J. E. Alexander, *Transatlantic Sketches* (London, 1835), II, 19; Achille Murat, *A Moral and Political Sketch of the United States of North America, With a Note on Negro Slavery,* by Junius Redivivous [*pseud.* of W. B. Adams] (London, 1833), p. 383; Charles Lyell, *Travels in North America, in the Year 1841–2* (New York, 1845), I, 134 f., 146; Frederick Douglass, *My Bondage and My Freedom* (New York, 1855), pp. 166, 185; Russell, *My Diary North and South,* p. 233; T. K. Cartmell, *Shenandoah Valley, Pioneers and Their Descendants* (Winchester, Va., 1909), p. 88; cf. N. Parker Willis, *Health Trip to the Tropics* (New York, 1853),

happy that Moses had joined what they called their band of angels.
The following song had grown from the time of the popularity of the
Moses theme, about 1824, to the army days of Negro soldiers during
the Civil War.

1. *If you look up* [See dat] *de'* road *you* see fader Mosey,
   Join [Jine] de angel band,
   If you look up [See dat] *de* road *you* see fader Mosey,
   Join [Jine] de angel band.

2. *Do, fader Mosey, gader your army,*

3. *O do mo' soul gader togeder.*

4. *O do join 'em, join 'em for Jesus,*

5. *O do join 'em, join 'em archangel.*[42]

In Africa from Sierra Leone to the Cameroons secret meetings
constituted powerful political, legal, and economic units for the separate training of males and females. The privileges of the individual
cultists depended upon the number of grades or degrees through
which they had advanced. Advances were almost invariably accompanied by the payment of fees to the society.[43] In the Americas the
institution of the African cult rather than the home (monogamy was
not too common) was relied upon by adult Negroes to train their
children to take every step of life. The spiritual abilities of slaves were
called forth in secret meetings in the woods of the Western Hemisphere under the slogan of getting religion:

[Chorus:]
My brudder (or Sister Katy, etc.), *want to* get religion?
Go *down* in de *lonesome* valley, etc.

1. Go *down* in de *lonesome* valley,
   Go *down* in de *lonesome* valley, *my Lord;*
   Go *down* in de *lonesome* valley,
   To meet my Jesus dere.

---

p. 83; *A Short Journey in the West Indies,* II, 59 f.; Dallas, *op. cit.,* II, 455;
R. Fitzroy, *Narrative of the Surveying Voyage of His Majesty's Ships "Adventure" and "Beagle"* (London, 1839), II, 61; Donnan, *op. cit.,* I, 358.

[42] *Slave Songs,* p. 39; Allen (comp.), *op. cit.,* p. xl.

[43] Wilfrid D. Hambly, *Culture Areas in Nigeria* (Chicago, 1935), p. 452.

2. *O feed on milk and honey.*

3. *O John he write de letter.*

4. *And Mary and Marta read 'em.*[44]

The valley in this song was heaven, which had moved out of the North and away from Africa and showed no influence of the Methodist hymn about the wilderness. The original singer was sure that the secret meetings of Negroes promoted their group solidarity and their fellowship of worship, that is, their prayer life. Negro prayer was described as a spontaneous song or chant in which stilted phrases were laid aside and individuals were "prayed for by name after humming over their particular sins." [45] One prayer song of the secret experiences of Negroes in Nashville, Tennessee, called upon some Civil War missionary to give help which the African cult did not supply.

> *As* I *went* [go] *down* in de valley to pray,
> Studying about dat good old way,
> *When you* [I] *shall* wear de starry crown,
> Good Lord, show me de way.
>
> O mourner (or Sister, etc.), *let's* go down,
> [O mourner], *let's* go down, *let's go down,*
> O mourner, *let's* go down,
> Down in de valley to pray.[46]

Pent-up energy was released in secret meetings. Rhythmic exercises or shouts were common in the woods, as in the Negro spiritual "Shout On, Chil'en, You Never Die." The song beginning with the words "I meet little Rosa early in de mornin'" was another shout song of the secret meetings. Negroes shuffled their feet and walked around "in slow time, keeping step to their song." Religion of the secret meetings was, for Negro devotees, occasions for shouting unlike the formal religion of the churches. A freedom medley told that the shouting of the African cult in the 1800's was the peculiar "rock" accompanying the singing of a "Deep River" spiritual like "Rain Fall

[44] *Slave Songs,* p. 5; Allen (comp.), *op. cit.,* p. xxxix.

[45] Newell Niles Puckett, *Folk Beliefs of the Southern Negro* (Chapel Hill, 1926), p. 62.

[46] *Slave Songs,* p. 84; Allen (comp.), *op. cit.,* p. xli.

and Wet Becca Lawton." Negroes spent much of their time away from plantations indulging in these religious joys.[47] They probably were without both timepieces [48] and ability to tell time, so that secret meetings might be prolonged indefinitely. These convocations of Negroes were not always for the purpose of making militant protests against American slavery. Divers "runaways" often returned to plantation labor after absences of a few days, weeks, months, or years.[49] Hercules of Jamaica, "the poor paralytic runaway" slave, died on his plantation.[50]

Negroes in general opposed bitter American slavery but not Oriental master-slave relationships. The words of the original "Hinder Me Not" song of Negroes of the Port Royal Islands, South Carolina, asked God to have mercy upon their souls while they met in the woods. Instead of tiptoeing around in their secret meetings, some slaves in Virginia got so reckless that they did not mind who knew that they were holding secret meetings. Those Negroes were in a frenzy, thinking it daytime when their meetings were at black night. They had shouted themselves out of this world:

> [Chorus:]
> O shout, O shout, O shout away,
> *And* don't you mind,
> *And* glory, glory, glory in my soul!

> 1. *And when 'twas* [It] night I *thought* [think] *'twas* [it] day,
>   I *thought* [think] I'*d* pray my soul away,
>   *And* glory, glory, glory in my soul!

> 2. *O Satan told me not to pray,*
>   *He want my soul at judgment day.*

> 3. *And every where I went to pray,*
>   *There some thing was in my way.*[51]

[47] See J. Rosamond Johnson, *Rolling Along in Song* (New York, 1937), pp. 60 f.

[48] Karl Scherzer, *Travels in the Free States of Central America* (London, 1857), II, 9.

[49] Matthew Gregory Lewis, *op. cit.,* pp. 82, 109, 115, 156.

[50] *Ibid.,* p. 224.

[51] *Slave Songs,* p. 71; Allen (comp.), *op. cit.,* p. xlii.

79

As this song says the difficulties in carrying on this abandon were quite real. It was hard to find an unfrequented place where they could carry on such devotions. Any attempt to dissuade them from adopting actions which led to violence were unpopular with the slaves before 1832. Negroes did not welcome whites who tried to persuade them not to adopt violent methods. Slaves sang that their warnings against militancy came from the devil, and they continued their course of action, for they thought they were divinely commissioned to act as they did:

> Wai', Mister Mackright, an' e yedde *what* Satan say;
> Satan *full me full of music, an'* tell me not to pray.

> Mister Macknight cry holy;
> O Lord, *cry holy* [hab mercy].[52]

Slaves around Augusta, Georgia, sang that any Negro who failed to frequent secret meetings showed that he was not "on de Lord's side":

> [Chorus:]
> *Let* me tell you *what is nat'rally de fac'* [he in de Lawd]
> *Who is on de Lord's side,* [Me tell you he in de Lawd,]
> *None o' God's chil'n nebber look back*
>   [Me tell you he in the Lawd],
> *Who is on de Lord's side* [He in de Lawd].

> 1. Way in de valley,
>   *Who is on de Lord's side,*
>   Way in de valley,
>   *Who is on de Lord's side.*

> 2. Weepin' Mary.

> 3. *Mournin' Marta.*

> 4. *Risen Jesus.*[53]

Southern states charged that all Negroes who met together were guilty of civil disobedience. South Carolina, the area in which many slave songs originated, re-enacted in 1819 her law against "all unlawful assemblies, of slaves, free negroes, mulattoes or mestizoes." Patrol officers were commanded to enter all secret meetings, exclu-

---

[52] *Slave Songs,* p. 43; Allen (comp.), *op. cit.,* p. xl.
[53] *Slave Songs,* p. 56; Allen (comp.), *op. cit.,* p. xl.

sive of churches where a warrant was needed, and to administer corporal punishment to the devotees. These enforcement officers were entirely from the male white nonslaveholding population between the ages of eighteen and forty-four years. Not only were these patrolmen, commonly referred to as "poor whites," recognized by law as being sometimes in an unfit condition to perform their duties, for which disorderly conduct fines were provided, but they also entertained an economic grudge against slaveholders. Slaveholders who objected to damage to their property had no legal redress except to bring suit, and failure to win their suit meant a fine amounting to three times the court costs. The law was not at all popular, and patrolmen were permitted to procure white substitutes between the ages of eighteen and sixty. Perhaps it was spite which made patrolmen crucify Negroes.

Spirituals also told the slaves what to do when they learned that the patrol was on their trail. They should run for their lives; for if they were caught, they knew they might meet death. "Run, Nigger, Run" became so popular that many white people sang it. It was, according to Dr. John A. Wyeth of New York City, "one of the oldest of the plantation songs." Of the circumstances under which it and similar songs were composed, Dr. Wyeth reported:

White people were always afraid of an insurrection among the Negroes, and so they had the rule that no Negro should be off his own plantation, especially at night, without a pass. They had patrols stationed along the roads to catch truant Negroes, and the slaves called them "patterrollers." The darkies sang many amusing songs about the patrols and their experiences in eluding them.[54]

William E. Barton preserved one such song which must have been close to its original form, for his spiritual began with "jine de band." Mary, who symbolized a weeping race, ran from an early morning secret meeting in order to escape the consequences of being at an unlawful assembly of slaves, as did little Rosa. A freedom variant in the earliest collection of spirituals confuses Mary fleeing an early morning secret meeting with Biblical Mary at the tomb of Jesus.

    1. O run, Mary run,
       Hallelu, hallelu!

---

[54] Scarborough, *op. cit.,* p. 23.

O run, Mary, run,
Hallelujah!

2. It was early in de mornin',
   Hallelu, hallelu!
   It was early in de mornin',
   Hallelujah!

3. *That she went to de sepulchre,*

4. *And de Lord he wasn't da.*

5. *But she see a man a-comin',*

6. *And she thought it was de gardener.*

7. *But he say, "O touch me not,"*

8. *"For I am not yet ascended.*

9. *"But tell to my disciples*

10. *"Dat de Lord he is arisen."*

11. *So run, Mary, run, etc.*[55]

One of many secular derivatives from this theme presumably during the Civil War was:

O some tell me that a nigger won't steal,
But I've seen a nigger in my cornfield;
O run, nigger, run, for the patrol will catch you,
O run, nigger, run, for 'tis almost day.[56]

Negro cultists did not see their behavior as either good or bad,[57] but they did know that they were prepared to accept death. It was not accidental that Negroes who so consistently envisioned the good life, as do all human beings, suddenly turned and sang about death in North America in the first half of the nineteenth century. Their vicarious accomplishments for Negroes were not without profound influence for the emancipation of slaves in the Western Hemisphere

[55] *Slave Songs,* p. 54; Allen (comp.), *op. cit.,* p. xl. Exact Biblical information among Negroes is a result of Civil War missionary activity.

[56] *Slave Songs,* p. 89; Allen (comp.), *op. cit.,* p. xli.

[57] [Bosman], "A New and Accurate Description of the Coast of Guinea," in Pinkerton, *op. cit.,* XVI, 401.

in the West Indies, South America, Central America, and North America. In the second verse of the spiritual beginning "Oh Deat' he is a little man," the singer says he wants to lie "out in de grave" and to stretch "out e arms." When Colonel Higginson heard his Negro soldiers singing about lying "in the grave" and stretching out their arms, he called the spiritual "most poetic" akin to the "Lyke-Wake Dirge" in Scottish minstrelsy. He exclaimed: "Never, it seems to me, since man first lived and suffered, was his infinite longing for peace uttered more plaintively than in that line." [58]

A postwar variant from Augusta, Georgia, also likened the deaths of African cultists to the crucifixion of Jesus [59] and asked the bearer to point out the crime which merited such punishment. The argument was obtained from the second verse of Watts's "Godly Sorrow at the Cross." The spiritual follows:

> [Chorus:]
> *One cold freezing morning*
> *I lay dis body down;*
> *I will pick up my cross an' follow my Lord*
> *All roun' my Fader's throne.*

> 1. *Every hour in de day cry holy,*
>   *Cry holy, my Lord!*
>   *Every hour in de day cry holy,*
>   *Oh show me de crime I've done.*

> 2. *Every hour in de night cry Jesus,* etc.[60]

"Lay dis body down" was the theme of a group of songs,[61] all of which probably derived from Isaac Watts's "Evening Reflection," with its third verse beginning, "I lay my body down to sleep." [62]

This theme came into Negro singing between 1828 and 1831. At that time an actor named Thomas Dartmouth Rice achieved fame by imitating the walk or dance of an odd-looking Negro called Jim

[58] Higginson, *Army Life in a Black Regiment*, pp. 55, 208 f.
[59] Brinckerhoff, *The Freedman's Book of Christian Doctrine*, pp. 21 f.
[60] *Slave Songs*, p. 58; Allen (comp.), *op. cit.*, p. xl.
[61] *Slave Songs*, pp. 19 f.; Allen (comp.), *op. cit.*, p. xxxix; Russell, *My Diary North and South*, p. 140.
[62] Baron Stow and S. F. Smith, *The Psalmist* (Boston, 1854), p. 605.

Crow.[63] One version of a "Lay dis body down" spiritual said: "O I reel (or shout, wheel) and I rock in de graveyard," referring to the Jim Crow song with the famous chorus:

> So I wheel about, I turn about
> I do just so,
> And ebery time I wheel about,
> I jump Jim Crow.[64]

In addition, a Negro spiritual that was sung two verses at a time recalled what happened at Jerusalem. Now, Jerusalem was another name for the town of Courtland, Southampton County, Virginia. There Nat Turner was lodged in jail pending his trial for stirring up a slave insurrection.[65] His life was so important in the story of antebellum race relations that the period might well be divided into "Before Nat Turner" and "After Nat Turner."

1. (Brudder Sammy) *Who* gwine to lay dis body,
   Member, O, shout glory (or Sing glory, Graveyard).
   And-a who gwine to lay dis body,
   Oh ring Jerusalem.

2. O call all de member to de graveyard.
   Member, etc.

3. *O graveyard, ought to know me,*

4. O grass grow in de graveyard

5. O I reel (or Shout, Wheel) and I rock in de graveyard.[66]

Nat Turner was a leader of the transplanted African cult, even though he was born and reared in Southampton County, Virginia. He held numerous secret meetings in the woods with four companions.[67] The Conservation and Development Commission of Virginia

---

[63] *Jim Crow Vagaries; or, Black Flights of Fancy* (London, [n.d.]), *passim;* Carl Wittke, *Tambo and Bones: A History of the American Minstrel Stage* (Durham, 1930), p. 21.

[64] *Jim Crow Vagaries,* p. 12.

[65] William Sidney Drewry, *The Southampton Insurrection* (Washington, 1900), pp. 94, 96 ff.

[66] *Slave Songs,* p. 15; Allen (comp.), *op. cit.,* p. xxxix.

[67] [Gray], *op. cit.,* p. 11.

has erected this iron marker in Southampton County on United States Highway 58 toward Norfolk:

U 122

SOUTHAMPTON
INSURRECTION

SEVEN MILES SOUTHWEST NAT TURNER, A NEGRO INAUGURATED, AUGUST 21, 1831, A SLAVE INSURRECTION THAT LASTED TWO DAYS AND COST THE LIVES OF ABOUT SIXTY WHITES. THE SLAVES BEGAN THE MASSACRE NEAR CROSS KEYES AND MOVED EASTWARD TOWARDS COURTLAND (JERUSALEM). ON MEETING RESISTANCE, THE INSUR- RECTION SPEEDILY COLLAPSED.

It is a small matter that scholars have found that not until October 31, 1831, was Nat Turner moved to Jerusalem jail. Turner's insurgents sang spirituals, possibly like their leader. Negro followers joined the band as it moved toward Jerusalem, sometime between August 21, 1831, and October 31. Here is one of their songs:

O *join* [jine] 'em all, *join* [jine] for Jesus, *Join* [Jine] Jerusalem Band.

Sister Mary, stan' up for Jesus.

Sixteen souls set out for Heaven.

O brudder an' sister, come *up for* [to] Heaven.

Daddy Peter set out for Jesus.

Ole Maum Nancy set out for Heaven.[68]

The verse beginning "sixteen souls . . ." is probably spurious because antebellum Negroes could seldom count above twelve. In the last verse Nancy is probably pseudonymous for Lucy, a slave who was put in jail on September 26, 1831, and hanged for trying to pre-

[68] *Slave Songs,* p. 39; Allen (comp.), *op. cit.,* p. xl.
"Sister Mary, stan' up for Jesus" suggests two famous hymns. Watts's *"The Christian Soldier"* contained the words, "Stand up my soul, shake off thy fears" (Stow and Smith, *op. cit.,* p. 720), with which Negroes were undoubtedly familiar. Duffield, the author of "Stand Up, Stand Up for Jesus" (1853), was thoroughly acquainted with the aspirations of slaves (Robert Elmer Smith, *Modern Messages from Great Hymns* [New York, 1916], p. 39). His hymn might have reflected their thought about liberty.

vent the escape of Mrs. John T. Barrows.[69] The whole song may have been the work of a female slave who recruited others of her sex for secret meetings, where the sexes were rigidly divided.

While "Jerusalem" was thus defined, and while Negroes in Georgia thrilled at its mention even in the 1850's,[70] "Jericho" is not so easily accounted for. In freedom it would be expected that Negroes would have exact Biblical information about a man who was shamefully beaten on the road from Jerusalem to Jericho and who was at length befriended by a good Samaritan. Yet during slavery this incident undoubtedly inspired the composer of the song given below. He felt that ultimate success would attend meetings of the Jerusalem band. His worry over Jericho may have been an expression of his anxiety about the activity of the white people who had been reinforced by militia in several counties of Virginia, Maryland, and North Carolina.[71] The singer himself had almost been caught once, but he had escaped, and he gave his god credit for it. At the secret meeting where plans were laid for the furtherance of the revolt, the pseudonymous Brother Hercules had told him and others that they had better "turn back." The singer had been determined to continue his work regardless of consequences:

1. Pray all de member (or True believer),
   O Lord!
   Pray all de member,
   Yes, my Lord!

2. *Pray a little longer,*
   O Lord!
   Pray a little longer
   Yes, my Lord!

3. Jericho da worry me,
   O Lord!
   Jericho da worry me,
   Yes, my Lord!

4. *Jericho, Jericho,*

5. I been to Jerusalem.

[69] Drewry, *op. cit.*, p. 98 n.

[70] Adolph B. Benson (ed.), *America of the Fifties* (New York, 1924), p. 150.

[71] Drewry, *op. cit.*, pp. 83 f.

6. Patrol aroun' me.

7. Tank God he no ketch me.

8. *Went* [Go] to de meetin'.

9. *Met* [See] brudder Hacless (Hercules).

10. *Wha' d'ye tink he tell me?*

11. Tell me for to turn back.

12. Jump along Jericho.[72]

This song is probably the earliest "yes, my Lord!" or "O yes, Lord" spiritual. Its last verse is a reference to the popular Jim Crow song, showing that Negroes were not disturbed by what was happening. They shouted or danced on the spiritual as each verse probably swung like this:

> Patter-roll 'roun' me,
> O Lawd!
> Patter-roll, 'round' me,
> Yes, my Lawd.

Originating in Virginia, the song migrated to the Port Royal Islands, South Carolina, where it was preserved. The editing of the song involved the omission of difficult constructions for a beginner in the language, like adjectival comparisons and questions.

The secret meetings of Negroes reached a climax under the militant leadership of Nat Turner. Nineteenth-century assemblies of the African cult in the United States had begun with the ambitious plans of Gabriel Prosser to take and fortify Richmond, Virginia. Slave plots continued through the daring scheme of Denmark Vesey to annihilate the white population of Charleston, South Carolina. Nat Turner fomented a slave insurrection of such significance as to cause England and the Americas to debate the greatest social problem of the century. *Slave Songs of the United States* emphasized this militant side of the secret meetings of Negroes, although not to the neglect of their peaceful and religious usefulness. Said the aged and feeble Gib Earnest Carter who some years ago conducted a "Slavery Museum" on a highway at Darien, Georgia: "In the old days about five o'clock in the morning you see forty or fifty of them in the road going to praise. That all the help they looked to get."

[72] *Slave Songs*, p. 35; Allen (comp.), *op. cit.*, p. xl.

"YOU'D BETTER MIN'"

You'd better min',
You'd better min',
For you got to give account in Judgment,
You'd better min'.[1]

THE African cult had gained the reputation of instigating those slave insurrections that characterized the nineteenth century. After Turner's terror, pacific Negroes seized racial leadership. These conservative slaves reminded one another in various songs with sentiments similar to the above spiritual that their disabilities would be relieved should Negroes prove that they were good people.

The militant minority among Negroes was, however, not convinced that it was not composed of good people, at least potentially, because it attempted to better the conditions of black folk by secret meetings. The resulting plots and revolts were periodic throughout the legal duration of slavery, even though they never attained the notoriety of Turner's insurrection in North America. Negroes sang that anybody who advocated the discontinuance of the African cult was not friendly but satanic. People were called upon to pay no attention to the talk that right racial attitudes came by persuasion and not by protests. Jesus Himself had whispered to a Negro who could sing that, should the local African cult in the southeastern slave states meet with violence, He would build it up again. A chief reason

[1] Work, *American Negro Songs*, p. 212. Used by permission of Theodore Presser Company, Bryn Mawr, Pa., from *American Negro Songs*.

for the continuance of secret meetings of Negroes was because these
laboring people had been cheated, as his song said:

1. *I* [Me] an' Satan *had* [hab] a race,
   Hallelu, hallelu,
   I [Me] an' Satan *had* [hab] a race,
   Hallelu, hallelu.

2. [Me] Win de race agin *de course* ['em].

3. Satan tell me to my face

4. *He will* [Him] break my *kingdom* [heab'n] *down.*

5. Jesus *whisper* [tell me] in my heart

6. *He will* [Him] build 'em up again.

7. *Satan mount de iron grey;*

8. *Ride half way to Pilot-Bar.*

9. *Jesus mount de milk-white horse.*

10. *Say* you cheat my fader children.

11. *Say* you cheat 'em out of glory.

12. Trouble like a *gloomy* [tunder] cloud.

13. *Gader dick an' tunder loud.*[2]

Turner's insurrection seemed to usher in the judgment day for the
entire Negro race. It would be of interest to know what became of an
original singer on the Port Royal Islands, South Carolina, who was
certain that he could not stand the fire of that judgment. At Coffin's
Point he sang:

> Can'*t* stand the fire,
> Can'*t* stand the fire,
> Can'*t*, etc.
> (*O Lord, I*) Can'*t* stand the fire.[3]

More than thirty years after Turner's terror a variant song was heard
on the Islands referring to this experience but saying that the Confederate cause was burning down:

[2] *Slave Songs,* p. 40; Allen (comp.), *op. cit.,* p. xl.
[3] *Slave Songs,* p. 42; Allen (comp.), *op. cit.,* p. xl.

> *Fier, my Saviour, fier,*
> *Satan's camp a-fire;*
> *Fier, believer, fier,*
> *Satan's camp a-fire.*[4]

Spirituals during the aftermath of Turner's insurrection remind one of the various descriptions of the judgment day in sacred literature. Perhaps a fitting theme for a spiritual of such an event would be, "What a mornin'!"[5] Although collectors marvel at the word "mornin'," "moanin'" or "mournin'" would be equally characteristic. A fuller and hence a later judgment song was heard in Charleston, South Carolina. It began with the words, "And de moon will turn to blood," and stated that people would wail "yoy" "in dat day."[6] Seemingly, the very stars fell:

> *I tink I hear my brudder (or Titty Nelly, De member, etc.) say,*
> *Call de nation great and small;*
> *I lookee on de God's right hand,*
> *When de stars begin to fall.*

> Oh *what a mournin'* (*sister*) [dat day, sister],
> Oh *what a mournin'* (*brudder*) [dat day, sister],
> Oh *what a mournin'* [dat day, sister],
> *When* de stars begin to fall.[7]

Spirituals on this theme also declare that in Turner's judgment insurrectionists found no place to flee to or to hide from their overlords. A variant song gathered momentum and ideas as it was preserved in the Reconstruction on the Port Royal Islands. Its reference to Monday was perhaps to Monday Gell of Vesey notoriety:

> 1. My Lord, my Lord, *what shall* I do?
>   And a heav'n bell a-ring and praise God.
>
>   or
>
>   *Timmy, Timmy, orphan boy,*
>   *Robert, Robert, orphan child.*

---

[4] *Slave Songs*, p. 27; Allen (comp.), *op. cit.*, p. xl.

[5] Cf. James Weldon Johnson, *The Book of American Negro Spirituals* (New York, 1925), pp. 162 f., with Marsh, *op. cit.*, p. 199.

[6] *Slave Songs*, p. 53; Allen (comp.), *op. cit.*, p. xl.

[7] *Slave Songs*, pp. 25 f.; Allen (comp.), *op. cit.*, p. xl.

2. *What shall I do for a hiding place? And a heav'n,* etc.

3. *I run to de sea, but de sea run dry.*

4. *I run to de gate, but de gate shut fast.*

5. No hiding place for sinner *dere* [here].

6. *Say you when you get to heaven say you 'member me.*

7. *Remember me, poor fallen soul (or When I am gone, For Jesus' sake).*

8. *Say when you get to heaven say your work shall prove.*

9. *Your righteous Lord shall prove 'em well.*

10. *Your righteous Lord shall find you out.*

11. *He cast out none dat come by faith.*

12. *You look to de Lord with a tender heart.*

13. I wonder *where* poor Monday *dere* [gone].

14. *For I am gone and sent to hell.*

15. *We must harkee what de worldy say.*

16. *Say Christmas comes but once a year.*

17. *Say Sunday come but once a week.*[8]

On the Port Royal Islands a singer asked over and over again whether his life, too, would be required in that judgment. This man had been instructed in the Christian religion, but what was most impressive to him was that Jesus died and would come back to earth again. He rejoiced that the dead revisited the earth:

1. Believer, O *shall* I die?
   O *my army* [Lord], *shall* I die?

2. Jesus die, *shall* I die?
   Die on de cross [Jesus die], *shall* I die?

3. Die, die, die, *shall* I die?
   Jesus da coming, *shall* I die?

[8] *Slave Songs,* p. 20; Allen (comp.), *op. cit.,* p. xxxix.

4. *Run for to meet him, shall I die?*
   Weep like a weeper, shall I die?

5. *Mourn like a mourner, shall I die?*
   Cry like a crier, shall I die?[9]

It was a naked truth that Negroes were in trouble. Not a few slaves were mentally confused like the singer on the Port Royal Islands who sang:

I *am* a-trouble in de mind,
O I *am* a-trouble in de mind;
I ask my Lord *what shall I do,*
I *am* a-trouble in de mind.

I'm a-trouble in de mind,
What you doubt for (or Titty Rosy, Brudder Johnny,
   Come along dere)?
I'm a-trouble in de mind.[10]

Since innocent slaves suffered death in post-Turner days, all that a singer in Florida was heard uttering about the judgment was that he, too, was in trouble. This variant song of freedom was still simple enough to fit the Nat Turner era although it later took on such difficult words as "sometimes" and "neither."

I*'m* in trouble, Lord, I*'m in trouble,*
I*'m* in trouble, Lord, *trouble about my grave.*

Sometimes I weep, sometimes I mourn,
I'm in trouble about my grave;
Sometimes I can't do neither one,
I'm in trouble about my grave.[11]

Peculiar non-Christian Negro burial rites employed a trouble spiritual even in the early days of freedom. Possibly, in African custom, the members of the family of a deceased person would sing as they

---

[9] *Slave Songs*, p. 41; Allen (comp.), *op. cit.*, p. xl.

[10] *Slave Songs*, pp. 30 f.; Allen (comp.), *op. cit.*, p. xl. This song was said to have originated with a slave in Tennessee who was so moved at being flogged by his master that he poured out this wail (Work, *Folk Songs of the American Negro*, p. 88).

[11] *Slave Songs*, p. 94; Allen (comp.), *op. cit.*, p. xli.

marched around the corpse in the order of age and relationship. The custom obtained in North Carolina, South Carolina, and elsewhere that the youngest child would then be passed over and under the coffin. Two strong men would afterward run to the grave with the remains. The song which was sung was:

> Dese all my fader's children,
> Dese all my fader's children,
> Dese all my fader's children,
> *Outshine de sun.*
>
> My fader*'s* done wid de trouble o' de world,
> [My fader done] wid de trouble o' de world,
> *wid de trouble o' de world,*
> My fader*'s* done wid de trouble o' de world,
> *Outshine de sun.*[12]

[12] *Slave Songs*, p. 101; Allen (comp.), *op. cit.*, p. xliii; see, also, I. M. Lowerey, *Life on the Old Plantation in Ante-Bellum Days* (Columbia, S.C., 1911), pp. 85 f. This song was sung with verses of family relations; see [Seward], *op. cit.*, pp. 54 f.; Pike, *op. cit.*, pp. 208 f.; Marsh, *op. cit.*, pp. 158 f.; Seward and White, *op. cit.*, pp. 54 f.

A strange freedom medley in *Slave Songs*, p 8; Allen (comp.), *op. cit.*, p. xxxix, was:

> "1. *I want to be (or O you ought to be) my Fader's chil'en,*
> *I want to be my Fader's chil'en,*
> *I want to be my Fader chil'en,*
> *Roll, Jordan, roll.*
>
> "[Chorus:]
> *"O say (or My Sister, My Mudder, etc.), ain't you done*
> *wid de trouble ob de world,*
> *Ah! trouble ob de world, Ah!*
> *Say ain't you done wid de trouble ob de world,*
> *Ah Roll, Jordan, roll.*
>
> "2. *I ask de Lord how long I hold 'em, (ter)*
> *Hold 'em to de end.*
>
> "3. *My sins so heavy I can't get along, Ah! etc.*
>
> "4. *I cast my sins in de middle of de sea, Ah! etc.*"

In freedom's "jubilee" Negroes of Savannah, Georgia, sang a medley made of the "wish" of "Deep River" and the "Roll, Jordan, Roll" of "When I Die":

> *"I wish I was in jubilee,*
> *Ha, jubilee;*

By the time of freedom and the ordeal of the Reconstruction Negroes sang a variant medley which told that no one could imagine what they endured except Jesus. The original singer was not greatly perturbed about it, however, for in his song he suggested that both berries and trouble are sweet in the end. Post-Civil War experiences were the second major crisis of the Negro race; the first crisis was presumably the aftermath of Turner's insurrection, after the "O yes, Lord" period. Negroes had survived that ordeal with distinction. They should take courage to live through the Reconstruction. "Glory hallelu!" a songster told Negroes to sing:

[Chorus:]
Nobody knows de trouble *I've had* (or I see),
Nobody knows but Jesus,
Nobody knows de trouble *I've had* [I see]
(Sing) Glory hallelu!

1. One morning I was a-walking down,
O yes, Lord!
I saw some berries a-hanging down,
O yes, Lord!

2. I pick de berry and I suck de juice, O yes, Lord!
Just as sweet as the honey in de comb, O yes, Lord!

3. Sometimes I'm up, sometimes I'm down,
Sometimes I'm almost on de groun'.

I wish I was in jubilee,
Roll, Jordan, roll."

In the mouth of another singer on the Port Royal Islands (Allen [comp.] *op. cit.*, p. xlii) the trouble of the world was caused by a certain Roman Catholic priest who would not endorse a certain Negro's religion, as was told in *Slave Songs*, pp. 99 f.

"*I ax Fader Georgy for religion,*
Fader Georgy wouldn't give me religion;
You give me religion for to run to my elder;
O dis is de trouble of de world.

"*Dis is de trouble of de world, O*
(or What you doubt for?), etc.
Dis is de trouble of de world.
(What you doubt [or shame] for?; take it easy; Titty 'Melia.)"

4. What make ole Satan hate me so?
   Because he got me once and he let me go.[13]

After Turner's insurrection southerners persisted in the illogical assumption that abolitionism was the cause of Negro unrest rather than admit that the ancient African cult was at work. Nat Turner had shocked slaveholders into attempting to stop all possible leakages in their containment of Negro liberty. So the slave codes of the South were revised, chiefly by forbidding Negroes to read and write and to be instructed from printed literature. Nearly everywhere in the South the independence of Negro churches was taken away, and Negro pastors, who were ordinarily free Negroes, were silenced. Southern people, of course, understood what Negroes wanted.[14] They simply had never dreamed of the changes involved in the introduction of Negroes into the Americas, and, whenever they thought seriously of the adjustments demanded, they became panicky. After the insurrection of Nat Turner, Colonel Dabney of the militia in Gloucester County, Virginia, had his men keep "their horses saddled and bridled in the stable every night for three weeks, ready for every alarm or emergency."[15] A lady in Virginia "often" heard her mother describe how the evenings were spent "starting and trembling when a leaf fell or a twig crackled on the gravel walk."[16] Said a son of a governor of Virginia: "It was part of my early education to learn of a fearful massacre, led by a desperate negro named Nat Turner."[17]

So Nat Turner caused many persons to look at the problems faced by Negroes. Visitors of many nationalities—English, French, German, Spanish, Scandinavian, and the like—came to North America in order to appraise the progress of this social movement. Citizens of the United States also discussed Negroes with considerable heat and wrote and acted according to their feelings. It was agreed that slaves did not want bitter slavery, and enlightened southerners began a movement for plantation missions without books. As a result, Wil-

[13] *Slave Songs*, p. 55; Allen (comp.), *op. cit.*, p. xli.
[14] Jones, *The Religious Instruction of Negroes in the United States*, p. 272.
[15] Smedes, *op. cit.*, p. 41.
[16] Sally [McCarty] Pleasants, *Old Virginia Days and Ways* (Menasha, [c. 1916]), p. 119.
[17] John S. Wise, *The End of an Era* (Boston, [1899]), p. 74.

liam Capers, Bishop Mead, Charles C. Jones, and other evangelists made themselves notable by teaching Negroes.

Faced with the stark reality of a most serious condition, cautious and conservative Negroes who exhibited a side of Africanism opposite to militancy captured racial leadership from militant ones. Such peace-loving Negroes had been trying to lead the black masses ever since Africans had left their native homes. In 1704, when a mutiny took place on shipboard among Negroes who were about to be transported to North America, a black boy of seventeen years caught the arm of the Negro who was about to strike the ship captain. In Virginia this lad was indentured to Colonel Carter until the youth could purchase freedom for himself. In 1750 at Boston, Massachusetts, a slave on a ship from the West Indies would not let his fellows throw another white man overboard after nine had been drowned. Some American slaves volunteered to check the militancy of North Carolina Negroes in the eighteenth century and lost their lives "in suppressing rebel slaves." Other Negroes consented to be made "very useful in suppressing insurrection" of slaves. The record of the loyalty of South Carolina Negroes toward slaveholders was indeed gratifying in the first half of the eighteenth century, and the conduct of slaves toward the colonists in the American Revolution drew this extravagant praise: "Perhaps the whole world cannot exhibit a history more remarkable, or more worthy of grateful remembrance." [18] At the turn of the nineteenth century slaves succeeded in disclosing the Gabriel Prosser plot. On June 7, 1802, a trusted house servant in Virginia wrote a letter "to the white pepil" in which he gave away a slave plot, because, as he said, he was friendly to his master's family. Negroes betrayed the Vesey plot. There were other examples of their allegiance to the ruling class. In fact, many Negroes were themselves slaveholders.[19]

[18] "Fidelity of Slaves," *De Bow's Review*, XXIX (November, 1860), 579 ff.

[19] Gilbert Farquhar Mathison, *Narrative of a Visit to Brazil, Chile, Peru, and the Sandwich Islands* (London, 1825), p. 158; Henry Benjamin Whipple, *Bishop Whipple's Southern Diary, 1843–1844*, ed. with an Introduction by Lester B. Shippe (Minneapolis, [c. 1937]), p. 113; James R. Creecy, *Scenes in the South* (Washington, 1860), p. 19; Carter G. Woodson, *Free Negro Owners of Slaves in the United States in 1830* (Washington, [c. 1924]), *passim;* Charles Henry Haynes, "Why Did Free Negroes Own Slaves?" (M.A. thesis, University of Chicago, 1928), *passim.*

White people relied upon nonmilitant Negroes for safety and gave considerable responsibility and freedom to those they trusted. Such slaves were allowed to take jobs away from plantations for long periods of time. During the ascendancy of secret meetings in the nineteenth century adventurous masters gave trusted Negroes full charge of plantations, the internal slave traffic, the punishment of slave crimes, and labor supervision, which was ordinarily under white overseers in order to meet legal requirements. Trusted Negroes had a monopoly of certain tasks like barbering and rowing, particularly where the lives of the whites might be in jeopardy.

The insurrection of Nat Turner would have been more savage had it not been for "faithful slaves." On United States Highway 58 in Southampton County, Virginia, the Conservation and Development Commission has erected this marker:

U 155
BUCKTHORN QUARTERS

ONE MILE NORTH WAS THE ESTATE OF MAJOR THOMAS RIDLEY, IN THE SERVILE INSURRECTION OF AUGUST, 1831, THE HOUSES WERE FORTIFIED BY FAITHFUL SLAVES AND MADE A PLACE OF REFUGE FOR FUGITIVE WHITES. IN THIS VICINITY NAT TURNER, THE LEADER OF THE INSURRECTION, SPENT THE NIGHT AFTER HIS DEFEAT, NEAR COURTLAND, AUGUST 28, 1831.

This period was the most crucial one for Negroes before the Civil War. A conservative Negro sang to his militant acquaintances to turn from the violence of their secret meetings. This song was "the most dramatic of all the shouts" in South Carolina. By the time of freedom this song carried reasons why a potential insurrectionist should turn to pacifism. First, the whole Negro population was suffering—"de worl' da gwine"; secondly, if the "sinner" did not care about his race, he should at least value his own life, which might be lost unless he turned from violence; and, finally, militant revolters against the living conditions of Negroes were not doing the will of heaven, as they said they were. A simple statement of this theme was uttered in post-Turner days in order to persuade Negroes to aid in keeping innocent ones from being penalized. Subsequent singers of this spiritual were certain that the wishes of the original songster were in accord with a heaven to which they were going.

1. Turn, sinner, turn to-day,
   Turn, sinner, turn O!
   Turn, sinner, turn to-day,
   Turn, sinner, turn O!

2. Turn, O sinner, de worl' da gwine,
   Turn, sinner, turn O!
   Turn, O sinner, de worl' da gwine,
   Turn, sinner, turn O!

3. *Wait not for to-morrow's sun. Turn, sinner, turn O.*

4. *To-morrow's sun will sure to shine.*

5. *The sun may shine, but on your grave.*

6. *Hark! I hear dem sinner say.*

7. *If you get to heaven I'll get there too.*

8. *O sinner, you make mistake.*

9. *While de lamp hold out to burn.*

10. *De wile' sinner may return.*[20]

[20] *Slave Songs*, pp. 36 f.; Allen (comp.), *op. cit.*, p. xl.

After Turner's terror a Negro dug a well to this theme and tune. Freedom verses of the song which are identical as in "Nobody Knows, etc." suggest how the spiritual was sung at that time:

"1. *Bro' Joe, you ought to know my name—Hallelujah.*

"2. *My name is written in de book ob life.*

"3. *If you look in de book you'll fin' 'em dar.*

"4. *One mornin' I was a walkin' down.*

"5. *I saw de berry a-hinging down.*

"6. *(Lord) I pick de berry, an' I suck de juice.*

"7. *Jes' as sweet as de honey in de comb.*

"8. *I wonder where fader Jimmy gone.*

"9. *My fader gone to de yonder worl'.*

"10. *You dig de spring dat nebber dry.*

"11. *De more I dig 'em, de water spring.*

"12. *De water spring dat nebber dry.*"

The methods which conservative Negroes decided would obtain for their race better treatment from the dominant people were simple enough. Numerous songs illustrate the fact that Negroes trained themselves always to be very polite to white people. They called each white person "Sir" or "Maum," as the sex might be, and even gave titles of "Miss" or "Mr." to little children. Negroes bowed and scraped. In the West Indies Uncle Tom kissed his master's shoes again and again and sang and showed extravagant joy.[21] In North America he halted his mistress in the middle of the road and bowed himself almost to the ground as he exclaimed, "Your most obedient." The white people shouted with laughter at so "sudden, grotesque, uncouth, and yet dexterous a gambado." [22] It must have been altogether pleasing to a slaveholder to be deified in a Negro song by the word "Lord," and the master was not unwilling to accept and defend his slave's inference that slaveholding was not sinful. Slaveholders caused division in the popular denominations of Presbyterians, Baptists, and Methodists rather than be convinced to the contrary, and they risked the lives of all southerners in the Civil War. A northern visitor looked at the southern people—and missed seeing that they were at the mercy of Uncle Tom—but wrote: "It often makes me feel disagreeably, when I pass a slave, to see him cringingly let off his hat, if he has any, and say—'servant, master'; and when he enters his master's door, to see him drop his piece of a cap outside and crouch along as if he were in the presence of his maker." [23] Thus Americans misinterpreted the emphasis of Negroes upon lowly virtues.

In George W. Clark's arrangement of C. G. Howard's song, "Uncle Tom's Religion," in the *Harp of Freedom*, a slave demonstrated not retaliation but love and patience and comfort. He had a religion which would take him to the shore where he would meet all of the faithful in the resurrection. The slave's forgiving love was said to illustrate his inferior position. Even when his family was auctioned and he himself had been flogged, he thought "of Him who died to save." For such conduct Uncle Tom was thought of as "still a boy in

[21] *A Short Journey in the West Indies*, I, 81.
[22] Francis Kemble, *Journal of a Residence on a Georgian Plantation in 1838–1839* (New York, 1863), p. 16.
[23] [Henry Cogswell Knight] (*pseud.* Arthur Singleton), *Letters from the South and West* (Boston, 1824), p. 80.

Southern parlance." Actually his unresisting humility was a considered choice between two evils.

In Virginia a nursery song counseled the rising generation of American Negroes that when they learned to live by their resourcefulness, they would be "toted," [24] and unlike Denmark Vesey, Nat Turner, and scores of other Negroes they would not be killed. God would "leave the old sheep alone," because they would not turn from their militant African heritage, but the young lambs would be toted in His bosom. The time of this warning is suggested by the mention of Abraham. Abraham as mentioned here, was not associated with the Biblical story of the lamb, but probably was a well-known Negro interpreter to the Florida Indians during the second Seminole War. [25] That made this counsel timely during the aftermath of Turner's insurrection:

1. Rock o' [a] my soul in de bosom of Abraham,
   Rock o' [a] my soul in de bosom of Abraham,
   Rock o' [a] my soul in de bosom of Abraham,
   Lord, rock o' [a] my soul. (*King Jesus.*)

2. He toted the young lambs in *his* [de] bosom [of Abraham], (*ter*)
   And leave the old sheep alone. [26]

A preacher in Virginia sang that the aftermath of Turner's insurrection was "almost over" at one of his baptisms held about 1835. This preacher thanked God that it was so. The last verse referred to a specific colonization event of that year, the probable time of the origin of the song. Converts to conservative Christianity waded through the snowy and ice-cold water to be baptized. One sister was afraid that she would be sick from such exposure, but that excuse was then as now brushed aside because of the lingering African belief that God would protect His own. The preacher himself had been immersed in the wintertime, and he knew that everything was all

[24] [Knight], *op. cit.,* p. 82; Buckingham, *The Slave States of America,* II, 293; Nathaniel Tillman, "A Possible Etymology of 'Tote,' " *American Speech,* XVII (April, 1942), 1289; cf. Thomas L. Broun, "The Word 'Tote,' " *Publications of the Southern History Association,* VIII (July, 1904), 295, 296.

[25] Frederick Marryat, *A Diary in America* (London, 1839), III, Part II, 238, 250.

[26] *Slave Songs,* p. 73; Allen (comp.), *op. cit.,* p. xli.

right if one was not playing with God. As the candidate was in the hands of the preacher for baptism, the congregation on the bank dramatically sang the chorus of this spiritual after each verse:

> [Chorus:]
> And I'*ll* thank God, almost over,
> [I thank God], almost over, *almost over,*
> (*My Lord*) And I'*ll* thank God, almost over.

While preparations were being made to immerse another candidate, the onlookers sang a verse of their song just as Negroes do on such occasions today.

1. *Some seek de Lord and they don't seek him right*
   Pray all day and sleep all night;

2. Sister, *if* your heart *is* warm,
   Snow and ice *will* do you no harm.

3. I done been down, and I done been tried,
   I been through the water, and I been baptized.

4. O sister, you *must* mind *how* you step *on the cross,*
   Your foot *might* slip, and your soul get lost.

5. *And when* you get to heaven, you'*ll be able for to* tell
   How you *shunned* [leave] the gates of hell.

6. *Wrestle* [Wrastle] with Satan and *wrestle* [wrastle] with *sin* [Satan]
   Step*ped* over hell and come back agin.[27]

The requirement that Negroes should "live 'umble" if they planned to live on this earth had been admirably met by the time of the Civil War. Army officers attributed the humility of Negro soldiers to the institution of slavery [28] rather than to the traditional Orientalism of Africans [29] and to the cautious counsel of peace-loving Negro leaders. The elaborate version of this "lost" spiritual theme which was sung in Colonel Higginson's regiment in South Carolina suggests a

[27] *Slave Songs*, p. 74; Allen (comp.), *op. cit.*, p. xli.

[28] Higginson, *Army Life in a Black Regiment*, p. 259; Benjamin F. Butler, *Autobiography and Personal Reminiscences of Major-General Benj. F. Butler* (Boston, 1892), p. 494; cf. pp. 273, 492.

[29] Batutah, *op. cit.*, p. 327; Leo Frobenius, *The Voice of Africa* (London, 1913), I, 265, Plate III.

simpler original. Even Higginson's song retained the "O yes" words, which point to its origin immediately following Nat Turner's insurrection. Likewise the ringing bell referred not to African but to North American meetings, and rang out that militant meetings of Negroes should stop. A "glory and honor" song cautioned young Christians to "live 'umble, 'umble, 'umble yourself" because the bell rang. Contemporary verses of "Steal Away" circulated with this song.[30] Fenner's "Glory and Honor" and Higginson's elaborate variant with "O yes" words and the ringing bell admonished Negroes to live humble lives:

> *Do my brudder, O yes, yes, member,*
> *De bell done ring.*
>
> *You can't get to heaben,*
> *When de bell done ring.*
>
> *If you want to get to heaven,*
> *Fo' de bell, etc.*
>
> *You had better follow Jesus,*
> *Fo' de bell, etc.*
>
> *O yes, my Jesus, yes, I member,*
> *De bell, etc.*
>
> *O come in, Christians,*
> *Fo' de bell, etc.*
>
> *For the gates are all shut,*
> *When de bell, etc.*
>
> *And you can't get to heaven,*
> *When de bell, etc.*[31]

[30] [Fenner], *Religious Folk Songs of the Negro*, p. 87.

[31] *Slave Songs*, pp. 34 f.; Allen (comp.), *op. cit.*, p. xl.

Still another slave song announced that the church bell was ringing for meeting on the Port Royal Islands.

> "[Chorus:]
> *"I know member, know Lord,*
> *I know I yedde de bell da ring.*
>
> "1. *Want to go to meeting,*
> *Bell da ring,*

A final requirement of Uncle Tom Negroes was that they should be sincere in the whole business of considering white people above themselves and of living humbly in their presence. Contemporary society wondered how sincerity was possible. Only occasionally did Uncle Tom take time to answer. He sang to his followers that, though the insurrectionists under the leadership of Nat Turner had invariably sworn their nonguilt,[32] mere words were not enough.

> Chorus:
> You *must* be *pure and* holy,
> You *must* be *pure an'-a* holy,
> You *must* be *pure and* holy
> To see God feed his lambs.

Collectors stated that this song was brought out of the South to Auburn, New York, where it was first heard. Its originator was possibly the fugitive slave, Harriet Tubman, who took her whole family to those parts and who composed original spirituals.[33] The words of this song were prolonged almost endlessly by adding freedom verses like the following:

> *Want to go to meeting,*
> *Bell da ring.*
>
> "2. *(Say) Road to stormy (or Boggy, Tedious),*
> *Bell da ring,*
> *(Say) Road so stormy,*
> *Bell da ring.*
>
> "3. *I can't get to meetin' (or 'ciety, Lecter, Praise-house).*
>
> "4. *De church mos' ober.*
>
> "5. *De heaven-bell a heaven-bell.*
>
> "6. *De heaven-bell I gwine home.*
>
> "7. *I shout for de heaven-bell.*
>
> "8. *Heaven 'nough for me one.*
>
> "9. *(Brudder) hain't you a member?"*

[32] Drewry, *op. cit.,* p. 97.

[33] Sarah H. Bradford, *Scenes in the Life of Harriet Tubman* (Auburn, 1869), p. 37; Earl Conrad, "General Tubman, Composer of Spirituals," *Etude Music Magazine,* IX (May, 1942), 305 f.

1. *When I was wicked an'-a prone to sin,*
   My Lord, bretheren, ah my Lord!
   I thought that I couldn't be born agin,
   My Lord, bretheren, ah my Lord.

2. *I'll run all round the cross and cry,*
   My Lord, bretheren, ah my Lord,
   Or give me Jesus, or I die,
   My Lord, bretheren, ah my Lord.
   You *must* be *pure and* holy, etc.

3. *The Devil am a liar and conjurer too.*
   My Lord, etc.
   If you don't look out he'll conjure you
         (*or cut you in two, cut you through*).
   My Lord, etc.

4. *O run up, sonny, and get your crown,*
   My Lord, etc.
   And by your Father sit you down,
   My Lord, etc.

5. *I was pretty young when I begun,*
   My Lord, etc.
   But, now my work is almost done,
   My Lord, etc.

6. *The Devil's mad and I am glad,*
   My Lord, etc.
   He lost this soul, he thought he had,
   My Lord, etc.

7. *Go 'way, Satan, I don't mind you,*
   My Lord, etc.
   You wonder, too, that you can't go through,
   My Lord, etc.

8. *A lilly (little?) white stone came rolling down,*
   My Lord, etc.
   It rolled like thunder through the town,
   My Lord, etc.[34]

The holiness movement among Negroes received great emphasis during post-Turner days. When, in 1837, some slaves gave up danc-

[34] *Slave Songs*, pp. 107 f.; Allen (comp.), *op. cit.*, p. xlii.

ing and secular singing, they taunted their mistresses with "You no holy. We be holy. You no in state o' salvation." [35] The music of holiness Negroes included a song which Negroes sang in Anne Arundel County, Maryland, in 1842. "In a somewhat different form" the spiritual was a Methodist hymn:

1. Sanctofy me, sanctofy me,
   Sanctofy me, sanctofy me,
   Sanctofy me, just now;
   Just now, just now;
   Sanctofy me just now.

2. Good religion, good religion, etc.

3. Come to Jesus, come to Jesus, etc.[36]

Within two or three years after Turner's revolt many social changes for the benefit of slaves had been inaugurated. Everybody was given credit for his share in initiating these gains except those people who used spiritual weapons instead of the material ones which they did not possess. A change in social ideals was attributed to the militant protests of Negroes [37] and to the efforts of abolitionists.[38] Southern people also took pride in remembering that certain slaves were well fed, well clothed, and well treated, both in areas far removed from Turner's insurrection and in the state of Virginia.[39] A complete explanation of the better treatment of Negroes after 1831 must include the fact that conservative Negroes made contributions to racial understanding even though they often had to endure being called handkerchief-headed Negroes and Uncle Toms. Many southern people responded favorably to their appeals.

"Uncle Tomism" was not applied to the behavior of all Negroes who wanted to exact less than the death penalty for anybody who

[35] Harriet Martineau, *Society in America* (4th ed., London, 1837), I, 386. See Olmstead, *A Journey in the Seaboard Slave States*, p. 128.

[36] *Slave Songs*, p. 67; Allen (comp.), *op. cit.*, p. xli.

[37] Martineau, *op. cit.*, I, 381; Bremer, *op. cit.*, II, 90.

[38] Kemble, *op. cit.*, p. 57; Wise, *op. cit.*, p. 74; John Allen Wyeth, *With Sabre and Scalpel* (New York, 1914), p. 77.

[39] Margaret Devereaux, *Plantation Sketches* (Cambridge, 1906), p. 30; Clayton, *op. cit.*, p. 124; Eliza Ripley, *Social Life in Old New Orleans* (New York, 1912), p. 193; Wyeth, *op. cit.*, pp. 52 f.

mistreated a black man. Only extremely conservative Negroes were generally criticized. In humble places, Uncle Tom did look bad with his unkempt clothes and his hat in his hand. In high places, he was not loved, for his motives were selfish.

Uncle Tom of the Port Royal Islands sang that he knew that he was too self-denying and humble for those Negroes who had not enjoyed his advantages of Christianization in South Carolina. These called him a boaster, a turncoat, and a destruction maker. He did not care what they called him, for he knew that he meant what he was about. During the period after the trial of Nat Turner his conduct had three noticeable results. After years of effort he was for the first time on his way to make money for himself, and he knew how to please his master and thus to get by. He claimed genuine interest in his people, "for Mary and Marta." The community, except the antagonistic Negro part, called him a success. He would, therefore, recommend his religion upon every occasion. It was *"so* sweet."

1. O walk Jordan long road,
   And religion *so* sweet;
   O religion *is* good for anyting,
   And religion *so* sweet.

3. Religion make you happy (or Humble).

4. Religion *gib* [make] me *patience* (or *Honor, Comfort*) [wait].

5. O member, get religion.

6. I long time been *a-huntin'* [seekin'].

7. I seekin' for my fortune.

8. O I gwine to meet my *Savior* [Jesus].

9. Gwine to tell him 'bout my trials.

10. Dey call me boastin' member.

11. Dey call me turnback (or Lyin', 'ceitful) Christian.

12. Dey call me 'struction maker.

13. But I don't care what dey call me.

14. Lord, trial 'longs to a Christian.

106

15. O tell me 'bout religion.

16. I weep for Mary and Marta.

17. I seek my Lord and I find him.[40]

Less-favored slaves showed that they were disgusted with the requirements which the South demanded of Negroes. They appropriated enough of American culture to know that the death penalty was too extreme a punishment for people who were not matured spiritually, as Negroes were. They chose to penalize themselves by fleeing to the North. To a partially Christianized Negro singer in North Carolina the aftermath of Turner's terror was just like the approaching winter season. There was one thing, he sang, which African cultists needed to do and that was to ask the Lord to turn them around. In an "O yes, Lord" spiritual, all of whose references were to events contemporaneous with Turner's insurrection, he asked the Lord "for wings to fly." (The verse describing those Negroes of Southampton County who revolted and who were arrested and tried at Jerusalem I have rejected because of its freedom adverbs, "so, so.") The closing months of 1831 were at hand; so the winter was approaching. After this winter was over Negroes sang devotionally that "de winter'll soon be over":

[Chorus:]
O de vinter, O de vinter, O de vinter'll soon be ober (or Am a-comin'),
    chilen,
[O] De vinter, O de vinter, O de vinter'll soon be ober [Am a-comin'],
    chilen,
[O] De vinter, O de vinter, O de vinter'll soon be ober (or Am
    a-comin'), chilen,
Yes, my Lord!

1. 'Tis Paul and Silas bound in chains, chains [jail, jail],
    And one did [Dey] weep (or Sing), and de oder one did [dey] pray!

2. You bend your knees (or I bend my knees, etc.) on holy [de] ground,
    ground,
    And [I] ask de Lord, Lord, for to turn you [me] around.
    For de vinter, etc.

[40] *Slave Songs*, p. 13; Allen (comp.), *op. cit.*, p. xxxix.

3. I turn my eyes to*wards* the sky, sky,
   And [I] ask de Lord, Lord, for wings to fly.

4. *For you see me gwine 'long so, so,*
   I has my tri-trials yer below.[41]

Thousands of Negroes easily became fugitive slaves as they gained ideas from their numerous songs about heaven and Canaan. Frederick Douglass gave the Jubilee Singers of Fisk University a song, called "Run to Jesus, Shun the Danger," with the statement that it first suggested to him the thought of escaping from slavery.[42] Said he in 1836:

We were at times remarkably buoyant, singing hymns, and making joyous exclamations, almost as triumphant in their tone as if we had reached a land of freedom and safety. A keen observer might have detected in our repeated singing of

> O Canaan, sweet Canaan,
> I am bound for the land of Canaan,

something more than a hope of reaching heaven. We meant to reach the North, and the North was our Canaan.[43]

Though Douglass tried his best to disparage the African cult with its conjuring, particularly after he became a Christian minister of the African Methodist Episcopal Zion Church, he was, nevertheless, indebted to secret meetings for his total ideology. In such meetings, with four male companions he planned his successful escape from slavery.[44]

A southern historian estimated that two thousand slaves were lost annually after 1831.[45] These people were among the most valuable Negroes and exhibited courage, daring, endurance, and skill in their

[41] *Slave Songs,* p. 78; Allen (comp.), *op. cit.,* p. xli.

[42] Marsh, *op. cit.,* p. 188.

[43] [Frederick Douglass], *Life and Times of Frederick Douglass* (Hartford, 1881), p. 179.

[44] [Frederick Douglass], *A Narrative of the Life of Frederick Douglass* (Boston, 1845), *passim.*

[45] John Spencer Bassett, *A Short History of the United States* (New York, 1921), p. 430.

escapes.[46] The escapes of Negroes were possible because owners were definitely unacquainted with individual slaves or were absentee proprietors, and because after working hours slaves were ordinarily left to themselves. Slaves simply walked away from many places in the South.[47] An added incentive to escape was the fact that runaway Negroes could receive needed help from their fellows, although an extreme Uncle Tom sometimes betrayed his companions.[48] If we omit the reference to the Civil War "soldiers," the following song is a good example of the fugitive theme:

Sister Rosy, you get to heaven before I go,
Sister, you *look out for me* [tell 'em], I'm on de way.
Trabel on, trabel on, *you heaven-born* (meaning *heaven-bound*) *soldier,*
Trabel on, trabel on,
Go hear-de *what* my Jesus say.[49]

After the Vesey plot was discovered in Charleston, South Carolina, only the adjoining Negro graveyard remained to tell where the local African Methodist church building had been located.[50] Morris Brown, who had joined the African Methodist Episcopal Church at Philadelphia in 1818, was the elder of this church. In the spring of the very year of the Vesey conspiracy (1822) he had been elected assistant to the venerable Bishop Allen. The city of Charleston exonerated him from any connection with the insurrectionary plot, and the general church elevated him as its second bishop in 1828,[51] con-

[46] Martineau, *op. cit.,* I, 358 f. The effects of slave escapes were noticed in George Combe, *Notes on the United States of North America during a Phrenological Visit in 1838–9–40* (Philadelphia, 1841), II, 34; Buckingham, *The Slave States of America,* I, 138, 571; Bristed, *op. cit.,* p. 197; W. Chambers, *Things As They Are in America* (Philadelphia, 1854), p. 362.

[47] [Josiah Henson], *The Life of Josiah Henson, Formerly a Slave, Now an Inhabitant of Canada* (Boston, 1849), pp. 48 f.; Charles Lyell, *A Second Visit to the United States of North America* (New York, 1849), II, 35.

[48] Robert Sutcliffe, *Travels in Some Parts of North America in the Years 1804, 1805 & 1806* (Philadelphia, 1812), p. 220; Matthew Gregory Lewis, *op. cit.,* p. 94.

[49] *Slave Songs,* p. 31; Allen (comp.), *op. cit.,* p. xl.

[50] Abel McKee Chreitzberg, *Early Methodism in the Carolinas* (Nashville, 1897), pp. 157 f.; Howell Meadows Henry, *The Police Patrol of the Slave in South Carolina* (Emory, Va., 1914), pp. 141 f.

[51] Payne, *History of the African Methodist Episcopal Church,* pp. 22, 26, 58.

nection was established between an African secret meeting and an American Negro church.

The exodus of Negroes from the South received its denominational character from its participants. Nat Turner was said to have been a preacher of Baptist persuasion.[52] After 1831 Negro Baptists enrolled such large groups of members in the North that their organizational life began there. In Ohio and in Illinois they organized their first associations in 1836 [53] and in 1839,[54] respectively. In New York they began their American Baptist Missionary Convention in 1840.[55] The flight of Negroes was so national in scope that a stringent federal fugitive law was required in 1850. That did not stop the matter, however. There were international angles to it. Nothing resulted from Congressional debate upon the several hundred slaves from Guatemala who had taken refuge within the United States, but the federal government demonstrated its concern over fugitive Negro slaves who were with the Indians of Florida, with the British of Canada, and with the Spaniards of Mexico.

Nevertheless, militancy was no more characteristic of Negroes than pacifism. In the United States Nat Turner had climaxed the efforts of Negroes to solve their problems by material methods, and the rulers of society had retaliated by showing Negroes that they did not possess sufficient material strength to cause satisfying changes in a nation. Then it was that pacific Negroes captured racial leadership and persuaded, in song, a majority of slaves to rely upon self-denial, humility, and sincerity. Other lowly spiritual possessions like patience, courtesy, obedience, and forgiveness were added to these basic virtues and explained why certain Negroes with such qualities developed unusual power in the antebellum South. Yet conservative Negroes did not claim that they had solved the problems of the black masses, but only their own. Thousands of other Negroes solved their problems by fleeing to free territories, leaving firsthand documents of their stories in slave songs.

[52] Drewry, *op. cit.*, p. 33.
[53] "Extracts of Minutes of Twenty-Fifth Anniversary of Providence Anti-Slavery Association of Ohio," in David Christy, *Pulpit Politics or Ecclesiastical Legislation on Slavery* (5th ed., Cincinnati, 1862), pp. 184 f.
[54] *Minutes of the Wood River Baptist Association, 1839*, I, 7.
[55] *American Baptist Year Book*, 1871, p. 26.

"I AM BOUND FOR
THE PROMISED LAND"

I am bound for the promised land;
I am bound for the promised land:
O who will come and go with me?
I am bound for the promised land.[1]

INSTEAD of resorting to violence after Nat Turner's insurrection, Negroes tried to get along with white people or became fugitives in the expectancy of benefiting from residence in free territories. They revived their hopes for African colonization and sang, "I can't stan' de fire, While Jordan da roll *so swif'* (dear sister)." [2] Liberia, called "home," "Canaan," and "heab'n" by Negroes in 1824, was still so

[1] "Boun' ter go" was an ambiguous Negro phrase which glorified the other world in Africa.

Rigdon McCoy McIntosh (1838–1899) wrote, "I am bound for the promised land" (*The Methodist Hymnal*, p. 551; *Negro Baptist Standard Hymnal* [Nashville, 1924], p. 581). Presumably the author was of age when he arranged this hymn with verses from Stennett's "On Jordan's stormy banks I stand." George Pullen Jackson, *Spiritual Folk Songs*, p. 238, ingenuously criticized the song and quoted it from the *Original Sacred Harp* (1844). McIntosh was but six years old when the first edition appeared, Jackson said. The difficulty was obviated in Jackson's *White Spirituals*, p. 219. McIntosh did not write this song; Miss M. Durham did. It appeared in the *Southern Harmony* of 1835.

[2] *Slave Songs*, p. 42; Allen (comp.), *op. cit.*, p. xl.

referred to during Turner's aftermath, but now it was also called "the promised land," "Zion," "Paradise," and the "new Jerusalem."

Francis Devany, who had lived in Liberia for more than seven years and who had been elected high sheriff of that country, returned to the United States in May, 1830, to appear before a Congressional committee and report that several emigrants had already made a fortune in Africa.[3] This information was comforting to Negro slaves, for there were no Sunday tasks over in Zion. With the mind's eye a Negro looked over into Zion and saw an angel segregated like himself, but this angel had a mark in his forehead and a harp in his hand. In Zion Negroes were going to "walk about" freely without having to obtain passes as they were compelled to do in the Americas. After they had walked as much as they pleased, Negroes sat right down at will. A fortune might even result from such idleness.

1. Gwine to walk about Zion, I *really do* believe;
   [Gwine to] Walk about Zion, I *really do* believe;
   [Gwine to] Walk about Zion, I *really do* believe;
   Sabbath has no end.

   [Chorus:]
   I *did view one* [see] angel
   In *one* [de] angel stand;
   Let's mark *him* [he] *right* down with the forehalf,
   With the harpess in *his* [he] hand

2. Gwine to follow *King* Jesus, I *really do* believe.

3. I love God *certain* [sho'].

4. My sister*'s* got *re*ligion.

5. Set down in *the kingdom* [heab'n].

6. *Re*ligion *is* a fortune.[4]

---

[3] M[atthew] Carey, *Letters on the Colonization Society . . . to Which Is Prefixed the Important Information Collected by Joseph Jones, a Coloured Man, Lately Sent to Liberia, by the Kentucky Colonization Society, to Ascertain the True State of the Country—Its Productions, Trade, and Commerce—and the Situation and Prospects of the Colonists* (11th ed., Philadelphia, 1838), p. 25.

[4] *Slave Songs*, p. 69; Allen (comp.), *op. cit.*, p. xli. The author of this song knew the "walk about Zion" in Psalm 48:12 and confused Revelation 13:16.

The transportation of Negroes to Zion was, however, more hazardous than anyone anticipated. When the *Harriet* sailed in 1829, the casualties among the emigrants were checked in red ink. There were 18 Negroes who were reported as having died on that vessel and 23 on the *Liberia*. No less than 56 out of 106 emigrants who started to Africa on the *Montgomery* in 1830 succumbed. That year colonizationists stopped recording the deaths of emigrants. Of the 382 Negroes who sailed to Africa that year, 143 of them died, over 37 per cent.

The name, age, occupation, residence in the United States, and time of emigration were recorded for each emigrant. A record was also kept giving the ship upon which each emigrant sailed. Negroes registered in advance for sailings to Africa and about 1832 asked questions, in song, about the ships upon which they were to embark. Questions similar to the facetious ones asked of Ohio flatboatmen were asked prospective emigrants: "Where from?" "How laden?" "Who is the captain?" etc.[5] About ten years later Negroes of Anne Arundel County, Maryland, sang:

1. *What* ship *is that* [be] you're *enlisted up*on?
   O glory hallelujah!

   [Chorus:]
   'Tis the old ship of Zion, hallelujah!
   'Tis the old ship of Zion, hallelujah!

2. *And who is* the Captain of the ship *that* you're on?—O glory, etc.
   My Saviour is the Captain, hallelujah! [6]

The American Colonization Society had originally been organized to send to Africa those free Negroes who chose to go from the United States. After the insurrection of Nat Turner, African colonization became a movement to rid the United States of its free Negro population. Pressure was put upon Negroes in the neighborhood of the Southampton insurrection to expatriate themselves in order that the safety of white people might be assured. The Racoonswamp Baptist Church of Southampton County, Virginia, drew up six lists of names of Negroes in the community and questioned each person on his ac-

---

[5] Flint, *op. cit.,* p. 31.
[6] *Slave Songs,* p. 102; Allen (comp.), *op. cit.,* p. xlii.

tivities during Turner's terror. If a slave broke the rules of the church, a master could chastise him without any liability of church discipline himself.[7] Churches as far removed as those in Georgia protested against this veritable ecclesiastical third degree.[8] Being closer to the scene of alarm in Virginia, the Portsmouth Baptist Association urged all of its churches, especially the Mill Swamp Church of Southampton County, to examine all of the Negro members and to instruct them in church government and in "their duty to their owners." If slaves refused this teaching, they were to be expelled.[9] The reverberations of such inquisitions were preserved by Negroes in North Carolina. It was probably in Virginia that a slave cried: "O mother I believe that Christ *was* crucified":

1. O mother I believe
   O mother I believe
   O mother I believe
   That Christ *was* crucified!

   [Chorus:]
   O don't you hear the Heaven bells a-ring*ing over me?*
   [Hear the Heaven bells] a-ring*ing over me? a-ringing over me?*
   O don't you hear the Heaven bells a-ring*ing over me?*
   It *sounds like the* judgment day! [10]

The Maryland Colonization Society sent thirty Negroes to Liberia on the *Orion* on October 22, 1831. This was sixteen emigrants less than had sailed on that Society's *Criterion* in July. When the *James Perkins* sailed for Africa under the auspices of the American Colonization Society on December 9, 1831, it carried out 339 emigrants. One might presume that militant Negroes would have been cleared from Southampton County by this time, but of those emigrants to Africa in December exactly 276 were freedmen from Southampton County alone, and the other emigrants were from neighboring counties in Virginia and North Carolina. From South-

---

[7] "Record Book of the Racoonswamp Baptist Church," MS, Virginia Baptist Historical Society.

[8] *History of the Baptist Denomination in Georgia* (Atlanta, 1881), p. 274.

[9] *Minutes of the Virginia Baptist Portsmouth Association* (1932), pp. 26 f., in the Virginia [Richmond] Baptist Historical Society.

[10] *Slave Songs*, p. 79; Allen (comp.), *op. cit.*, p. xli.

ampton County went two families of Turners: Peter, age 24; Julia, his wife, 23; Debborah, 4; Jacob, 3; and the infant, James. The names in the family of Andrew Turner, a shoemaker, 38, his wife, Milly, 40, and their children reveal perhaps that they were not as religious. There were William, 14; Bessy, 12; John, 9; Ely, 6; Dahley, 4; Vine, 3; and Lewis, 2.[11] On three colonization ships that sailed to Africa in 1832, forty-one other emigrants from Southampton County, Virginia, were included.

A Negro who kept hearing his fellows sing that their home was in the wilderness retorted that he knew when he was going home. He was bound for Africa, himself; he was afraid to die, having been convinced by Satan that the civil rights which Negroes sought would never be operative in the United States. This "O yes, Lord" song used concepts of the post-Turner era. This spiritual was preserved on the Port Royal Islands, but its place of origin was perhaps in Southampton County, Virginia:

> Old Satan *told* [tell] me to my face,
> O yes, Lord,
> De God I seek *I never find,*
> O yes, Lord.
> True believer, I know *when* I gwine home,
> True believer, I know *when* I gwine home,
> True believer, I know *when* I gwine home,
> I *been* afraid to die.[12]

One result of Turner's insurrection was that the trumpet of the patrol was continually sounding in the ears of Virginia Negroes who were being put in jail at Jerusalem. Undoubtedly Biblical information among Negroes was feverishly accelerated by Civil War missionaries, but the trend was begun in post-Turner days. So one Negro spiritual was based on Acts 16:23–40, which tells of the imprisonment of Paul and Silas at Philippi. Thinking of what he and his companions suffered, the author of the spiritual said the treatment of these missionaries was unjust. This conservative singer hoped constantly that he might be expatriated to Liberia, West Africa, his "new Jerusalem." This song was heard in Charleston, South Carolina, in

---

[11] "Emigrant Register," p. 48.
[12] *Slave Songs,* p. 30; Allen (comp.), *op. cit.,* p. xl.

1842, though it spoke of circumstances that had occurred in Southampton County, Virginia, more than ten years earlier:

> Paul and Silas, *bound* in jail,
> Christians pray *both* night and day,
> *And* I hope dat trump *might* blow me home
> To my new Jerusalem.
> *So* blow de trump*et*, Gabriel,
> Blow de trump*et*, loud*er*,
> *And* I hope dat trump *might* blow me home
> To my new Jerusalem.[13]

Negroes in Virginia probably sang this spiritual in words close to
the original, and the variant song was heard on the Port Royal Islands
"in nearly the same form," although its author was less Christianized.
He began his song with "the tall palm tree" of "Paradise." His spiritual expressed the plantation teaching that Christianity was in every
respect superior to the religion which the black masses possessed.
Hence in freedom it was the "talles' tree." The non-Christian "new
Jerusalem" and "Gabriel" were mentioned ahead of "Paul and Silas,"
but the song was climaxed by ending with the Lord's Prayer of praise
to God. It might have taken about a year for this spiritual to migrate
to South Carolina.

> 1. De tall*es'* tree in Paradise,
>   De Christian call de tree of life;
>   *And* I hope dat trump *might* blow me home
>   To de new Jerusalem.
>
> [Chorus:]
> Blow your trump*et*, Gabriel,
> Blow loud*er, louder;*
> *And* I hope dat trump *might* blow me home
> To de new Jerusalem.
>
> 2. Paul and Silas, *bound* in jail,
>   Sing God'*s* praise *both* night and day;
>   *And* I hope, etc.[14]

---

[13] *Slave Songs*, p. 3; Allen (comp.), *op. cit.*, p. xxxix.
[14] *Slave Songs*, p. 3; Allen (comp.), *op. cit.*, p. xxxix.

Jacob's ladder continued as a Negro concept of African colonization, denoting progress. In Wyer's Cave, Virginia, seventeen miles from Staunton, it was the name of a natural flight of steps.[15] Slaves in Florida sang a revived Jacob's ladder spiritual, adding that one reason why they had not been removed to Liberia any faster was because masters only manumitted a few Negroes for colonization. As much as one singer wanted to make progress in this direction, that is, "to climb *up* Jacob's ladder," he could not do so until he had won the esteem of "the Lord." Of course, this statement ambiguously meant either peace with his earthly master or the acceptance of Christianity. Possibly both were intended, although the singer swore that he would follow secret meetings until he died. The reference to Jerusalem in the song suggests its Virginia origin early in post-Turner days:

> I want to climb *up* Jacob's ladder.
> [I want to climb] Jacob's ladder, *O Jacob's ladder,*
> I want to climb *up* Jacob's ladder,
> *But* I can't climb *it* till I make *my* peace with the Lord.
> O praise *ye* the Lord,
> *I'll* praise *Him* till I die,
> *I'll* praise *Him* till I die,
> *And* sing Jerusalem.[16]

Negroes dreamed about what they were going to do when they got to Liberia. More than one of them had been reading holy books. This fitted in nicely with the instruction of colonizationists for emigrants to do the first necessary thing in Africa, namely, to build houses. Most likely it was original with a Negro from South Carolina to have such intentions, for on the Port Royal Islands more than one hopeful emigrant kept singing for many years that he was going to "build a house in Paradise." This song was prolonged by singing verses of the family relations. The one who originated this spiritual resented being called a heathen because, unlike the heathen mentioned in Jeremiah 10:4, who made and adorned his idol "with nails and with hammers," he intended to construct his home "widout a hammer *or* [and] a nail."

---

[15] Buckingham, *The Slave States of America,* II, 277, 366.
[16] *Slave Songs,* p. 96; Allen (comp.), *op. cit.,* p. xli.

[1.] My brudder build a house in Paradise,

> Build it widout a hammer *or* [and] a nail,
> Build it widout a hammer *or* [and] a nail.

[2.] [My] fader build a house in Paradise.

[3.] Ona build a house in Paradise.[17]

When this song reached Virginia during the next year, 1833, it was used for a work song. Mills were often floating affairs, mounted between two flatboats, and at one of these mills, say on the James River, the slave imagined that it was on the Jordan River in the heavenly land, in Africa, and that it ran "without wind *or* [and] water"—as his mill certainly did not. The first singer of this song probably had some contact with Biblical teachings, since he took his inspiration from Jeremiah:

> 1. Jerdan's mills a-grind*ing,*
>   Jerdan's a-hay;
>   Jerdan's mills a-grind*ing,*
>   Jerdan's a-hay.
>
> 2. Built without nail *or* [and] hammer.
>
> 3. Runs without wind *or* [and] water.[18]

Details like these in spirituals disprove both the belief of those who imagined that Negroes returning to Africa would become savage as soon as they could (such persons did not care as long as the Negroes were gotten rid of [19]) and the theory of "forgotten memories," which declared that Negro slavery dissolved the bonds of sympathy between men of the same blood and household.[20] The desire drive to return to Africa was prominent among Negroes who had been reared in the folkways of American culture.

Such a Negro on the Port Royal Islands had been Christianized enough to know Matthew 7:24–27 and to sing an "O yes, Lord" version of the Paradise-house concept in the light of the man who built his house on the rock. After considering all sides of the matter, he

[17] *Slave Songs,* p. 29; Allen (comp.), *op. cit.,* p. xl.

[18] *Slave Songs,* p. 68; Allen (comp.)ṣ *op. cit.,* p. xli.

[19] Murat, *op. cit.,* p. 107.

[20] Frazier, *The Negro Family in America,* p. 21.

wanted to go to Africa. This farewell spiritual coincided with the
sailing of South Carolina emigrants for Africa in December, 1832.
Its popularity did not end until it had incorporated the "Marching
Along" song which had been taught Negro troops by Civil War missionaries.[21]

> I build my house *upo*n a rock,
> O yes, Lord!
> No wind *nor* [and] storm *shall* blow dem down,
> O yes, Lord!
>
> *March on, member, Bound* [Want] to go;
> *March on, member, Bound* [Want] to go;
> *March on, member, Bound* [Want] to go;
> Bid 'em fare you well.[22]

Verses concerning the hanging berries of the "Nobody Knows"
spiritual when attached to the Paradise-house "O yes, Lord!" song,
label it a freedom variant. In it houses built on rock and sand were
contrasted in Biblical fashion. The hazards of sailing to Liberia and
the difficulty of building a house there, should one survive acclima-
tion, were looked upon as the preferable courses of a wise man. To
lay plans to remain in the United States was thought to be foolish by
not a few ex-slaves.

> 1. *I build my house upon de rock,*
>   *O yes, Lord!*
>   *No wind, no storm can blow 'em down,*
>   *O yes, Lord!*
>
>   [Chorus:]
>   *March on, member, Bound to go;*
>   *Been to de ferry, Bound to go;*
>   *Left St. Helena, Bound to go;*
>   *Brudder, fare you well.*
>
> 2. *I build my house on shiftin' sand.*
>   *De first wind come he blow him down.*
>
> 3. *I am not like de foolish man.*
>   *He build his house upon de sand.*

---

[21] Higginson, *Army Life in a Black Regiment*, p. 221.
[22] *Slave Songs*, pp. 22 f.; Allen (comp.), *op. cit.*, p. xl.

4. *One mornin' as I was walkin' along.*
   I saw de berries a-hanging down.

5. *I pick de berries and I suck de juice.*
   He sweeter dan de honey comb.

[6.] *I tuk dem brudder, two by two.*
   I tuk dem sister, tree by tree.[23]

Negro firemen around Savannah, Georgia, put logs into the boilers of boat engines on the river while they sang an African colonization song which the original singers in the 1830's had intended as their request for expatriation. "Each company of laborers," said Kane O'Donnell, describing this incident to the Philadelphia *Press,* "has its own set of tunes, its own leader, and doubtless in the growth of time, necessity and invention, its own composer." Their song told that they had "rather court a yellow gal than work for Henry Clay."

Heave away, heave away!
I'*d rather* court a yellow gal than work for Henry Clay,
Heave away, heave away!
Yellow gal, I want to go,
I'*d rather* court a yellow gal than work for Henry Clay,
Heave away!
Yellow gal, I want to go! [24]

Spirituals also told that slaves wanted to go to Africa to be rid of their Negro drivers. Man is inhuman to man whether he is black or white. Thus slaves hated their racial drivers although such overseers had been appointed on plantations to appease militant Negroes.[25] About 1832 a Negro driver and a particular master and mistress in the southeastern slave states were the objects of full condemnation in a Negro song:

[23] *Slave Songs,* p. 22; Allen (comp.), *op. cit.,* p. xl.
[24] *Slave Songs,* p. 61; Allen (comp.), *op. cit.,* p. xl.
[25] Pinckard, *op. cit.,* II, 121; R. Bickell, *The West Indies As They Are; or a Real Picture of Slavery, but More Particularly As It Exists in the Island of Jamaica* (London, 1825), p. 56; Basil Hall, *Travels in North America in the Years 1827 and 1828* (Edinburgh, 1829), III, 145; Kemble, *Journal,* pp. 42, 43, 172; [Lewis], *op. cit.,* p. 128; James Stirling, *Letters from the Slave States* (London, 1857), p. 288; Olmsted, *A Journey in the Back Country,* pp. 14–15.

1. Done wid driber's dribin',
   Done wid driber's dribin',
   Done wid driber's dribin',
   Roll, Jordan, roll.

2. Done wid massa's *hollerin'* [call].

3. Done wid missus' *scoldin'* [call].[26]

Negro soldiers in the regiment of Colonel Higginson expressed their desire to go to Africa in an "O yes, Lord!" spiritual. By going to Liberia, Negro slaves wanted to escape work in the falling rain and burning sun and "stormy weather" under harsh Negro drivers who cracked their whips of authority. Imagining that old loyalties would continue in Africa, one original singer contrasted the joy of being at home to the post-Turner trials of about 1832. Subsequent singers added the accompanying tribulations of Negroes in the United States.

1. Dere's no rain to wet you.
   O yes, I want to go home,
   Want to go home.

2. Dere's no sun to burn you,—O yes, etc.,

3. Dere's no hard trials.

4. Dere's no whips a-crackin'.

5. Dere's no stormy weather.

7. No *more* slavery in *de kingdom* [heaven].

8. *No evil-doers in de kingdom.*

9. *All is gladness in de kingdom.*[27]

Another reason why Negroes chose to go to Africa was that they were "an unwanted people." [28] A spiritual from the Port Royal Islands included the Civil War rumor that Negroes would be emancipated and then expatriated. This song was sung two verses at a

---

[26] *Slave Songs,* p. 45; Allen (comp.), *op. cit.,* p. xl.

[27] *Slave Songs,* p. 46; Allen (comp.), *op. cit.,* p. xl.

[28] Bassett, *A Short History of the United States,* p. 578; John Hope Franklin, *The Free Negro in North Carolina 1790–1860* (Chapel Hill, 1943), chap. vi.

time and stated that one day was as good as another for black people to decide to leave the United States since all of them sooner or later would be obliged to emigrate. Such a song combined several familiar Negro concepts. Its singer, of about 1833, was laboring under the belief that a "fortune" awaited him at "Wappoo." His leaving the United States would be a "new repentance" since he was probably a militant secret meeter. He would arrive in Africa in time to witness his "dying Saviour":

1. Oh *one* [a] day *as* anoder,
   Hallelu, hallelu!

2. *When* de ship is out a-sail*in'*,
   Hallelujah!

3. *Member walk and never tire.*

4. Member walk Jordan long road.

5. Member walk tribulation.

6. You go home to Wappoo.

7. Member seek new repentance.

8. I go to seek my fortune.

9. I go to seek my dying Saviour.

10. *You want to die like Jesus.*[29]

When one of the emigrants from South Carolina was about to embark on the transport ship of December, 1832, he sang his "goodbye." The song incorporated the familiar concept of absence in the body and presence in spirit. When in 1838 or 1839 a mistress was about to leave South Carolina for St. Simon Island, Georgia, slaves uttered their good wishes in a song which was interpreted to mean that they were "parted in body, but not in mind."[30] Once at a local conference of the Colored Methodist Episcopal Church, the presiding bishop recalled that on taking a short trip in his young manhood he was bidden adieu by Negroes who waved goodbye and hoped to

---

[29] *Slave Songs,* p. [50]; Allen (comp.), *op. cit.,* p. xl.
[30] Kemble, *op. cit.,* p. 159.

meet him in the spirit. Such a farewell might be said to be characteristic of Negroes.

1. Good-bye, brother, good-bye, brother,
   If I don't see you *more;*
   Now God bless you, *now* God bless you,
   If I don't see you *more.*

2. *We* [I] part in de body *but we* [I] meet in de spirit,
   We'll [I] meet in de heaben in de *blessed*
   (or *Glorious*) *kingdom* [glory].

3. *So* good-bye, brother, good-bye, *sister* [brother];
   Now God bless you, *now* God bless you.[31]

Another "good-bye" spiritual rejoiced that the singer was going home and encouraged other slaves to want to go.

> Good-bye, my brudder, good-bye,
> Hallelujah!
> Good-bye, *sister Sally,* [my brudder], good-bye,
> Hallelujah!
> Going home,
> Hallelujah!
> Jesus call me,
> Hallelujah!
> *Linger no longer,*
> *Hallelujah!*
> *Tarry no longer,*
> *Hallelujah!* [32]

Emigrants to Africa continued to sing their farewells:

> *When we do* [I] meet again,
> *When we do* [I] meet again,
> *When we do* [I] meet again,
> *'Twill* [It] be no *more to* part.
> Brother Billy, fare you well,
> Brother Billy, fare you well,
> *We'll* [I] sing hallelujah,
> *When we do* [I] meet again.[33]

[31] *Slave Songs,* p. 47; Allen (comp.), *op. cit.,* p. xl; Marsh, *op. cit.,* p. 215.
[32] *Slave Songs,* p. 52; Allen (comp.), *op. cit.,* p. xl.
[33] *Slave Songs,* p. 41; Allen (comp.), *op. cit.,* p. xl.

Disadvantaged Negroes were so anxious to leave cultured North America and go to Liberia that many of them secreted themselves in the holds of ships going to Africa and showed themselves only when it was too late to return them.[34] There can be no doubt that many leaders of Christian thought in the United States were in sympathy with the desire of the Negro masses to leave the country. It was not mere rhetoric when in 1831 Elliott Cresson, able agent of the American Colonization Society, declared in England that 100,000 American slaves were ready to go to Africa. Longfellow summarized this longing for expatriation in his poem "The Slave's Dream," which told of a Negro's wish to be by the banks of the Niger where he could roam and escape the lash of the Negro driver. Even before this, colonizationists had sent five vessels to Liberia in 1832 and five the next year. Only one ship sailed to Africa in 1834, but it carried 127 colonists. Four vessels went to Liberia in 1835, four in 1836, and thereafter two a year until 1841. From 1820 through 1853 at least 104 ships sailed for Liberia under the auspices of the American Colonization Society, carrying out 8,204 Negroes, not counting the additional 1,000 emigrants who had gone under the auspices of the Maryland Colonization Society.[35]

It appeared to unlettered slaves that their emancipation was in sight. Beginning about 1832, South Carolina Negroes sang about this multitude of ex-slaves who were being carried to Africa. In this song they also protested their weekly food allowances, expressed displeasure at the numerous and trivial calls for services by an overlord, and deplored their laboring conditions under merciless Negro drivers who illegally administered one hundred lashes.[36] One stroke of the lash was real punishment. The lash was a cowhide plaited around a handle of about a yard's length. Altogether it was about twice as long, and when well laid on brought blood and always left

[34] Flint, *Recollections of the Last Ten Years,* p. 343; Buckingham, *The Eastern and Western States of America,* I, 199; Higginson, *Travellers and Outlaws,* p. 201.

[35] "Register of Emigrants, 1835–1853," inside cover.

[36] Bremer, *op. cit.,* I, 297; Olmsted, *A Journey in the Back Country,* p. 61; Julian Ralph, *Dixie* (New York, 1895), p. 216. Slaves were given several hundred lashes in South America (W. Pettingill, tr., *Letters from America, 1776–1779* [Boston, 1924], p. 257; Pinckard, *op. cit.,* II, 46).

a permanent scar.[37] This antebellum slave's spontaneous farewell as he was on the gangplank of a ship bound for Liberia became so popular that in freedom Negroes were still singing:

1. No *more* peck o' corn for me,
   No *more,* [peck o' corn for me,] *no more;*
   No *more* peck o' corn for me,
   Many *tousand* [people] go.

2. No *more* driver's lash for me.

3. No *more* pint o' salt for me.

4. No *more* hundred lash for me.

5. No *more mistress'* [missus] call for me.[38]

The American Colonization Society was faced with certain insurmountable obstacles. Free Negroes were not being transported to Africa as fast as they naturally increased, opposition to the Society was widening, and slaves were experiencing real difficulties in obtaining manumissions for African colonization. Only 4,549 Negroes had been manumitted up to 1853, yet in 1850 there were 765,160 Negroes in the United States. William Lloyd Garrison's *Thoughts on African Colonization* had launched a telling attack upon the whole plan. Captain Charles Stuart's English writings relied upon the anticolonization sentiments of Nathaniel Paul, who was touring the British Isles in the interest of a Negro school in the United States.[39] Free

[37] [Amos Dresser], *Narrative of Amos Dresser* (New York, 1836), p. 21; Lyell, *A Second Visit to the United States,* I, 266; B. R. Carroll, *op. cit.,* I, 351.

[38] *Slave Songs,* p. 48; Allen (comp.), *op. cit.,* p. xl.

The collectors of this song, which was heard in Colonel Higginson's regiment of Negroes, remarked that it was a song "to which the Rebellion had actually given rise. This was composed by nobody knows whom though it was the most recent doubtless of all these 'spirituals' and had been sung in secret to avoid detection. The peck of corn and pint of salt were slavery's rations." Lt. Col. Trowbridge first heard the song when Beauregard took slaves from the Port Royal Islands to build fortifications at Hiltonhead and Bay Point. Notwithstanding, this song was not a spiritual of the Civil War period, for spirituals were called forth by contemporary and not past events.

[39] Gilbert Hobbs Barnes, *The Anti-Slavery Impulse, 1830–1844* (New York, [1933]), pp. 213 f.

Negroes in the North had never quit saying that the contributions of black folk to American culture warranted their assimilation by the United States. Spirituals told that even Negro slaves grew hesitant about the whole scheme during the terrible 1830's.

A slave around the Port Royal Islands who probably did not go to Liberia on any ship in 1832 sang:

1. O member, *will* you *linger* [wait]?
   See de chil'en *do linger* [wait] here.

2. I go to glory wid you,
   Member, *join* [jine]

3. O Jesus *is our* [de] Captain.

4. *He lead us on to glory.*

5. *We'll meet at Zion gateway* (or *Heaven portal*).

6. *We'll talk dis story over.*

7. *We'll enter into glory.*

8. *When we done wid dis world trials.*

9. *We done wid all our crosses.*

10. O brudder, *will* you meet us?

11. *When de ship is out a-sailin'.*

12. *O Jesus got de hellum.*

13. *Fader, gader in your chil'en.*

14. *O gader dem for Zion.*

15. *'Twas a beauteous Sunday mornin'.*

16. *When he rose from de dead.*

17. *He will bring you milk and honey.*[40]

The original spiritual of 1832 comforted the many Negroes who were not carried to Liberia at that time by saying that their expatriation delay was caused by the indecisiveness of Negro slaves and not by the will of colonizationists. Through the years this concept be-

---

[40] *Slave Songs*, p. 51; Allen (comp.), *op. cit.*, p. xl.

came a freedom medley declaring also that the expatriation of Negroes was indeed ready. In Africa Negro emigrants would see black folk whom they had known in the United States. A chief subject of their conversation would be the insurrection of Nat Turner.

Colonizationists acted as though Negroes themselves could defeat their plans unless the mouths of slaves were stopped. Leading Negroes from Liberia had been brought by the Society in "Deep River" days to declare themselves in favor of the expatriation of Negroes,[41] and later select Negroes of the United States were dispatched to Liberia to report the lay of the land to which they would return. Gloster Simpson, aged 43, and Archey Moore, aged 41, both of Natchez, Mississippi, were selected to make their report on Liberia for the Natchez branch of the Society. They sailed on the *Jupiter,* on May 9, 1832. Their report is not available, but one has been found from Joseph Jones of Winchester, who was sent "home" by the Kentucky Colonization Society. Jones left Louisville on March 23, 1833, and New Orleans on April 10. He reached Africa July 11 and spent nine months and twenty-three days visiting all five of the Liberian settlements. He then reported his visit to the Kentucky Board as well as to interested groups all over the state. He said that in Liberia there were five churches, seven schools, no capital crimes, and satisfied colonists, the majority of whom did not wish to return to the United States. He felt that the only drawbacks to a flourishing colony were the "inordinate desire for trade" in order that the former slave emigrants might make a fortune, the lack of promotion of agriculture, and the need for more male colonists to emigrate.[42]

Echoes of such tours caught the imaginations of southern slaves, who made spirituals of the events. In Charleston, South Carolina, one such spiritual had the refrain: "I can't stay away." In Edgefield another advised: "Don't stay away, my mudder." Colonel Higginson's regiment sang "I can't stay behind." In the time of freedom, Negroes of the Port Royal Islands sang about these investigating tours and concluded, in song, that there was "room enough in de heaven." The original singer needed just that much fact to add that he had sufficiently searched every room "in de heaven," in his mind, and that he had found one in which angels were singing all around

[41] *African Repository,* II (1826), 122 f.; Martineau, *op. cit.,* I, 89.
[42] Carey, *op. cit.,* pp. 1–4.

the throne. God was still calling for American Negroes to go to Africa, but these people were contributing so much to American culture that their colonization had become unthinkable. By the time of freedom all that Negroes could do was to look backwards to their hopes for African colonization and shout:

[Chorus:] (repeated)
I can't stay *behind* [away], my Lord,
I can't stay *behind* [away]!

1. Dere's room enough, Room enough
   Room enough in de heaven, my Lord (or For you).
   Room enough, Room enough,
   I can't stay *behind* [away].

2. I been all around, I been all around,
   [I] been all around de Heaven, my Lord.

3. *I've searched every room—in de Heaven, my Lord (or And Heaven all around).*

4. *De angels singin' (or Crowned)—all around de trone.*

5. *My Fader call—and I must go.*

6. *Sto-back* (meaning shout backwards), *member; sto-back, member.*[43]

Negroes made many adjustments to their thwarted desires for colonization. They not only demonstrated that they were excellent people, but they preserved the efforts of colonizationists to get rid of them in beautiful devotional spirituals which told about " 'Way in de kingdom." One of the earliest such songs was:

[Chorus:]
*God got plenty o' room, got plenty o' room,
'Way in de kingdom,
God got plenty o' room my Jesus say,
'Way in de kingdom.*

1. *Brethren, I have come again,
   'Way in de kingdom,
   To help you all to pray and sing,
   'Way in de kingdom.*

[43] *Slave Songs,* p. 6; Allen (comp.), *op. cit.,* p. xxxix.

128

2. *So many-a weeks and days have passed,*
   Since we met together last.

3. *Old Satan tremble when he sees,*
   The weakest saints upon their knees.

4. *Prayer makes the darkest cloud withdraw,*
   Prayer climbed the ladder Jacob saw.

5. *Daniel's wisdom may I know,*
   Stephen's faith and spirit sure.

6. *John's divine communion feel,*
   Joseph's meek and Joshua's zeal.

7. *There is a school on earth begun,*
   Supported by the Holy One.

8. *We soon shall lay our school-books by,*
   And shout salvation as I fly.[44]

Sending Negroes to Liberia on investigating tours proved to be an excellent idea. As a result of favorable reports, sixty-eight Negroes from Mississippi, including Simpson and Moore, and three from New Orleans sailed from that city to Zion on March 4, 1835, after having a farewell service in a New Orleans Baptist church, where the emigrants were organized into a temperance society.[45] Jones also was returned to Africa. Instead of singing that African emigrants were expatriating themselves from the United States forever, Negroes thought that a passage to Liberia would be a pleasure trip from which they, too, would soon return. They could then boast among their fellows that they had been to "heaven" (i.e., Liberia) once and that they were going back again. The original spiritual containing this thought is not available but a variant song was heard at Helena, Arkansas, where the news had traveled:

1. Little children, *then won't* you be glad,
   Little children, *then won't* you be glad,
   [Little children, you be glad,]
   That you *have* been to heav'n, *an' you're* gwine to go again.
   For to try on the long white robe, children,
   For to try on the long white robe.

[44] *Slave Songs,* p. 106; Allen (comp.), *op. cit.,* p. xlii.
[45] "Emigrants from New Orleans," New Orleans *Picayune,* March 30, 1835.

2. *King Jesus, he was so strong* (*ter*), *my Lord,*
   That he jarred down the walls of hell.

3. *Don't you hear what de chariot say?* (*bis*)
   De fore wheels run by de grace ob God.
   An' de hind wheels dey run by faith.

4. *Don't you 'member what you promise de Lord?* (*bis*)
   You promise de Lord that you would feed his sheep,
   An' gather his lambs so well.[46]

In spite of all that was said and done about removing Negroes from the United States to Liberia under the auspices of the American Colonization Society, this primary object was not fully accomplished. Some slaves were versatile enough to adapt their colonization songs to their unfulfilled hopes, while others still hoped that their dream of being transported to Africa would come true. At a baptismal service during the troubled days after Turner's revolt, a black preacher let everybody know in the first verse of his song that he would much prefer to have been baptizing over in Africa, in "Canaan land." To his song he attached what he knew about his patron saint, Moses, namely, that God one day told Moses to go into Egypt and to tell Pharaoh to let His people go. Pharaoh disobeyed; so God went to Moses' house. The preacher concluded his version of the "Go Down, Moses" spiritual with God and Moses walking and talking in a characteristic antebellum manner. This spiritual included the words "come along, Moses," but it began in the troubled period after Nat Turner.

> [Chorus:]
> Come *down* [along], angel, *and* trouble the water,
> Come *down* [along], angel, *and* trouble the water,
> Come *down* [along], angel, *and* trouble the water,
> *And* let God*'s saints come in* [chillun go].
> (*God say you must.*)

1. Canaan land *is* the land for me,
   And let God*'s saints come in* [chillun go],
   Canaan land *is* the land for me,
   And let God*'s saints come in* [chillun go].

[46] *Slave Songs,* p. 87; Allen (comp.), *op. cit.,* p. xli.

2. *There was a wicked man,*
   He kept them children in Egypt land.

3. *God did say to Moses one day,*
   Say, Moses go to Egypt land,

4. *And* tell *him* [Pharaoh] to let my people go.
   And Pharaoh would not let 'em go.
   [Tell Pharaoh to let my people go.]

5. *God did go to Moses' house,*
   And God did tell him who he was.

6. God and Moses walked and talked,
   And God did show him who he was
   [God and Moses walked and talked].[47]

Such songs do not suggest that their singers were frustrated and heartsick. In convention on July 26, 1847, twelve emigrants in Liberia told why they were led to expatriate themselves from the land of their nativity, to settle on the "barbarous coast" of Africa, and to organize an independent government. Their unanimously adopted Declaration of Independence declared:

We, the people of the Republic of Liberia, were originally inhabitants of the United States of North America.

In some parts of that country we were debarred by law from all rights and privileges of men—in other parts, public sentiment, more powerful than law, frowned us down.

We were everywhere shut out from all civil office.

We were excluded from all participation in the Government.

We were taxed without our consent.

We were compelled to contribute to the resources of a country which gave us no protection.

We were made a separate and distinct class, and against us every avenue of improvement was effectually closed. Strangers from other lands, of a colour different from ours, were preferred before us.

We uttered our complaints, but they were unattended to, or only met by alleging the peculiar institutions of the country.

[47] *Slave Songs,* p. 76; Allen (comp.), *op. cit.,* p. xli.

All hope of a favourable change in our country was thus wholly extinguished in our bosoms, and we looked with anxiety for some asylum from the deep degradation.

Unlike any other country in the world, Liberia became a separate nation guaranteeing to Negroes an "asylum from the most grinding oppression." Its motto was: "THE LOVE OF LIBERTY BROUGHT US HERE." [48]

Thus an Oriental race living under Occidental slavery took various ways of overcoming distasteful conditions. Some, like Nat Turner and his followers, rebelled, while others accepted the master-slave relationship. Some fled to free territories, while others were manumitted to go to Liberia. Through it all slave songs preserved in joyful strains the adjustment which Negroes made to their living conditions within the United States.

[48] Harry Hamilton Johnston, *Liberia* (London, 1906), I, 199 f., 219.

"WHEN I DIE"

O Lawd, when I die,
I want to get to heab'n
My Lord, when I die.[1]

PLANTATION missionaries declared that overlords had discharged their responsibilities when conditions for slaves had been made better. After Nat Turner's insurrection some effort was made to reach Negroes through family prayers, through sermons in white churches with Negro membership or in special chapels on plantations, and through instruction from laymen, women, children, and overseers, who followed the advice of books on slave management. Denominational schools were occasionally established for Negroes, and Bibles and religious tracts were distributed among them. Their teachings ordinarily stressed otherworldliness, which envisioned the full life as neither in the United States nor in Africa. Negroes combined these teachings with their belief that the good life would be enjoyed on earth and sang about their beliefs concerning the crucified Christ and the judgment in the spiritual, "O Mother I Believe." This song illustrated both a this-worldly interpretation, and, when hope for final residence in Africa was thwarted, an otherworldly meaning.

Slave evangelists had hindrances from many directions: from masters, the clergy, and even from Negroes themselves.[2] The "very

[1] Botume, *op. cit.,* p. 251.
[2] J. H. Cuthbert, *Life of Richard Fuller* (New York, 1879), p. 108; cf. William Cathcart, *The Baptist Encyclopaedia* (Philadelphia, 1881), I, 498 f.

133

palatable" doctrine that, because of their color and "the form and construction of their bones," Negroes had no claim on human relationships [3] was one of the first to be set aside. The secret meetings of Africans were cited as evidence that Negroes were not behaving like Europeans.

Uncle Toms helped to make Negro uplift a comparatively easy accomplishment when they deified their white masters in spirituals like "O de Vinter," "Can't Stan' de Fier," and "Turn, Sinner." It must have been pleasing to plantation missionaries, particularly to the Reverend Richard Fuller and to officials of his church around Beaufort, South Carolina, to hear their names called in a distinctive Negro song. Like many southern ministers who got started in Christian service by instructing Negroes, Fuller said: "I had resolved, when first called to the ministry, to confine my labors wholly to our colored population. I was prevented by the hands of God." [4]

"Parson Fuller," "Deacon Henshaw," and the great Lincoln were thus immortalized in a song in which slaves interpreted their teachings. If Negroes wanted to live out their natural days, this spiritual said, they had better learn to be obedient to their master or overlord, that is, "to fear de Lord." They were further exhorted not to lie or to be revengeful. Such conduct of slaves, plus the good graces of their spiritual advisers, had the power to grant them life or death. Although Negroes were disgusted with such mockery of religion, their benefactors could not detect it. Hearers of this song were led astray by an occasional reference to "Brudder Mosey" and other well-known slaves. Negroes sarcastically called Fuller and the rest of the white people who thought that they presided over the destinies of black folk simply birds of the air which sat on the limbs of a tree in a variant "Roll, Jordan, Roll" spiritual, in which slaves were all the while wishing that they could be at home in Africa. This song began with material about heaven characteristic of songs of 1825 and continued with the "Marching Along" song of Civil War days. The following variant dates from about 1835, at which time Pastor Fuller had been at the Beaufort church about three years.[5]

[3] Faux, *op. cit.*, p. 112.

[4] Cuthbert, *op. cit.*, p. 108; cf. Cathcart, *op. cit.*, I, 498 f.

[5] Cuthbert, *op. cit.*, pp. 75, 79, 81.

1. Parson Fuller, Deacon Henshaw, Brudder Mosey, Massa
          Linkum, etc. (or My brudder) sittin' on de tree of life,
    An' he [him] yearde *when* [de] Jordan roll.
    Roll, Jordan, Roll, *Jordan,*
    Roll, Jordan, roll.

    [Chorus:]
    O march de angel march,
    O march de angel march;
    O my soul arise in Heaven, Lord,
    For to yearde when Jordan roll.

2. Little chil'en, learn to fear de Lord,
    And let your days be long;
    Roll, Jordan, etc.

3. O, let no false nor spiteful word
    Be found upon your tongue;
    Roll, Jordan, etc.[6]

The terrible 1830's proved a convenient time in which to evangelize Negroes. William Meade of Virginia was among outstanding
slave missionaries. He had been the first agent of the American Colonization Society, disliking slavery before he was elevated to the assistant bishopric of the Protestant Episcopal Church in 1829. William Capers, the father of plantation missions and a slaveholder of
long standing in South Carolina, began two missions for slaves there
in 1829. These were augmented to six missions in 1834.[7] Down in
Liberty County, Georgia, Charles C. Jones was the guiding spirit in
1832 to lead Presbyterians to support his oral instruction of Negroes, and an association for this purpose was organized. In its
Eighth Report (1843), plantation schools for slaves had demonstrated "their practicality" and also "their necessity," besides "their
propriety and expediency." One happy slaveholder wrote: "We owe
our thanks to the All wise and Merciful God, for the efforts of the
Association in our time of need."

Both Capers and Jones were typical plantation missionaries who
taught Christianity to slaves in terms of what Negroes already knew.

[6] *Slave Songs,* p. 1; Allen (comp.), *op. cit.,* p. xxxix.
[7] Wightman, *op. cit.,* pp. 291, 297.

In 1834 Capers wrote that a convenient time for instructing Negroes, but a very inconvenient one for the missionaries, was "at midnight" and "at the break of day." [8] The *Catechism* of Jones, even though it contained Scriptural advice on the duties of husbands, wives, parents, and children, and though it gave about equal space to the "Duty of Masters," and to the "Duty of Servants," had been largely corrected in its questions and answers by Negroes. Part I began the book with a discussion of God, who was to be worshiped by slaves at least every morning and evening. Part II discussed angels, the two good ones, Gabriel and Michael, and the great number of evil ones. Part III, about man, gave instruction in unfamiliar doctrines, such as the atonement and the resurrection (reincarnation), with emphasis upon the Holy Ghost. Part IV discussed the Ten Commandments, and Part V, the church. Negro pupils paid small attention to these final sections of the book, not because their subjects were too obtrusive but because they had little influence in winning good treatment from overlords. Other plantation missionaries used the Apostles' Creed and the Lord's Prayer as lesson material. Jones's *Catechism* was hailed as a Christian book, written by a Christian minister for Negroes, and yet it did not consider a discussion of Jesus Christ important enough for a distinct section. Indeed, Negroes rarely experienced any Christianity in operation that was superior to their traditional religion. Slaves often referred to conversations which they had with holy ones and attributed "some of their actions" to "direct influence of the 'Holy Spirit' or of the devil." [9]

Not only does it seem that the life of Jesus was neglected in some antebellum teaching, but spirituals indicate that correct Biblical information was sometimes refused to Negroes. The "Run, Nigger, Run" song in the mouths of instructed Charlestonians in freedom referred no longer to weeping Mary escaping from early-morning secret meetings, but to weeping Mary announcing "dat de Lord he is arisen." This confused information was not corrected by plantation missionaries for the thirty or more years that this slave song was extant. Another song made it known that Mary would have no more occasion to weep over in Africa. Then the song immediately pro-

[8] Wightman, *op. cit.,* pp. 244 f.
[9] Olmsted, *A Journey in the Back Country,* p. 105.

ceeded to give as the reason that Jesus had risen from the dead on Sunday morning.

> *Weep no more, Marta,*
> *Weep no more, Mary,* (or *Doubt no more, Thomas*)
> *Jesus rise from de dead,*
> *Happy* (or *Glorious, Sunday*) morning.

> [Chorus:]
> *Glorious* (or *O what a happy Sunday*) *morning,*
>   *Glorious morning,*
> *My Saviour rise from de dead,*
>
> *Happy morning.*[10]

Negroes soon learned that their plantation teachers were interested primarily in making slavery more secure, and slaves paid their missionaries scant attention. At the end of a very active life in 1854 Capers annually employed thirty-two preachers at twenty-six stations. His yearly expenses had mounted from $300 to $25,000, but only 11,546 Negro Methodists had been evangelized.[11] There were 393,944 Negroes in South Carolina in 1850,[12] and yet, because of the influence of plantation missionaries, an otherworldly meaning was almost always attached to Negro beliefs. Actually, not one spiritual in its primary form reflected interest in anything other than a full life here and now.

Overlords did not see or care that field slaves dropped tears which watered the ground they cultivated. Indeed, the opinion of no less a person than George Washington was that slaves required brutal treatment.[13] In the internal slave traffic to the Far South coffles traveled to the tunes of fiddles, songs, and stories.[14] The vocal part of this African music enumerated the districts to which Negroes were

[10] *Slave Songs,* p. 10; Allen (comp.), *op. cit.,* p. xxxix.

[11] Wightman, *op. cit.,* p. 217.

[12] United States Bureau of Census, *Bulletin 8, Negroes in the United States* (Washington, 1904), p. 102.

[13] Parkinson, *op. cit.,* II, 240; also, Matthew Gregory Lewis, *op. cit.,* p. 119; H. Gregoire, *De la litterature des Nègres* (Paris, 1808), p. 89; cf. Stirling, *op. cit.,* p. 288.

[14] G. W. Featherstonhaugh, *Excursion through the Slave States from Washington on the Potomac to the Frontier of Mexico* (New York, 1844), p. 37.

moving. Said a traveler about the middle of the nineteenth century:

Arkansas, Louisiana, Tennessee, Carolina, "Old Virginny," all the melo-
dious names of the Southern States and places there, the abodes of the
slaves, are introduced into their songs, as well as their love histories, and
give a local interest and coloring not only to the song, but to the state
and to the place which they sang about.

A song originating in a slave coffle was sung in freedom like this:

1. I'm gwine to Alabamy, Oh,
   For to see my mammy, Ah.

2. She went from Ole Virginny,—Oh,
   And I'm her pickaninny,—Ah.

3. She lives on the Tombigbee,—Oh,
   I wish I had her wid me,—Ah.

4. Now I'm a good big nigger,—Oh,
   I reckon I won't git bigger,—Ah.

5. But I'd like to see my mammy,—Oh,
   Who lives in Alabamy,—Ah.[15]

Soon after slaves arrived in new territory, they speedily made use
of their internal resources. They were compelled to seek for a meaning for life within themselves and not in the outside world. In the
Sunbury section of Georgia one song leader expressed the soul of a
group of ex-slaves thus:

O massa take dat new bran coat
And hang it on de wall,
Dat *darkee* [nigger] take dat same ole coat
And wear 'em to de ball.

O don'*t* you hear my true lub sing?
O don'*t* you hear 'em sigh?
Away down in Sunbury
I'*m* bound to live and die.[16]

Negroes sang their wares on market days,[17] at festivities held on

[15] *Slave Songs*, p. 89; Allen (comp.), *op. cit.*, p. xli.

[16] *Slave Songs*, p. 99; Allen (comp.), *op. cit.*, p. xlii.

[17] William Wells Brown, *My Southern Home: or, the South and Its People*

holidays,[18] such as Christmas and Easter,[19] and at funerals.[20] The successful production of American crops was the occasion of great celebration [21] like the making of African crops. In the South corn was separated from the stalk when ripe but was left to be husked when needed. Thus, unlike husking occasions in the North, piles of unhusked corn were on hand to be shucked by moonlight or by the light of bonfires at a safe distance from the corn. In their husking Negro shuckers would tell many stories, part of which would be recited and part sung,[22] in African fashion. There was no rhyme to this singing.[23] While an army of shuckers would catch up a song, the plantation "captain," or song leader would improvise words and music "to a wild 'recitative.' " [24] One corn-husking song evolved from the "Deep River" spiritual, "Come Along, Moses," and told John to "shock along."

> Shock along, John, shock along.
> Shock along, John, shock along.[25]

The singing was likely to be enigmatical, like this freedom song with numbers:

> 1. Five can't ketch me and ten can't hold me,
>   Ho, round the corn, Sally!

(3rd ed., Boston, 1882), pp. 209 f.; Leiding, *op. cit., passim;* [Wood], *op. cit., passim.*

[18] [Knight], *op. cit.*, p. 77; Brown, *My Southern Home*, p. 43.

[19] Candler, *op. cit.*, XXIII, 190.

[20] Edwards, *op. cit.*, II, 104; Kemble, *op. cit.*, p. 114; [Knight], *op. cit.*, p. 77; Oliphant, *op. cit.*, p. 142; Brinckerhoff MS, *op. cit.*, pp. 30, 106.

[21] Olmsted, *A Journey in the Seaboard Slave States*, p. 668; William Howard Russell, *The Civil War in America* (Boston, 1861), p. 151; William Howard Russell, *Pictures of Southern Life, Social, Political, Military* (New York, [1861]), p. 96; Latham, *op. cit.*, pp. 221 f.; Anne Hobson, *In Old Alabama, Being the Chronicles of Miss Mouse, the Little Black Merchant* (New York, 1903), pp. 103–112.

[22] Matthew Gregory Lewis, *op. cit.*, p. 253.

[23] Oliphant, *op. cit.*, p. 43.

[24] Charles Augustus Murray, *Travels in North America during the Years 1834, 1835, & 1836* (New York, 1839), II, 176; Letitia M. Burwell (*pseud.* Page Thacker), *Plantation Reminiscences* ([Owensboro, Ky.], 1878), p. 46.

[25] *Slave Songs*, p. 67; Allen (comp.), *op. cit.*, p. xli.

> Round the corn, round the corn, round the corn, Sally!
> Ho, ho, ho, round the corn, Sally!

2. Here's your iggle-quarter and here's your count-aquils.

3. I can bank, 'ginny bank, 'ginny bank the weaver.[26]

Songs made work and the time required for it pass easily and quickly. It was not uncommon for slaves to sing pieces to the tunes of contemporary ditties. "Charleston Gals" furnished the tune of this piece:

1. As I walked down the new-cut road,
   I met the tap and then the toad;
   The toad commenced to whistle and sing,
   And the possum cut the pigeon-wing.

   [Chorus:]
   Along come an old man riding by:
   Old man, if you don't mind, your horse will die;
   If he dies, I'll tan his skin,
   And if he lives I'll ride him agin.
   Hi ho, for Charleston gals!
   Charleston gals are the gals for me.

2. As I went a-walking down the street,
   Up steps Charleston gals to take a walk with me.
   I kep' a walking and they kep' a talking,
   I danced with a gal with a hole in her stocking.[27]

American Negroes, whether African or native-born, made life situations their major song themes. So African colonization remained a primary desire of a large number of slaves. No doubt it was in freedom that early collectors of spirituals heard Negroes on the Port Royal Islands singing a colonization medley two stanzas at a time as they performed their rowing tasks. This song started with the "Hallelujah" of "Deep River" days but emphasized the post-Turner situation of about 1832. After this it progressed to freedom verses which questioned whether the white overlord would get home.

[26] *Slave Songs*, p. 68; Allen (comp.), *op. cit.*, p. xli.
[27] *Slave Songs*, p. 88; Allen (comp.), *op. cit.*, p. xli.

1. Michael row de boat ashore,
   Hallelujah!

2. *Michael boat a gospel boat,*
   Hallelujah!

3. I wonder *where* my mudder deh (there).

4. *See* my mudder *on de rock* gwine home.

5. *On de rock gwine home in Jesus' name.*

6. *Michael boat a music boat.*

7. Gabriel blow *de* [your] trump*et horn.*

8. O you mind your *boastin'* talk.

9. *Boastin' talk will sink your soul.*

10. *Brudder, lend a helpin' hand.*

11. *Sister, help for trim dat boat.*

12. Jordan *stream* [river] *is wide and* deep.

13. Jesus stand on t'oder *side* [sho'].

14. *I wonder if my maussa deh.*

15. My fader gone to *unknown land* [glory].

16. *O de Lord he plant his garden deh.*

17. *He raise de fruit for you to eat.*

18. *He dat eat shall neber die.*

19. *When de riber overflow.*

20. *O poor sinner, how you land?*

21. *Riber run and darkness comin'.*

22. *Sinner row to save your soul.*[28]

The words of this song as sung on Hiltonhead Island reflected freedom concepts:

> *Michael haul the boat ashore.*
>
> *Then you'll hear the horn they blow.*

[28] *Slave Songs,* pp. 23 f.; Allen (comp.), *op. cit.,* p. xl.

Then you'll hear the trumpet sound.

Trumpet sound the world around.

Trumpet sound for rich and poor.

Trumpet sound the jubilee.

Trumpet sound for you and me.[29]

Slaves were reminded by their transportation duties to sing their colonization desires. Thus the ark was named in a spiritual heard in Virginia. The reference, however, was not originally to the Bible but to family boats used for the transportation of easterners and their household goods to river settlements on the frontier early in the nineteenth century. These boats looked "very much in appearance like Noah's ark" [30] and were so called.[31] It was a laborious achievement to "keep the ark a-moving" or floating down western rivers by means of treelike rudders.[32] Calling to mind "O brudders, don't get weary" of "Deep River" days, one slave first, then many, sang out in those difficult days when the world seemed on fire, that they were not "weary and noways tired" from labor and that they had not abandoned their persistent efforts to get home. All of the first singers wanted to go to heaven, Africa, and the collectors understood those Negroes to want to be at another point in the world.

[Chorus:]
I don'*t* feel weary and noways tired,
O glory hallelujah.

1. Jest let me in the *kingdom* [heaben]
   While the world *is* all on fire.
   O glory hallelujah.

[29] *Slave Songs,* p. 24; Allen (comp.), *op. cit.,* p. xl.

[30] Faux, *op. cit.,* p. 241; Marryatt, *op. cit.,* II, 5 f.; Featherstonhaugh, *op. cit.,* p. 62.

[31] Sutcliff, *op. cit.,* p. 102; Charles Fenno Hoffman, *A Winter in the West* (2nd ed., New York, 1835), p. 15.

[32] François A. Michaux, *Travels to the Westward of the Alleghany Mountains,* trans. from the French (London, 1805), p. 31; Wellington Williams, *Appleton's Southern and Western Travellers' Guide* (New York, 1850), p. 134.

2. Gwine to live with God *forever, While,* etc.

3. *And* keep the ark a-moving, *While,* etc.[33]

The desire to escape also constituted a major Negro song theme. Slaves sang that if they could escape from slavery, they would experience all of the joys of freedom. In the days of trials and burdens, about 1832, they sent messages to their fellow slaves to prepare to aid them. The mansion idea was a good nineteenth-century thought [34] with which to express fugitive ideas. When slaves sang about the mansion, they were saying that they wanted to be elsewhere:

> [Chorus:]
> *Good* Lord, in de manshans *above,*
> *Good* Lord, in de manshans *above,*
> *My Lord,* I *hope* [want] to meet my Jesus
> [My Lord,] in de manshans *above.*

> 1. *If* you get to heaven before *I do* [me],
> Lord, tell *my Jesus* ['em] I'm *a-comin' too* [come],
> To de manshans *above.*

> 2. *My Lord, I've had many crosses an' trials here below;*
> *My Lord, I hope to meet you*
> *In de manshans above.*

[33] *Slave Songs,* p. 70; Allen (comp.), *op. cit.,* p. xli.

[34] Parkinson, *op. cit.,* I, 55; Edouard de Montule, *A Voyage to North America, and the West Indies, in 1817* (London, 1821), p. 8; Adlard Welby, *A Visit to North America and the English Settlements in Illinois in Early Western Travels 1748–1846,* ed. Reuben Gold Thwaites (Cleveland, 1904–1907), XII, 25; Bernhard, *op. cit.,* II, 65, 68, 81; Anne Royall, *Letters from Alabama on Various Subjects* (Washington, 1830), p. 61; J. K. Paulding, *Slavery in the United States* (New York, 1836), p. 197; Buckingham, *The Slave States of America,* II, 438; W. Williams, *op. cit.,* p. 95; John S. C. Abbott, *South and North; or, Impressions Received during a Trip to Cuba and the South* (New York, 1860), p. 66; J. Milton Mackie, *From Cape Cod to Dixie and the Tropics* (New York, 1864), p. 181; Rachel Wilson Moore, *Journal of Rachel Wilson Moore, Kept during a Tour to the West Indies and South America in 1863–64* (Philadelphia, 1867), p. 24.

   3. *Fight on, my brudder, for de manshans above,*
      For I hope to meet my Jesus dere
      In de manshans above.[35]

Possibly, the originals of otherworldly spirituals were not in existence when the first collectors made their search. There can be no doubt, however, that slaves, like other people, transferred their earthly desires to the other world when they were frustrated. Negroes expressed strong desires to be reincarnated in Africa.[36] To make sure that inhuman masters would be cheated, slaves often committed suicide.[37]

This almost inextinguishable hope of Negroes to be returned to Africa was included with a "Deep River" theme about Jacob. One song which said, "I'm on my way," would be considered a fugitive song were it not for the fact that the colonizing Jacob was mentioned in it. This song retained the one necessary prerequisite for slave manumission, which was for the slave to receive the favor of the overlord. Yet the overlord had nothing to do with one going to heaven when he died. The abode of the reverent and faithful was reserved for those who "do love de Lord" and not for those who ironically said this. The author of this song was not thinking of getting to a spiritual resting place but to Africa, where he had friends whom he desired to greet:

   1. Wake up, Jacob, day *is* a-breaking,
      I'*m* on my way;
      O, wake up, Jacob, day *is* a-breaking,
      I'*m* on my way. O!

      [Chorus:] (repeat)
      I want to go to heaven *when I die,*
      Do love de Lord!
      I want to go to heaven *when I die,*
      Do love de Lord!

   2. [I] Got *some* friends on de oder shore
      Do love de Lord!
      I want to see 'em *more an' more* [when I die],
      Do love de Lord!

[35] *Slave Songs,* p. 59; Allen (comp.), *op. cit.,* p. xli.
[36] Basil Hall, *op. cit.,* III, 128.
[37] Montule, *op. cit.,* p. 59; Matthew Gregory Lewis, *op. cit.,* p. 100.

Wake up, Jacob, etc.[38]

Negroes developed a popular song about their reincarnation in Africa which began with the words, "swing low, sweet chariot." A chariot was a French sledlike vehicle used to transport tobacco in the Carolinas. After Turner's revolt slaves wanted a chariot to swing out of the skies from Africa low enough for their souls to mount and to be carried many miles from North America.[39] A singer from Florida was one of the first persons to use this concept when he thought of his African heritage of secret meetings, which he desired to join over "yonder":

> *What is* that *up* yonder I see?
> *Two* little angels comin' a'ter me;
> I want to jine the band,
> I want to jine the band, (*Sing together*)
> I want to jine the band.[40]

In conclusion, two typical reactions to slavery became apparent during this period. On the one hand, some Negroes developed spiritual resources upon which they drew heavily when things went against them. The behavior of these singing people contrasted sharply with that of contemporary ruling society in the Western Hemisphere which took no time from its pioneering work to cultivate the expression of the soul.[41] Americans quickly recognized the color

---

[38] *Slave Songs,* p. [65]; Allen (comp.), *op. cit.,* p. xli.

[39] According to Edward A. Pollard, *Black Diamonds Gathered in the Darkey Homes of the South* (New York, 1859), p. 115. In 1858 Aunt Matilda at Green Mountain, Virginia, was singing:

> "*Swing low chariot!* Pray let me in!
> For I don't want to stay behind.
> Swing low chariot! Pray just let me in!
> For I don't want to stay here no longer."

There is a legend that Mrs. Hannah Shepard of Tennessee was the originator of "Swing Low, Sweet Chariot" (Work, *Folk Songs,* pp. 79 f.).

[40] *Slave Songs,* p. 95; Allen (comp.), *op. cit.,* p. xli.

[41] Grandfort, *op. cit.,* p. 69; Thomas Colley Gratton, *Civilized America* (2nd ed., London, 1859), I, 125; Frederick Von Raumer, *America and the American People,* trans. from the German, William W. Turner (New York, 1846), p. 490.

and warmth which Negro music added to life. Some white people, therefore, blackened their faces and went about playing instruments and singing songs as much as possible like Negro productions. These minstrels [42] were adjudged quite inferior to Negro performers by many contemporaries who heard them.[43] When the religious part of white society ascetically proscribed the emotional expressions of Negroes, which were vehicles of their religion, an artificial distinction was made between secular and religious music. The rhythmic and instrumental parts of it were called "balls" or dances, although the vocal scores also retained characteristics of the spirituals.[44]

On the other hand, thousands of Negroes were so depressed by the conditions under which they were forced to live in America that they viewed Liberia as a place where they would be rid of their hardships.

After Nat Turner's insurrection Negroes were taught to believe that the only place where they would have a safe and free abode was heaven. Negro slaves ordinarily believed that Africa was heaven, but if one were required to locate heaven within the limits of the United States, heaven was in the North in preference to the South. There, many Negroes sought an abundant life which everywhere had its human problems. Contemporary society saw slaves holding up so well under most adverse conditions that it tried to imitate Negroes. The Negroes seemed so unwearied in bearing their burdens that they actually gained spiritual strength.

[42] Buckingham, *The Eastern and Western States of America*, II, 27; Jacques Offenbach, *America and the Americans* (London, [1877]), p. 33; John Tasker Howard, *Stephen Foster, America's Troubador* (New York, [c. 1934]), pp. 83, 194, 300.

[43] Bremer, *op. cit.*, I, 327, 369 f.; Latham, *op. cit.*, p. 221; Lewis W. Paine, *Six Years in a Georgia Prison* (New York, 1851), p. 184; Russell, *My Diary North and South*, p. 140; John Mason Brown, "Songs of the Slave," *Lippincott's Magazine*, II (December, 1868), 618; "Wandering Negro Minstrels," *Leisure Hour*, XX (1871), 600.

[44] *Slave Songs*, pp. 109–113.

"LOOK WHAT A WONDER JEDUS DONE"

Look what a wonder Jedus done; sinner believe.
Look what a wonder Jedus done; sinner believe.
Look what a wonder Jedus done; sinner believe.
King Jedus had died for me.[1]

AN EX-SLAVE used his former master's German word, *wunder*, in telling the unconverted, in song, that emancipation was a miracle. So prevalent was this thought among Negroes that a missionary had to stress that emancipation was no miracle but the objective of the Civil War.[2]

The strategy of both the South and the North was to use Negroes in that conflict. Southern slaves were solicitous of the welfare of their masters and incidentally of themselves. They held midnight meetings of praise, which included singing and praying for their masters who were in the Confederate forces,[3] and a legion of slaves went along as servants. Undoubtedly, the accompanying Negroes inspired the warriors with martial music according to African custom, since the fife and drum corps of the Confederacy made poor music.[4] Unfortu-

[1] Ballanta, *Saint Helena Island Spirituals,* p. 69.
[2] Brinckerhoff, *Advice to Freedmen,* pp. 31 f.
[3] J. William Jones, *Christ in the Camp; or, Religion in Lee's Army* (Richmond, 1887), p. 25.
[4] T. C. DeLeon, *Four Years in Rebel Capitals* (Mobile, Ala., 1892), p. 299.

nately their songs were not preserved, though it is suspected that none of them would have been outside the concepts and vocabularies of antebellum Negroes. In June, 1862, slaves were seized to work upon southern fortifications as laborers. One who wrote the story of Negroes in the Civil War said that "the Negro's love of music and song taught him the poetry of movement, and his grace, under the influence of music, was quite captivating in a laborer." [5] The South seriously debated the employment of Negroes as Confederate soldiers,[6] although slaves had requested such service since March, 1863.[7] The outcome was that many slaves were emancipated and armed as Confederate soldiers in 1864.

Sergeant C. T. Trowbridge of the New York Volunteer Engineers was detailed, on May 7, 1862, to organize the "Hunter Regiment" of the Union forces from slaves of South Carolina. Not a few persons, even missionaries, felt that Negroes were unfit for military duties.[8] After four months in camp on Hiltonhead the Hunter Regiment was forced to disband, except the one company under Trowbridge, which, on August 5, had been sent to garrison St. Simon Island off the coast of Georgia. Conscription without pay and desertions proved the regiment's undoing.[9] One Negro soldier was heard weeping, in song, because something within him forbade that he remain longer in the detachment. He regretted that he did not measure up to the description of a "valiant soldier," and hoped that his act of desertion would therefore not be disciplined by his commanding officer. The man thought of the traditional "praise" theme which called for "mercy." This was not later than September, 1862, when the Hunter Regiment was disbanded.

[5] George W. Williams, *A History of Negro Troops in the War of the Rebellion, 1861–1865* (New York, 1888), p. 168.

[6] Chesnut, *op. cit.*, p. 224; Wirt Armistead Cate (ed.), *Two Soldiers* (Chapel Hill, 1938), pp. 16 f.

[7] Chesnut, *op. cit.*, p. 147; Joseph T. Wilson, *The Black Phalanx* (Hartford, 1888), p. 483, stated that in September, 1861, Tennessee had two regiments of Negro soldiers and 1,000 Negro laborers.

[8] Elizabeth Ware Pearson (ed.), *Letters from Port Royal Written at the Time of the Civil War* (Boston, 1906), pp. 40, 41, 42, 43, 96, 102.

[9] Pearson, *op. cit.*, pp. 29, 38, 42, 96; Higginson, *Army Life in a Black Regiment*, pp. 15, 273.

> Oh Lord, I want some valiant soldier,
> I want some valiant soldier,
> I want some valiant soldier,
> To help me bear de cross.
>
> *For* I weep, I weep,
> I can*'t* hold *out* [no more];
> *If* any mercy, Lord,
> O pity poor me.[10]

Perhaps other songs of Negro soldiers recorded the threats, the fears, and the hardships of exposure without tents endured by the First South Carolina Volunteer Regiment. In some places local plantations were emptied of young men by a draft which was executed with excessive severity, if not with horrible cruelty.[11]

As Roman Catholic Negroes cast in their lots with South Carolinians, the songs of the soldiers gave large place to Mary. A variant spiritual was a longer song than the one above. Lest one should think that weeping Mary [12] was meant, Colonel Higginson stated that it was the Virgin Mary of Roman Catholicism. On January 13, 1863, he wrote in his journal that "we have recruits on their way from St. Augustine, where the negroes are chiefly Roman Catholics; and it will be interesting to see how their type of character combines with that elder creed." The African cult knew no denominationalism. Possibly no one of the recruits recalled the "Hail Mary" of his prayer book. A prominent Negro minister reported that many slaves were Roman Catholics but said that he had found "no melody of the slave singing divine praises to the Virgin Mary." [13] However, the Roman Catholic recruits who joined the First South Carolina Volunteer Regiment sang a spiritual of the Virgin Mary. They shouted "O hail, Mary!" as a refrain to their song about the "valiant soldier here":

> I want some valiant soldier here,
> I want some valiant soldier here,

[10] *Slave Songs,* p. [50]; Allen (comp.), *op. cit.,* p. xl.
[11] Pearson (ed.), *op. cit.,* pp. 98, 108, 172, 174, 249, 283.
[12] See above, pp. 136 f.
[13] Henry Hugh Proctor, *Between Black and White, Autobiographical Sketches* (Boston, 1925), p. 86.

I want some valiant soldier here,
To help me bear de cross.

O hail, Mary, hail!
O hail, Mary, hail!
O hail, Mary, hail!
To help me bear de cross.[14]

The ignorance of ex-slaves handicapped them in service. So Union Army leaders trained Negroes in the fundamentals of American living as in army tactics. Active in this program were Brigadier General Rufus Saxton and Colonel Thomas Wentworth Higginson in South Carolina, Chaplain John Eaton in Mississippi, General N. P. Banks in Louisiana, Private Henry Martin Tupper in North Carolina, General Clinton B. Fiske of Tennessee, General Samuel Chapman Armstrong of Virginia, and General O. O. Howard of the Freedman's Bureau.[15] Accuracy in countersigns taxed the "distressingly limited" vocabularies of ex-slaves. When Negroes got through struggling to pronounce *ambulance,* it sounded like *amulet* or *epaulet* or *omelet.* Colonel Higginson wrote that his Negro soldiers knew Saxton and himself respectively as "de General" and "de Cunnel." So the Polish Gurowski wrote Stanton, the Secretary of War, on January 30, 1863, eight suggestions respecting Negro soldiers, including the one that the drill manual be revised "to free it as far as possible from needless technicalities, and to reduce it to the most urgently needed and most readily comprehended particulars." This was done.[16]

Congregationalists in 1861 helped Negroes through a denominational agency. Within two years the United Presbyterians of Ohio, the Baptists, the United Brethren, and the Reformed Presbyterians had organized agencies for this purpose. The Protestant Episcopalians began their specific freedmen's work in 1865, the same year that Congregationalists called upon their churches to raise a quarter of a million dollars annually for freedmen's work. The Methodists followed the next year. In 1862 the Methodist Episcopal Church,

[14] *Slave Songs,* p. 45; Allen (comp.), *op. cit.,* p. xl.
[15] Dwight Oliver Wendell Holmes, *The Evolution of the Negro College* (New York, 1924), pp. 24–30.
[16] Adam Gurowski, *Diary* (New York, 1863), II, 115, 117, 125, 133.

followed in 1864 by other non-Negro denominations, received official permission from Secretary of War Stanton to follow the flag.[17] All Civil War missionaries were encouraged to increase their endeavors on behalf of ex-slaves, who in African fashion often sang about information to which they were exposed for the first time. These benefactors received the thanks of Negroes in spirituals.

The initial training of Negro soldiers was on the drill fields, where ex-slaves demonstrated that they could master the English words which differentiated left from right. In the fall of 1862 one missionary said: "About half didn't know which their right foot was, and kept facing to the left when I told them to face to the right. They seemed to enjoy it, however." They learned directions within a short time, and, on January 19, 1863, when the band of the Eighth Maine escorted the regiment to town, one soldier remarked: "We didn't look to de right nor to de leff. I didn' see notin' in Beaufort. Eb'ry step was worth a half dollar." [18]

Negroes felt that they were making progress. As evidenced by songs of this time, their vocabularies were increasing, although this was surprising to many white people. Because Negroes' knowledge was not self-evident, even Colonel Higginson got no sensible explanation from Negroes that they had mastered the difference between right and left. One soldier blushingly told him that "dat means if you go to de leff, go to 'struction, and if you go to the right, go to God for sure," and Colonel Higginson believed him. Likewise a Miss Morton saw Negroes "jumping Jim Crow" on this song, heard the word "wheel" in it, and concluded that the song's reference to right and left meant that "I hop on my right and catch on my leff." The spiritual medley which combined the ancient "praise" and the newer "valiant soldier" themes with the hymn "On Jordan's Stormy Banks I Stand" simply showed that about 1863 Negro soldiers used the directions which had been taught them, and they knew some points on the compass. They got enough joy from singing that Negroes were going to hold secret meetings as long as they lived to "jump Jim Crow":

[17] William Warren Sweet, *The Story of Religion in America* (New York, 1939), pp. 459–461.
[18] Higginson, *Army Life in a Black Regiment*, p. 254.

[Chorus:]
Praise, member (or Believer), praise God,
I praise my Lord *un*til I die;
Praise, member, praise God, (or Religion so sweet)
And reach de heavenly home. (or Shore)

1. O Jordan'*s* bank (or Stream, Fight) *is* a good old bank.
   And I hain'*t* but one more river to cross;
   I want some valiant soldier
   To help me bear the cross.

2. O soldier'*s* fight *is* a good old fight,
   And I hain'*t,* etc.

3. O I look to de East, and I look to de West.

4. O I wheel to de right, and I wheel to de left.[19]

By application Negro soldiers progressed to the difficult stage of
using comparisons in their speech, as illustrated by the words "one
more river to cross" in the song above. The "loud" blowing of the
trumpet and the "tall" palm tree of the "I Am Bound for the Promised Land" period became, respectively, "louder" and "talles'." Negroes learned to count, as was seen in the corn-husking song. Such
new knowledge augmented the Negro's limited vocabulary and from
it emerged combinations of spirituals. Negroes knew what to call
the sailors who would take them to Africa: they were the crew. A
contemporary Civil War song showed their knowledge of the difference between night and day and made reference to their current instruction about hell and about lying:

1. O come my brethren and sisters too,
   We'*ve* gwine to *join* [jine] the heavenly crew;
   To Christ our Saviour let us sing,
   And make our loud hosannas ring.

   [Chorus:]
   O hallelu, O hallelu,
   O hallelujah to the Lord.
   O hallelu, O hallelu,
   O hallelujah to the Lord.

[19] *Slave Songs,* p. 4; Allen (comp.), *op. cit.,* p. xxix.

2. Oh, there's Bill Thomas, I know him well,
   He's got to work to keep from hell;
   He's got to pray by night and day,
   If he wants to go by the narrow way.

3. There's Chloe Williams, she makes me mad,
   For you see I know she's going on bad;
   She told me a lie this arternoon,
   And the devil will get her very soon.[20]

Negroes were willing, brave, and daring enough to make good soldiers. The Civil War was over when an original singer looked back over the whole thing and sang that he successfully crossed rivers, but when the opposing forces attempted to cross streams, they were actually drowned like Pharaoh's army:

1. My army cross ober,
   My army cross ober,
   O Pharaoh's army drownded,
   My army cross ober.
   My army, my army, my army cross ober.

2. We'll cross de riber Jordan.

3. We'll cross de danger water.

4. We'll cross de mighty Myo.[21]

Their songs showed that Negro soldiers were being trained for actual combat duty. A longer and hence a later variant of this song also told what success was achieved:

[20] *Slave Songs,* p. 66; Allen (comp.), *op. cit.,* p. xli.
The editors were tempted to doubt the genuine Negro character of this song, but they were informed that it was sung at camp meetings a quarter of a century before. It illustrated the kind of influence "brought to bear upon the wavering" during the Civil War. The pamphlets of the missionary Brinckerhoff were circulated to check the unwholesome developments of Negroes. His teachings concerned hell and heaven (Brinckerhoff, *The Freedman's Book of Christian Doctrine,* pp. 8 f.). In *Gambling and Lotteries* (New York, 1865), Brinckerhoff warned against telling lies.

[21] *Slave Songs,* p. 38; Allen (comp.), *op. cit.,* p. xl.
Colonel Higginson found no explanation of "Myo." An old man thought that it meant the river of death. Editor Allen supposed that it was an African word. Lt. Col. Trowbridge was confident that it was a corruption of "bayou."

1. My brudder, tik keer Satan,
   My army cross ober,
   My brudder, tik keer Satan,
   My army cross ober.

2. Satan bery busy.

3. Wash 'e face in ashes.

4. Put on de leder apron.

5. Jordan riber rollin'.

6. Cross 'em, I tell ye, cross 'em.

7. Cross Jordan (danger) riber.[22]

A soldier from Georgia used the "weary" concept to describe a skirmish with the Confederates. The cannon ball which was aimed to keep him from the enjoyment of his freedom, he sang, went to "hell" and left him for "heaven."

[Chorus:]
O me no weary yet,
O me no weary yet.

1. I have a witness in my heart,
   O me no weary yet. (Brudder Tony) (or Sister Mary)

2. Since I been in de field to (or Been-a) fight.

3. I have a heaven to maintain.

4. De bond of faith are on my soul.

5. Ole Satan toss a ball at me.

6. Him tink de ball *would* hit my soul.

7. De ball for hell and *I* [me] for heaven.[23]

The choice of song themes of ex-slave soldiers revealed their most prominent concepts. Songs about the secret meetings of the "Sinner, Please" and of the "Steal Away" periods came first. A favorite marching song of the singing soldiers was about the "wilderness." This

[22] *Slave Songs*, p. 38; Allen (comp.), *op. cit.*, p. xl.
[23] *Slave Songs*, p. 12; Allen (comp.), *op. cit.*, p. xxxix.

spiritual with the chorus about "walk 'em easy round de heaben" was sung "in such an operatic and rollicking way that it was quite hard to fancy it a religious performance, which, however, it was." The song was interpreted to be "one of the most singular pictures of future joys, and with a fine flavor of hospitality about it." The men kept up their spirits with the jubilant marching song of the "You'*d Better Min'* " period which said that the "bell da ring." [24]

Missionary teaching about the other world definitely prepared the 178,795 Negroes who bore Union arms for possible death. That did not alarm them, for "death was a little man." A son of a Virginia governor wrote of the slaughter of Negro troops at the Crater by saying that "our men, inflamed to relentless vengeance by their presence, disregarded the rules of warfare which restrained them in battle with their own race, and brained and butchered the blacks until the slaughter was sickening." [25] Negro soldiers were "stripped" and "starved" and "reviled" in a Charleston, South Carolina, jail,[26] but they sang their "melodies till late in the evening." Negro soldiers had their backs to the walls and were forced to fight their way out. Acting Chaplain Private Thomas Long preached a sermon in the spring of 1864 in which he imagined what might have been said had Negroes refused to remain unpaid soldiers:

Suppose you had kept your freedom without enlisting in dis army; your children might have grown up free and been well cultivated so as to be the equal to any business, but it would have been always flung in dere face—"Your fader never fought for he own freedom"—an what could they answer? Never can say that to dis African race any mo'. . . .[27]

In the spring of 1864 Colonel Higginson noticed that his men relayed general orders in a strange fashion, such as, "Headquarters No. 1; General Order No. 162; Heretofore no man must fry he meat, must always boil he." So one soldier sang that, when he met death and after he had been reincarnated, his general order was going to be to tell Jesus "howdy":

[24] Higginson, *Army Life in a Black Regiment,* pp. 113 f., 207, 211.

[25] Wise, *op. cit.,* p. 366; cf. *ibid.,* pp. 368 ff.; also, [John Francis Campbell], *A Short American Tramp in the Fall of 1864* (Edinburgh, 1865), p. 338.

[26] Luis F. Emilio, *History of the Fifty-Fourth Regiment of Massachusetts Volunteer Infantry* (2nd ed., Boston, 1894), pp. 393 ff.

[27] Higginson, *Army Life in a Black Regiment,* p. 245.

1. In de mornin' when I rise,
   Tell my Jesus huddy, oh (or Morning);
   I wash my hands in de mornin' glory,
   Tell my Jesus huddy, oh.

2. Mornin' Hester, mornin', gal,
   Tell my Jesus, etc.

After the Civil War this spiritual was used to greet each person present by name as in African chants.[28] A variant spiritual has these verses:

[1.] Pray Tony, pray boy, you got de order,
   [Tell my Jesus, etc.]

2. Say, brudder Sammy, you got de order,
   Tell my Jesus, etc.

3. You got de order, and I got de order.[29]

Negroes did not clearly understand otherworldliness even as late as the Civil War. References of southern slaves to heaven might refer to escape to the North or to colonization in Africa. Negroes found refuge within the Union Army lines in such numbers that, on June 5, 1862, Brigadier General T. Williams of the Second Brigade, with headquarters at Baton Rouge, Louisiana, ordered his commanders to "turn all such fugitives in the camps or garrisons out beyond the limits of their respective guards and sentinels." [30] The drastic Confiscation Act of July 17, 1862, bestowed freedom upon slaves of masters who were disloyal to the Union, forbade their reclamation, and proposed their colonization. The black masses thought that now their chance to get home had come.

"Deep River" spirituals sounded all through the camps. There were the usual ones about "Canaan." The difficulties in getting home were sung about under the caption of "O Yonder's My Ole Mother." Another song referred to Jacob. Work songs which were also spirituals condemned both Negro drivers and living conditions of antebellum Negroes. Negro soldiers sang several versions of the protest spiritual about working in the rain.

[28] Park, *op. cit.* (1800), pp. 268 f.
[29] *Slave Songs,* p. 15; Allen (comp.), *op. cit.,* p. xxxix.
[30] Edward Bacon, *Among Cotton Thieves* (Detroit, 1867), p. 22.

They also sang the Old Ship of Zion spirituals in "three wholly distinct versions, all quite exuberant and tumultuous." When Colonel Higginson heard "I Can't Stay *Behind* [Away], My Lord," he wrote in his diary on December 5, 1862:

One of their favorite songs is full of plaintive cadences; it is not, I think, a Methodist tune, and I wonder where they obtained a chant of such beauty. It always excited them to have us looking on, yet they sing songs at all times and seasons. I have heard this very song dimly droning on near midnight, and, tracing it into the recesses of a cook-house, have found an old fellow coiled among the pots and provisions, chanting away with his "Can't stay behind, sinner," till I made him leave his song behind.

The version sung in Colonel Higginson's regiment follows:

> O, my mudder is gone! my mudder is gone!
> My mudder is gone into heaven, my Lord!
> I can't stay behind!
> Dere's room in dar, room in dar.
> Room in dar, in de heaven, my Lord!
> I can't stay behind.
> Can't stay behind, my dear,
> I can't stay behind!
>
> O, my fader is gone! etc.
>
> O, de angels are gone! etc.
>
> O, I'se been on de road! I'se been on de road!
> I'se been on de road into heaven, my Lord!
> I can't stay behind!
> O, room in dar, room in dar,
> Room in dar, in de heaven, my Lord!
> I can't stay behind! [31]

Negroes were nurtured in the finest traditions of American Christianity, and yet their benevolent chaplains and missionaries submitted ex-slaves to the evils of a narrow denominationalism. They attempted to destroy every vestige of slavery, even the spirituals which they admired. Singing classes were established in which, apparently, no spirituals were used. Negroes sang songs which they did not originate. A war song of the Fifty-fourth Massachusetts Regi-

[31] *Slave Songs*, p. 6; Allen (comp.), *op. cit.*, p. xxxix.

ment was "When This Cruel War Is Over," to which the white South lays claim.[32] There were "Old John Brown," "Hail, Columbia," "Homeward Bound," "Joyfully," "Freedom's Era," "The Star-Spangled Banner," "Yankee Doodle," and other songs. It appears that Colonel Higginson introduced the John Brown song among his soldiers. That Colonel Higginson was Brown's friend is attested by a farewell note from Brown on November 22, 1859.[33] On December 5, 1862, when Higginson had been in camp less than a month, his regiment was singing about John Brown with a new verse added: "We'll beat Beauregard on de clare battlefield." [34] On February 18, 1864, the Colonel described his regiment's singing in Florida, where "Glory, Hallelujah" had preceded him, as follows: "Down we marched, the men singing 'John Brown' and 'Marching Along' and 'Gwine into the wilderness'; women in tears and smiles lined the way."

"Marching Along" was taught the First South Carolina Volunteer Regiment by Quartermaster Bingham. The words of the song, "Gird on the armor," were stumbling blocks "until some ingenious ear substituted, 'Guide on de army,' which was at once accepted, and became universal." So "We'll guide on de army, and be marching along" was the official version of the song on the Sea Islands. This song was repeatedly sung when the regiment returned to the Port Royal Islands encampment in April and when the troops moved to Florida. Negro soldiers combined "Marching Along" with many spirituals, for example, with "My Brudder Build a House in Paradise," and the medley, "Gwine to March Away in de Gold Band."

1. Gwine to march away in de gold band,
   In de army, bye-and-bye;
   Gwine to march away in de gold band,
   In de army, bye-and-bye.

[32] Myrta Lockett Avary, *Dixie after the War: An Exposition of Social Conditions Existing in the South, during the Twelve Years Succeeding the Fall of Richmond* (New York, 1906), p. 9. Sawyer and Thompson of Brooklyn, New York, held the copyright of this song (*Frank Converse's "Old Cremona" Songster* [New York, 1863], p. 5).

[33] Mary Thacker Higginson, *op. cit.,* p. 196.

[34] Higginson, *Army Life in a Black Regiment,* p. 22.

[Chorus:]
Sinner, what you gwine to do dat day?
Sinner, what you gwine to do dat day?
When de fire's a-rolling behind you,
In de army, bye-and-bye.

2. Sister Mary gwine to hand down the robe,
   In the army, bye-and-bye;
   Gwine to hand down the robe and the gold band,
   In the army, bye-and-bye.[35]

Negroes did not take readily to singing the minstrel ditties to which they were exposed, but they used to deacon or repeat Psalms line by line from memory "in a sort of wailing chant." They sang the long and short meters of the hymnbooks. Since the days of plantation missionaries, they had been taught "to lay aside the extravagant and nonsensical chants of their own composing." [36] During the Civil War, Missionary I. W. Brinckerhoff added the words of twelve songs to both editions of his *Advice to Freedmen,* published by the American Tract Society. With two exceptions these songs received popular acceptance in Negro churches and their hymnbooks, such as the *New Hymn and Tune Book for the Use of the African M. E. Zion Church* (1878, 1909), the *Baptist Standard Hymnal* (1924), the revised *Hymnal* (1927) of the African Methodist Episcopal Church, and the *A. M. E. Hymn and Tune Book* (1938). In 1867 *Slave Songs of the United States,* in referring to the decline of Negro devotion, quoted Harriet Beecher Stowe as follows:

Even the "spirituals" are going out of use on the plantations, superseded by the new style of religious music, "closely imitated from the white people, which is solemn, dull and nasal, consisting in repeating two lines of a hymn and then singing it, and then two more, *ad infinitum.* They use for this sort of worship that one everlasting melody, which may be remembered by all persons familiar with Western and Southern camp-meetings, as applying equally well to long, short or common metre. This style of proceeding they evidently consider the more dignified style of the two, as being a closer imitation of white, genteel worship—having

[35] *Slave Songs,* p. [83]; Allen (comp.), *op. cit.,* p. xli.
[36] Jones, *The Religious Instruction of the Negroes,* pp. 266 f.

in it as little soul as most stereotyped religious forms of well instructed congregations."

This kind of singing among Negroes was approved and continued in singing conventions which came into the South with the Reconstruction.

Both the Civil War and the Reconstruction period produced acculturated Negroes who laid aside their old spirituals or combined the new songs with the old. They cried, "My soul wants something that's new," since in freedom ex-slaves were singing that everything was new, including their hands, their feet, their names, their world, and their status. The African spiritual heritage became a "forgotten memory" upon this level. In this connection a Negro soldier of Virginia about 1863 preserved in song what he knew about the twenty-third Psalm. The second verse of the spiritual added the thought of a line from Watts's "Godly Sorrow at the Cross," and the third verse the thought of Ryland's "Hinder Me Not," but the whole song depended upon "Marching Along" as well as on the Bible. Negro soldiers did not sing that they would walk through the valley until about 1866.[37]

1. We will march thro' the valley in peace,
   We will march thro' the valley in peace;
   If Jesus himself be our leader,
   We will march thro' the valley in peace.

2. We will march, etc.
   Behold I give myself away, and
   We will march, etc.

3. We will march, etc.
   This track I'll see and I'll pursue;
   We will march, etc.

4. We will march, etc.
   When I'm dead and buried in the cold silent tomb,
   I don't want you to grieve for me.[38]

In January, 1866, the Thirty-third Regiment (formerly the First South Carolina Volunteers) was mustered out at the same time that

[37] Marsh, *op. cit.*, p. 194; Seward and White, *op. cit.*, p. 8.
[38] *Slave Songs*, p. 73; Allen (comp.), *op. cit.*, p. xli.

the Twelfth and Thirteenth Tennessee Negro regiments were discharged. Public sentiment had not planned for the assimilation of Negroes within the limits of the United States but favored their colonization at various places outside the United States.[39] The ex-soldiers, however, had another place to which they suggested their expatriation. A variant of an African colonization spiritual on the Jacob theme in which Negroes made known their desires was called by Colonel Higginson "one of the wildest and most striking" of their songs. Said he:

There is a mystical effect and a passionate striving throughout the whole. The Scriptural struggle between Jacob and the angel, which is only dimly expressed in the words, seems all uttered in music. I think it impressed my imagination more powerfully than any other of these songs.

Ex-soldiers were trembling for fear that they would be sent elsewhere than to Africa:

1. I hold my brudder (or My sister, Brudder Jacky,
       All de member) wid a tremblin' han',
   De Lord will bless my soul (or I would not let him go).

   [Chorus:]
   Wrastl' on, Jacob,
   Jacob, day is a-breakin',
   Wrastl' on, Jacob.
   Oh he (or Lord, I) would not let him go.

2. I will not let you go, my Lord.

3. Fisherman Peter out at sea.

4. He cast (or Fish) all night, and he cast (or Fish) all day.

5. He (or I) catch no fish, but he (or I) catch some soul.

6. Jacob hang from a tremblin' limb.[40]

The singing of this spiritual in Virginia showed its African colonization intention. One verse was about the old ship of Zion:

[39] Adam Gurowski, *Diary* (Boston, 1862), I, 187, 227; Butler, *op. cit.*, p. 908; John G. Nicolay and John Hay, *Abraham Lincoln* (New York, 1890), VI, 354–367.
[40] *Slave Songs*, pp. 4 f.; Allen (comp.), *op. cit.*, p. xxxix.

I looked to the East at the breaking of the day,
The old ship of Zion went sailing away.[41]

Though some Negroes sang an increasing number of new songs or combined new songs and old, the black masses as a whole thrilled to the singing of their old spirituals in spite of acculturation.[42] They expressed dissatisfaction with the northern white missionaries of the Civil War, feeling that they were forcing Negroes to accept their standards and yet they represented sections of the United States which did not practice civil rights for everybody. It took Missionary Brinckerhoff just thirty days after he had gone to South Carolina in 1862 to conclude that some " 'niggers' can measure us men just like that (a Negro fitting a board in a fence), and when we just fill our place, say 'That's him, that's him.' " [43] Negroes confessed in song that they were confused, bewildered, and did not know what to do. Many slaves did not desire and would not accept freedom, but remained to carry on the work of the plantations about as usual and to protect the valuables and persons of southern people, or to permit themselves to be carried to places in the South for safe keeping. Those Negroes who were counting upon revived African colonization and who were going northward and westward and southward in droves encouraged one another, in song:

[Chorus:]
Don't be weary, traveller,
Come along home to Jesus;
Don't be weary, traveller,
Come along home to Jesus.

1. My head got wet with the midnight dew,
Come along home to Jesus;
Angels bear me witness too,
Come along home to Jesus.

[41] *Slave Songs*, p. 5; Allen (comp.), *op. cit.*, p. xxxix.

[42] Higginson, *Army Life in a Black Regiment*, p. 220; Daniel A. Payne, *Recollections of Seventy Years* (Nashville, 1888), pp. 253–256, was an enlightened Negro's criticism of the masses using so-called "cornfield ditties."

[43] Brinckerhoff, "Mission Work among the Freed Negroes," p. 30, MS, American Baptist Historical Society.

2. Where to go I did not know.
   Ever since he freed my soul.

3. I look at de worl' and de worl' look new,
   I look at de worl' and de worl' look new.[44]
   I look at my hands an' they look so, too.[45]

Christianity in operation showed such weaknesses that only a few favored ex-slaves were encouraged to accept its compensatory doctrines as presented by Civil War missionaries. One such Negro was a nurse on the Port Royal Islands. She wanted Jesus to anoint her head with the anointing vial and then to "drop on the crown." She would roll in His arms just like southern white children were rolling in hers. The second judgment, the Reconstruction, was happening to Negro peoples:

1. Meet, O Lord, on de milk-white horse,
       An' de nineteen wile (meaning the anointing vial)
           in his han';
   Drop on, drop on de crown on my head,
   An' rolly in my Jesus' arm.

   [Chorus:]
   In dat mornin' all day,
   In dat mornin' all day,
   In dat mornin' all day,
   When Jesus de Chris' been born.

2. Moon went into de poplar tree,
   An' star went into blood;
   In dat mornin', etc.[46]

After the war a milk-white horse was associated with Jesus, who was asked to come into the South. One song included this idea with a reference to morning and evening, the difference between which Negroes had learned by the end of the war:

You ride dat horse, you call him Macadoni,
Jesus, won't you come bumby?

[44] *Slave Songs,* p. [75]; Allen (comp.), *op. cit.,* p. xli.
[45] [Fenner], *op. cit.,* p. 127.
[46] *Slave Songs,* p. 43; Allen (comp.), *op. cit.,* p. xl.

You ride him in de mornin' and you ride him in de evenin'.
Jesus, won't you come bumby?

De Lord knows de world's gwine to end up,
Jesus, won't you come bumby? [47]

The reception of seceded states once again into the Union presented problems for Negroes also. Local churches of black folk suffered many hardships, but more than one ex-slave planned to live through it all. The uncertain status of Negroes during the Reconstruction was reflected in the "many ups and downs" of this song. These exact words, descriptive of this troubled era, characterized the theme of "Nobody Knows":

All dem Mount Zion member, dey have many ups and downs;
But cross come or no come, for to hold out to the end.

Hold out to the end, hold out to the end,
It is my 'termination for to hold out to the end. [48]

The trials of the Reconstruction were like a judgment at hand for that generation of Negroes. Civil War missionaries did not realize that they were calling upon Negroes to forsake their ancient African heritage of looking for the good life here and now. Some ex-slaves correspondingly did not make necessary preparations to live in this troubled world. The missionaries were nevertheless sure that freedmen would endure hardship like good soldiers. A recently emancipated Negro from the Port Royal Islands, South Carolina, partially accepted the missionary doctrine and sang that different relationships from current ones would truly obtain in the resurrection. Yet, after each verse he remembered traditional "Deep River" words, saying that he and his fellow singers would like to be domiciled in Africa.

1. Wai', my brudder (or All de member), better true
     believe (or Long time seeker 'gin to believe.)
   Better true be long time get over crosses;
   Wai', my *sister* [brudder], better true believe,
   An' 'e get *up* to heaven at last.

[47] *Slave Songs,* p. 60; Allen (comp.), *op. cit.,* p. xl.
[48] *Slave Songs,* p. 57; Allen (comp.), *op. cit.,* p. xl.

[Chorus:]
O my body rock 'long fever,
O! wid a pain in 'e head!
I wish I been to de kingdom, to sit along side o' my Lord!

2. By de help ob de Lord we rise *up* again,
   O de Lord he comfort de sinner;
   By de help ob de Lord we rise *up* again,
   An' we'll get to heaven at last.[49]

The black masses asked for such spiritual guidance as their secret meetings did not provide. One ex-slave felt that missionaries did not even know how to pray the right prayer for Negroes. This freedman from the Port Royal Islands was also sure that "heaven," "home," or Africa was the best place for him rather than other residences upon which Negroes were agreeing. His Christian instruction had taught him about the "Archangel," possibly of Isaiah or of the Book of Revelation, whom he wanted to "open the door" to heaven. This was at the time when Negro soldiers were being honorably discharged from the Union Army and when colonization was being proposed for them:

[Chorus:]
I ax all dem brudder (or *Sister*) roun',
Brudder (or *Sister*), *why* can't you pray for me?
I ax all dem brudder roun',
Brudder, *why* can't you pray for me?

1. I'm gwine to my heaven, I'm gwine home,
   Archangel open de door;
   I'm gwine to my heaven, I'm gwine home;
   Archangel open de door.

2. Brudder, *tuk* [tak] off your knapsack, I'm gwine home;
   Archangel open de door.[50]

White people did not unlock the racial situation with the key of understanding. Southerners were generally unresponsive to the needs of ex-slaves, and northerners had unsatisfactory doctrines. The black masses criticized the Christian religion in terms of what they

[49] *Slave Songs*, pp. 32 f.; Allen (comp.), *op. cit.*, p. xl.
[50] *Slave Songs*, p. 32; Allen (comp.), *op. cit.*, p. xl.

had learned about the Prodigal Son of Luke 15 and the resurrection of Jesus. The whole thing was hypocrisy.

> 1. Hypocrite and the concubine,
>   Livin' among the swine,
>   They run to God with the lips and tongue,
>   And leave all the heart behind.
>   Aunty, did you hear when Jesus rose?
>   Did you hear when Jesus rose?
>   Aunty, did you hear when Jesus rose?
>   He rose and he 'scend on high.[51]

Black people sang cynically that Jesus indeed had come, but He had locked up racial attitudes and presumably had put the keys in His pockets afterward. When Colonel Higginson heard them sing that freedmen were expected to humble themselves as formerly, he commented merely that the song was "very graceful and lyrical, and with more variety of rhythm than usual." To the tune of "Sail, O Believer" discouraged freedmen were actually singing that they longed to be in Africa:

> Bow low, Mary, bow low, Martha,
>
> [Chorus:]
> For Jesus come and lock de door,
> And carry de keys away.
>
> Sail, sa[i]l, over yonder,
> And view de promised land,
>
> For Jesus come, etc.
>
> Weep, O Mary, bow low, Martha,
>
> For Jesus come, etc.
>
> Sail, sail, my true believer;
> Sail, sail, over yonder;
> Mary, bow low, Martha, bow low,
> For Jesus come and lock de door,
> And carry de keys away.[52]

[51] *Slave Songs*, p. 70; Allen (comp.), *op. cit.*, p. xli.
[52] *Slave Songs*, p. 24; Allen (comp.), *op. cit.*, p. xl.

Militant Negroes resorted to violence rather than adjust themselves to conditions in the United States.[53] They also sang songs of
the African cult. Yet light was appearing, as one preacher from the
Port Royal Islands, at the time when southerners were rejoining the
Union, told his baptismal audience to keep on praying:

> Pray on, pray on;
> Pray on dem light us over;
> Pray on, Pray on,
> De union break of day.
>
> My sister, you come to see baptize,
> In de union break of day;
> My 'loved sister, you come to see baptize,
> In de union break of day.[54]

An increasing number of Negro missionaries went into the South
during the Civil War. Negro Baptists received permission to go
within the Union lines from President Lincoln on August 21, 1863.[55]
Secretary Stanton gave approval to the African Methodist Episcopal
Zion Church in 1864 [56] and the African Methodist Episcopal Church
in 1865 [57] to follow the Union Army. So many missionaries endorsed the programs of the independent Negro denominations that
certain Negro communities in the North declined after 1865.[58] These
missionaries gave status to meetings of the African cult by calling
them independent Negro denominational churches. For example,
the first missionary of the African Methodist Episcopal Zion Church,
James Walker Hood of Bridgeport, Connecticut, traveled annually
about 15,000 miles and organized fully 600 churches in North Carolina, South Carolina, and Virginia.[59] These churches differed only

[53] Aptheker, *op. cit., passim.*

[54] *Slave Songs,* p. 97; Allen (comp.), *op. cit.,* p. xli.

[55] Edmund Kelly, "Diary," p. 9, MS, Sunday School Publishing Board,
Nashville, Tennessee.

[56] Bishop E. D. Jones, *Comprehensive Catechism of the A. M. E. Zion
Church* (Charlotte, 1934), pp. 25 f.

[57] Payne, *History of the A. M. E. Church,* p. 71.

[58] Carter G. Woodson, *A Century of Negro Migration* (Washington,
1918), p. 124; predicted in 1862 by Gurowski, *op. cit.,* I, 149 f.

[59] William J. Simmons, *Men of Mark* (Cleveland, 1887), pp. 133 ff.

in minor details from other independent Negro churches. The traditional institution of praise was continued in independent Negro churches as prayer meetings. When the African cult was not absorbed by Negro churches, it was institutionalized separately in praise houses.[60] In a praise house in Memphis, Tennessee, ex-slaves were asking Negro missionaries to guide them "home":

> [Chorus:]
> Brudder, guide me home an' I *am* [be] glad,
> Bright angels biddy me to come;
> Brudder, guide me home an' I *am* [be] glad,
> Bright angels biddy me to come.

> 1. What a happy time, chil'n,
>   What a happy time, chil'n,
>   What a happy time, chil'n,
>   Bright angels biddy me to come.

> 2. Let's go to God, chil'n, (*ter*)
>   Bright angels biddy me to come.[61]

White missionaries were astonished that Negroes did not readily accept Christianity as preached in established denominations.[62] They did not understand that there were different emphases and practices in white churches and black ones; some people declared that segregation rather than deliberate retention of African customs was the cause of the differences. When Negro missionaries went among freedmen, dependent churches for Negroes lost most of their membership: in 1860 there were 207,766 Negroes connected with the Methodist Episcopal Church, South; in six years only 78,742 of them remained. The majority had joined independent Negro churches. So southern Methodism helped to organize the remnant into the independent Colored Methodist Episcopal Church in 1870.[63] At the

---

[60] Rossa B. Cooley, *School Acres* (New Haven, 1930), pp. 148 ff., 154; Weatherford, *Present Forces in Negro Progress*, p. 30, quoted in Puckett, *op. cit.*, p. 531; investigations by author at St. Helena Island, South Carolina, May 21–22, 1941.

[61] *Slave Songs*, p. 86; Allen (comp.), *op. cit.*, p. xli.

[62] Brinckerhoff MS, pp. 182, 184, 186, 196.

[63] J. M. Buckley, *A History of Methodists in the United States* (New York, 1896), pp. 597 f.

time of emancipation Roman Catholic Negroes were said to have been about as numerous as Methodist Negroes in the South. These Catholic Negroes joined independent Negro churches by the thousands.[64] The present-day estimate of a half-million Negro Protestants in dependent churches for Negroes contrasts strikingly with the estimated 7,500,000 Negroes in independent churches of their own. Through the years missionaries have left the relatively inexpensive field of Negro evangelism to Negroes themselves and have practically confined their activities to expensive schools for Negroes.

Another contribution of white missionaries to Negroes was a Christian vocabulary in which the latter might express their Africanisms. A Negro of Danville, Virginia, made a song about Missionary Brinckerhoff's popular booklet of doctrines of 1864, singing "I *had* [hab] a little book, an' I read it through." Other freedmen made spirituals of each of its theological concepts. The earliest collection of slave songs contained two spirituals on the doctrine that "all men are sinners" on "account of the sin of our first parents, Adam and Eve." One song came from Virginia, where freedmen sang "a most compendious account of the fall." It appeared first in *Slave Songs of the United States:* [65]

1. O Adam, where *are* [is] you?
   Adam, where are you?
   Adam, where are you?
   O what a trying time!

2. Lord, I *am* [be] in the garden.

3. Adam, you *ate* [eat] that apple.

4. Lord, Eve she *gave* [gib] it to me.

5. Adam, it *was* [be] forbidden.

6. Lord said, walk out de garden.[66]

The Adamic fall was so challenging to a South Carolina mammy on the Port Royal Islands during the "jubilee" period of 1865 that,

[64] John Thomas Gillard, *The Catholic Church and the American Negro* (Baltimore, 1929), pp. 33 f.

[65] R. W. Gordon, "Old Songs That Men Have Sung," *Adventure,* May 10, 1924, p. 191.

[66] *Slave Songs,* p. 74; Allen (comp.), *op. cit.,* p. xli.

while nursing white children and rocking the babies on her knees to the singing of a spiritual about Adam, she jubilantly told her opponents to stand back and let her go by. She sang that she could not stay at home, in her mind, for God had opened up the door.

1. O rock o' jubilee, poor fallen soul,
   (or To mercy seat, To de corner o' de world)
   O Lord, (or Yes) de rock o' jubilee!

2. O rock o' jubilee, and I rock 'em all about,
   O Lord, de rock o' jubilee!

3. Stand back, Satan, let me come by.

4. O come, titty Katy, let me go.

5. I have no time for stay at home.

6. My Fader door wide open now.

7. Mary, girl, you know my name.

8. Look dis way an' you look dat way.

9. De wind blow East, he blow from Jesus.[67]

Missionary Brinckerhoff advised freedmen to study the life of Jesus. He said that "in the Scriptures many names are given him, every one indicating some feature of his divine character. . . . He was called IMMANUEL . . . Jesus . . . and Christ." Negroes made many songs out of this information. One song coming from the Port Royal Islands about 1865 said that, with all the hindrances to prevent freedmen from fleeing the trials of the Reconstruction, should any Negro be fortunate enough to escape to his brethren, he should forever sing glory to "my King Emanuel":

1. O my King Emanuel, my Emanuel *above,*
   Sing glory to my King Emanuel.

2. If you walk de golden street and you *join* [jine] de golden band,
   Sing glory *be* to my King Emanuel.

3. If you touch one string, den de whole heaven ring.

[67] *Slave Songs,* p. 25; Allen (comp.), *op. cit.,* p. xl.

4. O the great cherubim, O de cherubim *above*.

5. O believer, ain*'t* you glad *dat* your soul *is* converted? [68]

Negroes were free in body. "How surprising of God." [69] Indeed, some ex-slaves had expected their freedom before the outbreak of the Civil War. Abolitionists had a pre-Civil War song entitled "I'll Be Free" sung to the air of "Flow Gently, Sweet Afton." [70] Many slaves therefore held that their freedom provoked the Civil War. Around Georgetown, South Carolina, Negroes were put in jail for the assertion. After soldiers went South and announced freedom to the slaves,[71] perhaps after Negroes had catechetical materials with questions and answers of missionaries, asking "How long was Noah building ob the ark?" "How long was Jonah in the *bowels* [belly] of the whale?" and "How long will the righteous [be] in heaven *be?*" [72] and after Lincoln issued his celebrated Emancipation Proclamation on September 23, 1862, probably after that very day Negroes sang with all their might that they soon expected to be free. They preferred to leave the United States and to "walk de *miry* [muddy] road" "of de new Jerusalem," in Africa:

[Chorus:]
My father, (or Mother, etc.) how long,
My father, how long,
My father, how long,
Poor sinner suffer here?

1. And it won*'t* be long,
   And it won*'t* be long,

---

[68] *Slave Songs*, p. 26; Allen (comp.), *op. cit.*, p. xl.

[69] Sermon on Luke 9:43 by the Rev. C. Marshall Muir, pastor of the Bellfield Presbyterian Church, Pittsburgh, Pennsylvania, in *Christian Century Pulpit*, VII (October, 1936), 231–234.

[70] William Wells Brown, *The Anti-Slavery Harp* (2nd ed., Boston, 1849), p. 19; Henry Gloucester, *The Songs of Freedom* (Portland, 1855), p. 22.

[71] James D. Lockwood, *Life and Adventure of a Drummer Boy* (Albany, N.Y., 1898), p. 99; Avary, *op. cit.*, pp. 85 f.; cf. *ibid.*, p. 183.

[72] Barton, *op. cit.*, pp. 38 f.; Kennedy, *Mellows,* pp. 83 f.; James Weldon Johnson, *The Second Book of Negro Spirituals* (New York, 1926), pp. 90 f.; Dett, *op. cit.*, p. 62.

And it won't be long,
Poor sinner suffer here.

2. We'll soon be free. (*ter*)
De Lord will call us home.

3. We'll walk de *miry* [muddy] road
Where pleasure never dies.

4. We'll walk de golden streets
Of de New Jerusalem.

5. My brudders do sing
De praises of the Lord.

6. We'll fight for liberty
When de Lord *will* call us home.[73]

The permanent abolition of Negro slavery in the United States is specifically attributed to political and social events of the country between 1861 and 1865. A first step occurred on May 23, 1861, when Major General Benjamin F. Butler protected three Negroes who went within Union lines at Fortress Monroe, Virginia, as "contraband of war." [74] The federal government did not disapprove of this act, but on August 6 and more dramatically on July 17, 1862, bestowed freedom upon deserting slaves. A second step was on August 25, when the Secretary of War instructed Brigadier General Rufus Saxton to emancipate Negro laborers and Negro soldiers serving in the war. A third step was President Lincoln's Emancipation Proclamation, which became effective on January 1, 1863. Finally, the Thirteenth Amendment to the Constitution of the United States confirmed Negro emancipation in 1865.

Ex-slaves sang that the cause of their freedom was explained wholly by the religion of Negroes. They declared that their secret meetings had wrought the miracle of emancipation. It had never failed to accomplish seemingly impossible tasks, except perhaps African colonization. This, no doubt, was not the will of God. A Christianized Negro on the Port Royal Islands, was heard singing a spiritual of two stanzas and a chorus telling that a "kind" and a "sweet" and a wonder-working Jesus whom no man could hinder

[73] *Slave Songs*, p. 93; Allen (comp.), *op. cit.*, p. xli.
[74] Butler, *op. cit.*, pp. 256–265.

had made Negroes like other folk. His song said that before emancipation the testimony of black folk was not counted as evidence, but in freedom they spoke out as witnesses; that ex-slaves had been crippled up and had sometimes been maimed by the slave system,[75] but since emancipation they had been enabled to walk; that antebellum slaves were blind, but freedmen could see; and that in slavery the black masses were impotent like dead Lazarus, but in freedom Negroes had life. The singer believed that Jesus was superior to Satan and that with Him people could do most anything. Therefore, Negroes joined in singing:

[1.] Walk in, kind Saviour,
No man can hinder me!
Walk in, sweet Jesus,
No man can hinder me!

2. See what wonder Jesus done,
O no man can hinder me!
See what wonder Jesus done,
O no man can hinder me!

[Chorus:]
O no man, no man, no man can hinder me!
O no man, no man, no man can hinder me!

3. Jesus make de dumb to speak.

4. Jesus make de cripple walk.

5. Jesus give de blind his sight.

6. Jesus do most anyting.

7. Rise, poor Lajarush, from de *tomb* [grave].

8. Satan ride an iron-gray horse.

9. King Jesus ride a milk-white horse.[76]

Some North American ex-slaves had daily evidence of the value of Christianization. Their denominations looked away to native

---

[75] Botume, *op. cit.*, p. 79; John H. Aughey, *Tupelo* (Lincoln, Neb., 1888), p. 418.

[76] *Slave Songs*, pp. 10 f.; Allen (comp.), *op. cit.*, p. xxxix.

Africans who were denied the opportunities of residence in the United States. After the Civil War Liberia appealed to Negroes not so much as a home but as a unique missionary challenge. This urge assumed missionary proportions first among Negro Baptists of South Carolina in 1877,[77] who were possibly inspired at least a decade earlier by a spiritual of that section about sending the light to the heathen:

> De sun give a light in de heaven all round,
> De sun give a light in de heaven all round,
> De sun give a light in de heaven all round,
> Why don't you give up de world?

> [Chorus:]
> My brudder, don't you give up de world?
> My brudder, don't you give up de world?
> My brudder, don't you give up de world?
> We must leave de world behind.

> De moon give a light.

> De starry crown.[78]

In conclusion, it has been shown how during the war period spirituals gave a broad outline of the recruiting and of the training of Negroes as soldiers. Freedmen were taught new songs, which they not only sang separately but in combination with old spirituals. Ex-slaves said in song that they wanted to go to Africa, yet white people permitted all schemes of expatriation for Negroes to collapse, for almost everywhere Negroes were proving to be valuable American citizens. The return to the Union of seceded states was not without problems which affected Negroes. It was an alarming fact that the whole United States was being Africanized.[79] So citizens did their utmost to bring the African cult to terms with American institutions. A host of missionaries sought to evangelize Negroes. The federal

[77] "Minutes of the Board of Managers of the Baptist Education, Missionary and Sunday School Convention (South Carolina, 1877)," p. 1, MS, in the possession of Miles Mark Fisher.

[78] *Slave Songs*, pp. 27 f.

[79] H. Gannett, "Are We to Become Africanized?" *Popular Science Monthly*, XXVII (June, 1885), 145–150.

government put an end to its sanction of polygamous marital relations for Negroes in 1865 by decreeing that legal marriage, singling out Negroes, existed only where one man and one woman lived together under license.[80] The Ku Klux Klan applied such force to Negroes as they thought necessary to make Negroes accept American culture. Just like the African cult, Klan demonstrations were held privately and publicly. Just like the African cult, klansmen wore hoods over their faces. Just like the African cult, Klan ideals were sometimes propagated by violence. Negroes were so outraged by the Klan that northern whites guided federal legislation against it in 1871.[81]

[80] M. French, *Address to Masters and Freedmen, with Marriage Code for Freedmen* (Macon, Ga., 1865), p. 8.

[81] Bassett, *A Short History of the United States,* p. 329.

9

UNDERSTANDING
SPIRITUALS

THE one hundred thirty-six slave songs in the earliest collection, with its thirty-six variant songs, were products of a particular time and place and were meaningless outside of that frame of reference. Negro songs collected at a later date infrequently added fresh spirituals but never altered the story of Negroes in the Western Hemisphere.

A spiritual may be defined as the utterance of an individual Negro about an experience [1] that had universal application at whatever time that song was popular. An enlightened freedman responded to the query of J. McKim as to how spirituals were made in these words:

I'll tell you; it's dis way. My master call me up and order me a short peck of corn and a hundred lash. My friends see it and is sorry for me. When dey come to de praise meeting dat night dey sing about it. Some's very good singers and know how; till dey work it in, work it in, you know; till dey get it right; and dat's de way.

An observer was on hand to note the birth of a spiritual in 1940. Negro hands were starting out to work when a fellow suddenly returned to the quarters for his coat. In wild glee, "even the boy joined in the shouting":

[1] *Slave Songs*, pp. xvi f.

He los' he coat
An' he los' he hat,
An' he los' he pants
An' shoeses! [2]

Such a euphonious response included facts with which the singer was acquainted. Derivative or variant spirituals are independent or borrowed reactions to similar environmental circumstances. A combination of several songs which a person might call upon to express his soul upon a particular occasion may form a spiritual medley. The English-speaking people consider as spirituals only Negro songs which incorporate religious terminology, even though differing types of Negro songs often grow from identical experiences.

When the black masses had few thoughts which they could express understandingly about a given situation, their songs were necessarily very brief and often repetitive. As the store of information of an original singer increased, primary themes became the subject of derivative or variant spirituals by the change of just a single word or concept. New stanzas were thus created. Freedmen inherited a meager vocabulary. As they grew in knowledge, they added new themes to their songs, largely by combining existing spirituals with new material into medleys.

The originators of spirituals would hardly have believed their ears had they heard Marian Anderson on Easter, 1939, sing their songs to an estimated 75,000 people at the base of Lincoln's Monument, in Washington, D.C.[3] Spirituals with formal titles are now to be found listed on programs of artists, to be sung either by groups or by soloists, in *a cappella* fashion or with orchestra, piano, or organ accompaniment. All approximations of the original language of the spirituals simply provide transportation for the thoughts of Negroes. These songs were used by the black masses, and their incorrect grammar is not exaggerated. Only the historical classification of spirituals preserves their primary emphases. Without concern for the music of the masters Negroes employed rhythmical songs to provide creature comforts, to accompany menial labor, to learn facts, to sell commod-

---

[2] Esther McTaggart, "I Saw a Spiritual Born," *Etude Musical Magazine*, LVIII (April, 1940), 236. Reprint by permission of *Etude, The Music Magazine*. Copyright 1940 by Theodore Presser Company.

[3] "Anderson Affair," *Time*, XXXIII (April 17, 1939), 23.

ities, and to share religion. In all life situations Negroes expressed themselves euphoniously. The originators of spirituals would be most surprised to find their musical reactions to their environments catalogued and preserved in libraries purporting to tell this or that about black folk.

Spirituals, though orally transmitted, were actually history. The book, *Slave Songs of the United States,* was advertised and widely sold as illumining the history of Negro people in the United States. The collectors of these songs substantiated their assertions with contemporary data. Internal evidence attests that all the songs were developmental. For example, Moses was understood in the eighteenth century to be Bishop Francis Asbury. Later he stood for a Negro and frequently attended camp meetings. All at once he was transported to Africa. There he again assumed religious significance as referred to in sacred literature, and Negroes begged him to come back to the United States and miraculously to stretch out his rod in order that slaves might walk to Africa on dry land. One of his main commissions in the United States was to tell Pharaoh to let the slaves go to the promised land. In spirituals no distinction was made among the various Biblical Marys. Weeping Mary was ejected from white churches for shouting, was colonized in Africa, and was mysteriously returned to the secret meetings of American slaves. She was at the tomb of Jesus on the resurrection morning. Likewise, heaven was located up north, in Africa, in secret meetings, or up above. Such evolution gave color to spirituals.

Besides giving impressions of real occurrences, spirituals are at the same time contemporary historical documents of these events. Spirituals gave the Negro's side of what happened to him. The original singers did not have enough knowledge to dissemble. No song seemed to have originated without possessing an author, date and place of composition, message, and kindred accompaniments.

At least eight kinds of material went into the making of spirituals. (1) First came the *African.* Traces of the ancient institution of the secret meetings survived in Negro spirituals. In spirituals African beliefs and customs were preserved. The way in which Africans passed on the traditions of their ancestors from generation to generation through music, instrumental and vocal, and through rhythm or dancing and emotionalism was clearly evident. Professional people, prophets, and "doctors" were the human transmitters of the tradition.

(2) Among those who noticed the influence of *nonhymnal European airs* upon Negro spirituals was Fanny Kemble, who mentioned Scotch and Irish tunes. The former were later noticed by Higginson, the various Fisk collectors, Barton, and Wallaschek. Negroes printed original songs and others for distribution and called them "ballets." This Scotch influence came into Negro singing about 1755 when Presbyterian ministers around Hanover, Virginia, distributed Scotch songbooks among slaves, and Scotch-Irish slaveholders might have continued the process.

(3) About the same time in the eighteenth century *hymns* were introduced among slaves by Samuel Davies. The *Psalms and Hymns* of Isaac Watts and the songs of Charles Wesley, Samuel Davies, John Leland, Lemuel Burkitt, Richard Allen, and others helped to create waves of revivalism.[4] These hymn writers and others through the Civil War period permanently influenced spirituals both in their arrangements, with verses first and then chorus, and in their theology, vocabulary, meter, rhythm, and tunes. Spirituals rendered without part singing show Oriental influence.

(4) *White songs* of the North American nineteenth century possibly influenced spirituals. Many secular songs but no religious ones are cited in *Slave Songs of the United States.*

(5) *Christianity* rarely occurred as an element in antebellum spirituals.[5] The characters mentioned in slave songs were, to be sure, Oriental. The prominence of Moses might be due to Jewish theology. A Haitian has suggested, however, that Moses was a main character of voodooism. When Moses came from the mountain, he found the people worshiping a golden calf, which in that French-speaking country is *veau d'or,* possibly giving a name to voodooism. Negroes have testified to the presence of supernatural voices and of angels ever since their introduction into the Americas.

(6) Spirituals about *Pilgrim,* the chief actor of Bunyan's allegorical *Pilgrim's Progress,* were omitted from the earliest collection but

[4] See Edward Summerfield Ninde, *The Story of the American Hymn* (New York, [1921]), *passim.*

[5] Barton, *op. cit.,* p. 1; the opposite view is accepted by most people, including Newman I. White.

not from other songbooks published since Reconstruction days.[6]

(7) *Representative Christians* were not mentioned by spirituals until the nineteenth century, when Richard Fuller and officials of his Beaufort church were definitely named along with the great Lincoln. General Hawley was the only benefactor of Negroes in the Union Army who was mentioned in a slave song. Not one of the numerous missionaries was so honored.

(8) The great spiritual events of *American history* were frequent subjects of spirituals. Slave songs throw light upon camp meetings, African colonization, the oral instruction of Negroes after 1831, work and leisure-time activities of Negro slaves, the Civil War with its soldiers, education, and evangelism, and the Reconstruction. How Negroes accepted Americanization is told with some color. Had every spiritual been preserved, a complete story of every emotion of American Negroes would be available.

The fact that, around New Orleans, spirituals were heard mostly in Baptist churches led one collector to observe that their originators were primarily of that denomination.[7] This conclusion appeared to be rather generally true of freedom spirituals, which coincided *in minutiae* with the development of that denomination. Pre-Civil War spirituals were not denomination-conscious, being scattered among all the popular Protestant denominations and among Roman Catholic Negroes. To claim that most spirituals were Baptist would be logical as that denomination included the greatest number of the illiterate black masses who had no other means to make known the longings of their hearts.

The nondenominational spirituals express the individuality of their author. As a matter of fact, all except perhaps five slave songs refer to the singer, if no more than to his body, his clothing, his family relations, and his words to an audience. Ordinarily, they are in the first person, using "I," "my," "me," and "we." By this use of the first person in the songs an attempt was made "to find concrete expressions for the origin of a tribe or community" by using personifica-

[6] Fenner, "Cabin and Plantation Songs," in Armstrong and Ludlow, *op. cit.*, p. 178; Dett, *op. cit.*, pp. 8 f., 191; Ballanta, *Saint Helena Island Spirituals*, p. 48.

[7] Kennedy, *Black Cameos, passim; Mellows, passim; More Mellows* (New York, 1931), *passim*.

tion, as was done in the Old Testament in the case of the Semites.[8]

These individual authors of spirituals described themselves. Some of them were persons who held tenaciously to their African heritage; others of them accepted acculturation; some were slaves; others were freedmen. Perhaps the people of Liberia, either actual or hopeful colonists, emerged as leading makers of spirituals with their themes of "home," "Jacob's ladder," and "roll, Jordan, roll" and with their words "no mo' " rainfall to wet you or "no mo' " peck of corn for me, "I can't stay behind [away]," and "swing low, sweet chariot," as well as songs about the ship of Zion. Not one of the originators of spirituals was a preacher in the Christian sense of the word as a person publicly set apart for the ministry. Songsters were lay leaders though "professional" people. They lined or deaconed hymns as was done with the colonial Bay Psalm Book of 1640, which used mostly common meter, although some Psalms were in long or hallelujah meter. Among Negroes, who never had sufficient books of praise, this custom proved very convenient. Almost everywhere in the South and in some places in the North, Negro churches lined hymns. Dr. Barton mentioned a "Sister Bumaugh" who was such a song leader; James Weldon Johnson named two more; and the author's Uncle Mark was another. It seems probable that Denmark Vesey, Nat Turner, and Harriet Tubman were authors of specific spirituals.

At first blush, it might appear that these leaders of song were simply furthering the function of American church deacons. They did further their work, but they also continued their African heritage. They originated spirituals to help along their hymns. In song, these leaders would state the theme about which they were singing in a short chorus, the last line of which was the key to what the group should say after each utterance:

Leader: There's a union in the heaven where I belong.
There's a union in the heaven where I belong.
There's a union in the heaven where I belong.
I belong to the Union band.

By that time the group knew what the leader was saying:

[8] William Rainey Harper, The Priestly Element in the Old Testament (Chicago, 1905), p. 240, citing William Robertson Smith, Kinship and Marriage in Early Arabia (Cambridge, [Eng.], 1885), pp. 20 f.

Leader:	O brother, didn't I tell you so?
Congregation:	I belong to the Union band.
Leader:	O brothers, didn't I tell you so?
Congregation:	I belong to the Union band.

The chorus sometimes followed two or more utterances of the leader, who made verses about the deacon, sister, preacher, and so forth. This song was originally sung by a Methodist,, who used the words, "There's free grace a-plenty where I belong." [9]

There are several objections to the popular Lorenz-White-Johnson-Jackson theory that Negro spirituals were copied from white revival songs of the nineteenth century. The internal and external evidences of slave songs point to conditions under which only Negroes lived and died. The exponents of the white-to-Negro song trend were not familiar with the special historical field to which spirituals belong.

Derivative devotional song material of Negroes, though it might embody musical and folkloristic characteristics and evidence of the behavior of Negroes, is not considered here. The internal evidence of slave songs, shows, first, that they preserve the reactions of Negroes to contemporary situations. As a rule, the Negro occasion for a spiritual antedated the no-occasion of a similar white song. For example, the earliest white song on the "home" concept was printed (probably soon after its origin) nine years after the Negro spiritual on that theme. Sometimes white songs came to life as long as thirty-six years after the occasion for a Negro spiritual. Secondly, only Negroes in the Americas experienced hereditary slavery or the racial emancipation which produced spirituals. Thirdly, Negroes did not sing other-worldly songs like white people, or, if they did, their meaning expressed frustrated this-worldly desires. Finally, simple historical documents are not developed from extended ones, just as the Gospel of Mark did not come from the Gospel of Matthew.

The external evidence of spirituals also disproves the white-to-Negro song trend. Annanias Davisson, the American founder of the so-called "white spirituals," initiated choral church singing by white

---

[9] Learned from an ex-slave and sung at the White Rock Baptist Church, Durham, North Carolina, by Mrs. Zula Mae Priscilla Belle Taylor Floyd.

people because mountain white people protested against slaveholding Presbyterians of Virginia using adult Negro slaves and rearing slave children for choir duty. The whites sang spiritual songs like the Negroes just like the later minstrels invaded the stage. White choral singers frowned upon the "shouting" with which Negroes accompanied their songs, but white people soon incorporated this feature as characteristic of their own efforts. Aristocratic southerners paid no attention to criticisms of their actions and used Negroes for their choirs until the Civil War. It is not known just when untrained white singers were first invited, as were Negroes, to sing to cultivated white audiences.

The earliest and latest spirituals have not been included in this study, which has been limited chiefly to songs of the eighteenth and nineteenth centuries, which outline the history of the residence of Negroes in the United States through the Civil War. Spirituals tell how Negroes attempted to spread brotherhood by the sword, took flight to "better" territory when possible, became pacific in the United States, and laid hold upon another world as a last resort. While constantly keeping in mind their ancient African cult, under the influence of Civil War missionaries Negroes sang old and new songs. Some old, songs are in African languages, suggesting that Africans transplanted their native song heritage into the Americas. As a matter of fact, the customs of secret meetings and of elaborate dress for worship arrived with transplanted Africans not later than the sixteenth century. With culture available to the black masses, Negroes seized more literate means of appraising contemporary happenings, keeping records, and promoting religion.

The first areas into which the religious cries of the black masses were introduced were the West Indies and South America, but the same types of Negro song flourished everywhere in the Americas. Spirituals came into North America in Virginia probably with the first Negroes of 1619. As more and more labor came to be supplied by Negroes, spirituals found places in other early settlements along the Atlantic coast. Variant songs followed the population across the Alleghenies, to the Far South, and eventually beyond the Mississippi to the Far West. In the earliest collection of slave songs there seem to be primary historical songs from the West. Spirituals are available particularly from places where something extraordinary in Negro life occurred. These songs outlined the significant developments of the Negro people, which would hardly have been different if every Negro song were found. Knowable facts of life do not vary with environments.

The chief reason for continuing the African institution of the secret meetings upon American soil was to initiate Negro youth into life processes. At first this was done peacefully, until the cult found that it must plan local resistance against those who sought to defeat the religious ideals of Negroes. Virginia legislators were afraid of the insurrectionary possibilities of such meetings as early as 1676. Vocal and instrumental music and bodily rhythm accompanied the ritual and orientation of such meetings. Insurrections practically ceased in the years immediately prior to the American Revolution, for it appeared that all of the slaves would be manumitted. If songs of this epoch in North America were available, some of them would, no doubt, be joyous.

Slave songs reveal the saddened condition of Negro life and the hardships of slave labor after the cotton gin was successfully put into operation. Christian churches did not help the situation when they ejected slaves from their services for demonstrating their religious emotion by shouting. Some Negroes still hoped for a happy solution to their problems in the scheme of the American Colonization Society (1816) to send free Negroes outside the United States, with their consent. Others successfully made their escape from slavery, first with the help of other Negroes and then aided by underground sympathizers along the route to freedom. Still others were militant and plotted local rebellion against white people.

Nat Turner and his associates killed scores of white people in Southampton County, Virginia, in 1831. His revolt left unforgettable memories in the minds of black and white people alike and caused international repercussions. The Negro race was penalized. For the first time conservative leadership gained ascendancy among Negroes and cautioned slaves to do their best to get along with their white overlords in North America. The black masses were not impressed with the kind of life which was expected of them in the South, and thousands ran away annually to escape the terror of retribution after Turner's insurrection. Many of them again hoped for African colonization. This racial and national crisis developed songs of otherworldly yearning. Then it was that abolitionism entered the field. Public opinion debated the merits of the slave system, and the South improved conditions. Not only did Negroes generally receive better treatment, but they were permitted to share somewhat in the administration of the slave system, in which they made a grand success even though the black masses hated their Negro drivers.

The two sections of the United States only drifted farther and farther apart in the dispute over abolition, while the West Indies, South America, and Central America granted Negroes statutory freedom. The Civil War between the North and the South over the slavery issue lasted from 1861 to 1865. In this, the black masses fought heroically both with the North and with the South and in the end gained emancipation. The benefits of education and evangelism both in and out of the army were gratuitously furnished the new freedmen by Yankee soldiers and missionaries, but a reaction against freed Negroes set in all over the South. In an effort to better their conditions, some ex-slaves accepted the Christianity of the missionaries, and some of them went to free territory—most frequently to Canada, the North, and Africa. With their backs to the wall some others resorted to violence, while the black masses of the South suffered and could but rely upon God. This story was reflected in slave songs.

Derivative devotional songs of the black masses, popularly labeled Negro spirituals, do not illustrate unmistakably that the primary historical purpose of the songs was to recite the story of Negroes in their reactions to incidents in their environment. True spirituals originated shortly after the chief incidents which gave rise to them had passed over, and all the songs derived from them fulfill a threefold secondary purpose: to preserve the outline of the religious development of Negroes, to supply basic songs which could be adapted to other uses, and to describe the conditions under which Negroes had to live.

First, spirituals trace the evolution of the religious institutions of Negroes. This may be illustrated by the following chart:

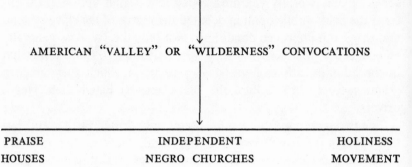

NEGRO SLAVE SONGS IN THE UNITED STATES

ANCIENT AFRICAN SECRET MEETINGS

AMERICAN "VALLEY" OR "WILDERNESS" CONVOCATIONS

| PRAISE | INDEPENDENT | HOLINESS |
| HOUSES | NEGRO CHURCHES | MOVEMENT |

African secret meetings were transplanted to colonies in the Americas. These convocations, sung about in spirituals of the "valley" or the "wilderness," were prohibited by law in North America at Virginia from about 1642. Not only were these secret meetings of "praise" institutionalized in island communities of North America as praise houses, but also these assemblies gave rise to independent Negro churches. David George, pastor of the earliest known Negro church in North America, at Silver Bluff, South Carolina, in about 1773 wrote an account of his first awakening to religion at a secret meeting, saying, "A man of color, named Cyrus, who came from Charleston, South Carolina, to Silver Bluff, told me one day in the woods, that if I lived so (unconverted), I should never see the face of God in glory. . . . I thought then that I must be saved by prayer." [10] Later in the eighteenth century the Bethel African Methodist Episcopal Church and the St. Thomas Protestant Episcopal Church, both of Philadelphia, sprang from the benevolent Free African Society of male members only and dedicated their first houses of worship in 1794.[11] The mother church of the African Methodist Episcopal Zion denomination was instituted in New York City in 1796 in praise services of ten men.[12] The holiness movement

[10] John Rippon, *The Baptist Annual Register for 1790–1800* (London, [n.d.]), p. 475.

[11] Wesley, *op. cit.,* pp. 61, 78.

[12] Christopher Rush, *A Short Account of the Rise and Progress of the African M. E. Church in America* (New York, 1843), p. 10.

among black people was contained within established churches, as Wesley intended it, until 1889, when the Church of the Living God, Christian Workers for Fellowship, emerged on the Arkansas frontier at Wrightsville with "fraternal points of doctrine known only to members of the organization." [13]

The doctrines of Negro churches were, of course, superficially Christian, but in truth they were the traditional beliefs of the secret meetings. Spirituals stressed the parts of their devotional services which were more important than their denominational tenets, namely, music, reading from a sacred book, preaching, and emotional devotion.

(1) The more emphasis placed upon music, the more attractive have been the praise houses, the independent Negro churches, and the holiness movement. A piano or an organ and musical instruments have come to be substituted for native African instruments. If, at a time of silence in the worship, those modern instruments should strike up a familiar spiritual in rhythm, one would most likely hear feet beating out the time in place of African drums. Syncopated gospel choruses have carried rhythmic singing in Negro churches to the extreme since 1933, while trained choirs have come to supply the music in more conservative areas. The popular hymns of Watts and other hymn writers are retained to this day in the hymnals of independent Negro churches.

(2) Reading from a sacred book has been an element of traditional importance in Negro meetings.

(3) Preaching, or the utterance of a leader of worship, has occupied a unique place. This element obtained from the beginning of spirituals. Preaching to the black masses has in many cases remained a singsong affair with a deep guttural accompaniment like in "a-weeping or -moaning." It is interesting to note that those independent Negro preachers who can "moan" their gospel, a method now dignified by its resemblance to the intonation and chanting of Roman Catholicism and to the head resonance taught in public speaking, are the pastors of the larger and more influential churches of the black masses, while those who intellectualize the gospel must remain in smaller churches, if at all, or in classrooms denouncing

[13] *United States Census of Religious Bodies: 1936, Bulletin II*, Part I (Washington, 1941), p. 491.

the administrations of independent Negro churches. The pay of a preacher is largely dependent upon his ability to please his audience.

(4) Emotionalism or shouting was once a happy part of devotion to which almost any spiritual was adapted. Summer "revivals" were fixed shouting times for the majority of rural churches. Even urban ones ordinarily included one or two annual revivals in their programs. If a preacher who sang was secured to conduct these revivals, the occasion was successful from the start. Shouting might or might not be serious business for Negroes; it certainly was happy recreation for many people.

Secondly, spirituals were developed first, and then so-called secular songs followed. Spirituals gave rise to syncopated rhythm. A Negro dance band in Wheeling, now West Virginia, in the early nineteenth century, consisted of three pieces—"two bangies" and "a lute, through which a chicksaw breathed with much occasional exertion and violent gesticulations." [14] The development of this syncopated rhythm may be traced further in the exploitation of Negro worship on Congo Square in New Orleans for secular purposes. It has been said that jazz sprang from spirituals; [15] swing music also in the nineteenth century has been described as "relatively brief, spontaneous, full of improvisation. . . ." This description coincides precisely with the characteristics which spirituals reveal.

"Blues" originated during the first quarter of the nineteenth century. The black masses used blues "as a vehicle for expressing the individual mood of the moment." [16] This commentator, after the thought of W. C. Handy, wrote that their three lines (instead of two or four) are a structural peculiarity, but spirituals of three lines [17] and with other structural irregularities exist which do not show hymnal influences. It has been admitted that blues are woven from the same stuff as work songs, love songs, and so forth. They are all, in fact, developments from spirituals. A teen-ager once remarked

[14] Thomas Ashe, *Travels in America, Performed in 1808* (Newburyport, 1808), p. 100.

[15] Frederic Ramsey, Jr. and Charles Edward Smith (ed.), *Jazzmen* (New York, 1939), p. 7; Wilder Hobson, *American Jazz Music* (New York, 1937), p. 16.

[16] Abbe Niles, "Introduction," in W. C. Handy (ed.), *Blues, an Anthology* (New York, 1921), p. 1.

[17] *Slave Songs*, pp. 19, 26, 59, 98, 102 f., 104.

that jazz made one pat his feet and swing on the outside while a spiritual might create the same emotion on the inside.

Spirituals have furnished the initial tune vocabulary for all kinds of Negro songs.[18] Songs about "de fiel' " and other work songs were developed from spirituals. "Deep River" spirituals about slaves having to work in the burning sun and chilling rains were work songs, as were the spirituals "Rain Fall and Wet Becca Lawton" and "Wai', Poor Daniel." "Poor Rosy, Poor Gal" was a spiritual and also a love song. The "You'*d Better* Min' " song about "rock *o'* [a] my soul in a de bosom of Abraham" was a spiritual and a nursery song before there were Negro lullabies. A variant of "Turn, Sinner" was sung while digging a well. In the "I Am Bound for the Promised Land" period, "Jerdan'*s* mill*s* a-grinding" was originated at tasks at the mill. Railroad songs came about after Negroes worked on railroads during the Civil War period.[19] Spirituals have indeed supplied themes for other Negro music.

Finally, spirituals have reflected the social conditions under which Negroes were forced to live. Civil War missionaries in North America found two classes of Negroes in the South. In one class were house servants who had been used to the "white" bread of their masters. In the other were field hands, representatives of the black masses, who were half-fed, poorly housed, ignorant, licentious, and sometimes maimed. Because of their lack of opportunity and abject poverty they looked as badly as they were treated. Casual observers could not detect that they were brokenhearted, for they appeared lighthearted. When the thorn pricked them too much, they showed defiance. They found much to laugh at when Americans did not even smile.

The black masses have preserved the spirituals. Acculturated Negroes have generally neglected them unless they were edited. Alexander Payne, during his ministry, about 1845, might be said to have represented the type of educated Negro who opposes the singing of spirituals. Bishop Payne commonly wrote of them as "rings," songs of "fist and heel worshipers," "cornfield ditties," and voodoo dances.

---

[18] White, *American Negro Folk-Songs*, p. 455; Kennedy, *Mellows*, pp. 20–23, 25, 26 f.

[19] Barton, *op. cit.*, pp. 33 f.; White, *American Negro Folk-Songs*, pp. 189 ff., 261 ff.

He said: "The time is at hand when the ministry of the A.M.E. Church must drive out this heathenish mode of worship or drive out all the intelligence, refinement, and practical Christians. . . ."

Uneducated Negroes were so attached to their old songs, their spirituals, that in freedom old spiritual themes were combined with the new songs taught to Negroes by Civil War missionaries. The masses were unprepared, however, to commit to writing the songs which they were singing, and so William Francis Allen, Charles Richard Ware, Lucy McKim, and certain other white people published *Slave Songs of the United States*. In the first sentence of their book the editors wondered "why no systematic effort has hitherto been made to collect and preserve their [Negroes'] melodies." Outside of this collection, the public was content to forget these creative songs. Many Civil War missionaries were unresponsive to them. Later, however, the Fisk University singers met with little success upon concert platforms until they startled their audiences with spirituals. Collectors promptly wrote out the music, rhymed the words, and cheaply sold booklets containing these songs. (The editing done by these collectors fortunately did not completely destroy the spirituals.) Spirituals thereafter were feverishly collected but edited almost out of recognition.

Negroes evidently had something that offset the wretched and unmoral pictures that were usually drawn of their total situations, something that gave them the strength to survive overwhelming hardships. Help from the federal government in preventing starvation and persecution by the Ku Klux Klan in the Reconstruction period and the noble efforts of missionaries, handicapped by lack of workers and means, cannot entirely explain why the turmoil of emancipation did not create a worse reaction in the Negro people. One of the reasons why it did not was the uncommon strength of the Negro spirit, and a major source of this strength was the spirituals. Spirituals were the safety valve of the Negro people through which they permitted pent-up energies to escape, and because of this they saved their souls and did not insist upon unconditional surrender to their ideals even though other Americans did.[20] Many Negroes succumbed to the rigors of American slavery, and all of them might per-

[20] Paul Hutchinson, " 'Unconditional Surrender'—Again," *Christian Century*, LXV (June 9, 1948), 567–568.

haps have become dispirited and have died out, according to expectations, had they not had their songs in the night.

The Negro spirit as displayed through spirituals has permeated and colored the entire United States. Spirituals have introduced certain barbarisms into the American language and they have spread abroad the Negro dialect. The popularity of spirituals in Europe is too well known to need rehearsal here. In both the Eastern and the Western hemispheres have the spirituals captured their listeners. Perhaps never before have the songs of a people woven such charms.

BIBLIOGRAPHY

MANUSCRIPTS

Brinckerhoff, I. W. "Mission Work among the Freed Negroes." MS, American Baptist Historical Society, Chester, Pennsylvania.

"Emigrant Register, 1820–1835." MS, Library of Congress.

[Kelly, Edmund]. "Diary of Edmund Kelly." MS, Sunday School Publishing Board, Nashville, Tennessee.

"Letter from Mrs. Sarah Williamson Shields Coleman, New Orleans, February 13, 1940." MS, in the possession of Miles Mark Fisher.

"Minutes of the Board of Managers of the Baptist Education, Missionary, and Sunday School Convention (South Carolina, 1877)." MS, in the possession of Miles Mark Fisher.

"Minutes of the Hanover Presbytery, Vol. II." MS, Presbyterian Historical Society, Philadelphia, Pennsylvania.

"Minutes of the Manumission Society of North Carolina." MS, Guilford College, North Carolina.

"Minutes of the North Carolina Yearly Meeting of Quakers." MS, Guilford College, North Carolina.

"Proceedings of the Board of Managers, American Colonization Society, Vol. I." MS, Library of Congress.

"Record Book of the Racoonswamp Baptist Church," MS, Virginia (Richmond) Baptist Historical Society.

"Register of Emigrants, 1835–1853." MS, Library of Congress.

Treatt, C. Court. "Swahili Hunt Song." MS, Library of Congress.

——. "Swahili Laboring Song." MS, Library of Congress.

att, C. Court. "Swahili Lament." MS, Library of Congress.
. "Swahili Lion Hunt Chant." MS, Library of Congress.

SONG COLLECTIONS

Allen, Richard. *A Collection of Hymns & Scriptural Songs from Various Authors*. Philadelphia, 1801.

[Allen, William Francis, Ware, Charles Pickard, and Garrison, Lucy McKim (comp.)]. *Slave Songs of the United States*. New York, 1867.

Allen, William Francis, Ware, Charles Pickard, and Garrison, Lucy McKim. *Slave Songs of the United States*. New York, 1929.

Marian Anderson [Program.] New York, 1947–1948.

Ballanta, Nicholas George Julius. *Saint Helena Island Spirituals*. New York, [c. 1925].

Baptist Standard Hymnal. Nashville, 1924.

Barton, William E. *Old Plantation Hymns; A Collection of Hitherto Unpublished Melodies of the Slave and the Freedman, with Historical and Critical Notes*. Boston, 1899.

Bowman, Laura, and Antonin, Le Roy. *The Voice of Haiti; an Unusual Collection of Original Native Ceremonial Songs, Invocations, Voodoo Chants, Drum Beats and Rhythms, Stories of Traditions, etc. of the Haitian People*. New York, [n.d.]

Brown, John Mason. "Songs of the Slave," *Lippincott's Monthly Magazine,* II (December, 1868), 617–623.

Brown, William Wells. *The Anti-Slavery Harp*. 2nd ed. Boston, 1849.

Burlin, Natalie [Curtis]. *Song and Tales from the Dark Continent*. New York, [c. 1920].

Chauvet, Stéphen. *Musique Nègre*. Paris, 1929.

Clark, George W. *The Harp of Freedom*. New York, 1856.

Cohen, Lily Young. *Lost Spirituals*. New York, 1928.

Davisson, Annanias. *Kentucky Harmony; or a Choice Collection of Psalm Tunes, Hymns, and Anthems: in Three Parts Taken from the Most Eminent Authors and Well Adapted to Christian Churches, Singing or Private Societies*. 2nd ed. Harrisonburg, 1817. Other eds., 1821, 1824, 1826.

Dett, R. Nathaniel (ed.). *Religious Folk-Songs of the Negro as Sung at Hampton Institute*. Hampton, 1927.

Fenner, Thomas P. (arr.). "Fifty Cabin and Plantation Songs." In Armstrong, Mrs. M. F., and Ludlow, Helen W., *Hampton and Its Students*. New York, 1874.

[——]. *Religious Folk Songs of the Negro.* Hampton, 1924. Reprinted from ed. of 1909.

Frank Converse's "Old Cremona" Songster. New York, 1863.

Gloucester, Henry. *The Songs of Freedom, A Collection of Songs for Anti-Slavery Meetings.* Portland, 1855.

Gordon, R. W. "Palmettos Folksongs of Georgia Negroes," *Golden Book Magazine,* IX (May, 1929), 76–77.

Higginson, Thomas Wentworth. *Army Life in a Black Regiment.* Boston, 1870.

Hobson, Anne. *In Old Alabama; Being the Chronicles of Miss Mouse, the Little Black Merchant.* New York, 1903.

Jim Crow Vagaries; or, Black Flights of Fancy Containing a Collection of Nigger Melodies. To Which Is Added the Erratic Life of Jim Crow. London, [n.d.].

Johnson, James Weldon. *The Book of American Negro Spirituals.* New York, 1925.

——. *The Second Book of Negro Spirituals.* New York, 1926.

Johnson, J. Rosamond. *Rolling Along in Song.* New York, 1937.

——. *Utica Jubilee Singers Spirituals As Sung at the Utica Normal and Industrial Institute of Mississippi.* Boston, 1930.

Kennedy, R. Emmet. *Black Cameos.* New York, 1924.

——. *Mellows.* New York, 1925.

——. *More Mellows.* New York, 1931.

Leiding, Harriette Kershaw. *Street Cries of an Old Southern City.* Charleston, 1910.

Marsh, J. B. T. *The Story of the Jubilee Singers, with Their Songs.* Rev. ed. Boston, 1880.

The Methodist Hymnal. New York, 1905.

Murphy, Jeannette Robinson. *Southern Thoughts for Northern Thinkers and African Music in America.* New York, [1904].

The New Negro Forget-Me-Not Songster. . . . As sung by Sable Harmonists. Cincinnati, [n.d.].

Ninde, Edward Summerfield. *The Story of the American Hymn.* New York, 1931.

Odum, Howard, and Johnson, Guy B. *Negro Workaday Songs.* Chapel Hill, 1926.

Pike, G. D. *The Jubilee Singers, and Their Campaign for Twenty Thousand Dollars.* Boston, 1873.

Pollard, Edward A. *Black Diamonds Gathered in the Darkey Homes of the South.* New York, 1859.

Rankin, Jeremiah Eaves. *Hymns Pro Patria and Other Hymns Christian and Humanitarian.* New York, 1889.

[Seward, Theodore F.]. *Jubilee Songs: Complete with an Introduction by E. M. Cravath.* New York, 1872.

Seward, Theodore F., and White, George V. *Jubilee Songs: As Sung by the Jubilee Singers.* New York, 1884.

Stow, Baron, and Smith, S. F. *The Psalmist. . . . With a Supplement by Richard Fuller and J. B. Jeter.* Boston, 1854.

Talley, Thomas W. *Negro Folk Rhymes.* New York, 1923.

[Wood, Samuel]. *The Cries of New York.* New York, 1822. Reprinted, Chicago, 1926.

Work, John W. *American Negro Songs: A Comprehensive Collection of 230 Folk Songs, Religious and Secular.* New York, [1940].

Work, John Wesley, *Folk Songs of the American Negro.* Nashville, 1915.

Wyeth, John Allen. *With Sabre and Scalpel.* New York, 1914.

DISCUSSIONS OF NEGRO SONGS

Allen, Cleveland G. "The Negro and His Songs," *Musical Courier,* CIII (October 3, 1931), 7.

——. "The Negro's Contribution to American Music," *Current History,* XXVI (May, 1927), 245–249.

"Anderson Affair," *Time,* XXXIII (April 17, 1939), 23.

Ballanta, Nicholas George Julius. "Gathering Folk Tunes in the African Country," *Musical America,* XLIV (September 25, 1916), 3.

Beckham, Albert Sidney. "The Psychology of the Negro Spirituals," *Southern Workman,* LX (September, 1931), 391–394.

Beckwith, Martha Warren. *Black Roadways: A Study of Jamaican Folk Life.* Chapel Hill, 1929.

——. *Folklore in America.* ("Publications of the Folklore Foundation.") Poughkeepsie, [c. 1931].

"Black Voices," *Nation,* CXIX (September 17, 1924), 278.

Blalock, John V. "Marian Anderson in Recital at North Carolina College," Durham *Morning Herald,* November 15, 1947.

"The Blight of Jazz and the Spirituals," *Literary Digest,* CV (April 12, 1930), 20.

Bradford, Sarah H. *Scenes in the Life of Harriet Tubman.* Auburn, 1869.

Bradford, Roark. "Swing Low, Sweet Chariot," *Collier's,* XCVI (September 21, 1935), 16–17.

Calverton, V. F. "The Negro and American Culture," *Saturday Review of Literature,* XXII (September 21, 1940), 3 ff.

Conrad, Earl. "General Tubman, Composer of Spirituals," *Etude Music Magazine,* LX (May, 1942), 305 f.

Correa de Ozevedo, L. H. "Folk-Lore in the Musical Curriculum in Brazil," *Proceedings of the Music Teachers Association,* 36th series (1914).

Couch, W. T. (ed.). *Culture in the South.* Chapel Hill, 1934.

Courlander, Harold. *Haiti Singing.* Chapel Hill, 1939.

D. C. P. "Nathaniel Dett," *Musical Standard,* XV (January 1, 1920), 38–39.

Densmore, Frances. "Traces of Foreign Influence in the Music of the American Indians," *American Anthropologist,* new series, XLVI (January–March, 1944), 152 ff.

DuBois, W. E. Burghardt. *The Souls of Black Folk.* Chicago, 1903.

Elam, William Cecil. "Lingo in Literature," *Lippincott's Monthly Magazine,* LV (February, 1899), 286–288.

Foote, William Henry. *Sketches of North Carolina, Historical and Biographical.* New York, 1846.

——. *Sketches of Virginia: Historical and Biographical.* 1st–2nd series, Philadelphia, 1850–1855.

Gielow, Martha S. *Mammy's Reminiscenses and Other Sketches.* New York, 1898.

Gillum, Ruth H. "The Negro Folksong in American Culture," *Journal of Negro Education,* XII (Spring, 1943), 173–180.

Gomme, George Lawrence. *Folklore as an Historical Science.* ("The Antiquary's Books.") London, [1908].

Gordon, R. W. *Folk Songs of America.* New York, 1938.

——. "Old Songs That Men Have Sung," *Adventure,* May 10, 1924.

Grew, Eva Mary. "The Colour Bar," *British Musician and Musical News,* VII (November, 1931), 229.

——. "The Sense of Pitch," *British Musician and Musical News,* VII (May, 1931), 112 f.

Grew, Sidney. "Random Notes on the Spirituals," *Music and Letters,* XVI (April, 1935), 105 f.

Handy, Sara M. "Negro Superstitions," *Lippincott's Monthly Magazine,* XLVIII (December, 1891), 735–738.

Hare, Maud Cuney. "Africa in Song," *Metronome,* XXXVIII (December, 1922), 61.

Helm, MacKinley. *Angel Mo' and Her Son, Roland Hayes.* Boston, 1942.

Henry, Mellinger Edward. *A Bibliography for the Study of American Folk-Songs with Many Titles of Folk-Songs (and Titles That Have to Do with Folk-Songs) from Other Lands.* London, 1937.

Herzog, George. "Research in Primitive and Folk Music in the United States," *American Council of Learned Societies, Bulletin No. 25,* April, 1936.

Hobson, Wilder. *American Jazz Music.* New York, [c. 1939].

Howard, John Tasker. *Stephen Foster, America's Troubador.* New York, [c. 1934].

Jackson, George Pullen. *Down-East Spirituals and Others.* New York, 1943.

——. *Spiritual Folk Songs of Early America.* New York, [1937].

——. *White and Negro Spirituals, Their Life Span and Kinship.* New York, [1943].

——. *White Spirituals in the Southern Uplands.* Chapel Hill, 1933.

Johnson, Guy B. *Folk Culture on St. Helena Island, South Carolina.* Chapel Hill, 1930.

——. "The Negro and Musical Talent," *Southern Workman,* LVI (October, 1927), 439–444.

Johnson, James Weldon. "Negro Folk Songs and Spirituals," *Mentor,* XVII (February, 1929), 50–52.

Journal of American Folk-Lore, I (April, 1888), 1, 5.

Kennedy, R. Emmet. "The Poetic and Melodic Gifts of the Negro," *Etude Musical Magazine,* XLI (March, 1923), 159–160.

Knapp, William. "An Interview with H. T. Burleigh," *Baton,* V (March, 1926), 2.

Krappe, Alexander Haggerty. *The Science of Folk-Lore.* London, [1930].

Krehbiel, Harry Edward. *Afro-American Folksongs.* New York, [c. 1914].

Laubenstein, Paul F. "An Apocalyptic Reincarnation," *Journal of Biblical Literature,* LI (December, 1932), 238–252.

——. "Race Values in Aframerican Music," *Musical Quarterly,* XVI (July, 1930), 378–403.

Leigh, J[ames] W[entworth]. *Other Days.* London, [1921].

"Letter Lucy McKim, Philadelphia, November 1, 1862," *Dwight's Journal of Music,* XXI (November 8, 1862), 254–255.

Locke, Alaine. *The Negro and His Music.* ("Bronze Booklet, No. 2.") Washington, 1936.

——. "The Negro's Contribution to American Art and Literature," *Annals of the American Academy,* CXL (November, 1928), 234–247.

Lorenz, Edmund S. *Church Music: What a Minister Should Know about It.* New York, [c. 1923].

Lovell, John. "The Social Implication of the Negro Spiritual," *Journal of Negro Education,* VIII (October, 1939), 636–643.

Mactaggart, Esther. "I Saw a Spiritual Born," *Etude Musical Magazine,* LVIII (April, 1940), 236.

"Mammy Song: A Negro Melody As Taken Down by Mrs. Julia Neely Finch," *Music,* XIII (March, 1899), 604–605.

Metfessel, Milton. *Phonophotography in Folk Music: American Songs in New Notation.* ("The University of North Carolina Social Study Series.") Chapel Hill, 1928.

Moderwell, Hiram Kelly. "The Epic of the Black Man," *New Republic,* XII (September 8, 1917), 154 f.

Murphy, Jeannette Robinson. "The Survival of African Music in America," *Popular Science Monthly,* LV (September, 1899), 660–672.

Nathanson, Yale S. "The Musical Ability of the Negro," *Annals of the American Academy,* CXL (November, 1929), 186–190.

"Negro Folk Song," *Music Student,* XI (September, 1919), 518.

"Negro Folk Song, Acclaimed as America's Musical Treasure," *Musical America,* XXVIII (September, 1918), 20.

"Negro Songs," *Dwight's Journal of Music,* XXI (August 9, 1862), 148.

Niles, Abbe. "Introduction," in Handy, W. C. (ed.), *Blues; an Anthology.* New York, 1926.

Odum, Howard W. "Folk-Song and Folk Poetry as Found in the Secular Songs of the Southern Negroes," *Journal of American Folk-Lore,* XXIV (July–October, 1911), 255–294, 351–396.

——. *Religious Folk-Songs of the Southern Negro.* Reprinted from *American Journal of Religious Psychology and Education,* III (July, 1909), 265–365.

Oliphant, Laurence. *Patriots and Filibusters.* London, 1860.

Osgood, H. G. "Sperichils," *Musical Courier,* XCIII (August 12, 1926), 14.

Owens, William. "Folklore of the Southern Negro," *Lippincott's Magazine,* XX (December, 1877), 748–755.

Pierce, Edward L. "The Freedman at Port Royal," *Atlantic Monthly,* XII (September, 1863), 291–315.

Proctor, Henry Hugh. *Between Black and White, Autobiographical Sketches.* Boston, 1925.

Puckett, Newell Niles. *Folk Beliefs of the Southern Negro.* Chapel Hill, 1926.

Ramsey, Frederic, Jr., and Smith, Charles Edward (eds.). *Jazzmen.* New York, [1939].

Scarborough, Dorothy. *On the Trail of Negro Folk-Songs.* Cambridge, 1925.

Seashore, Carl E. "Three New Approaches to the Study of Negro Music,"

Annals of the American Academy, CXL (November, 1928), 191–192.

75 Years of Freedom, Commemoration of the 75th Anniversary of the Proclamation of the 13th Amendment to the Constitution of the United States. The Library of Congress, December 18, 1940.

Shepard, Eli. "Superstitions of the Negro," *Cosmopolitan,* V (March, 1888), 47–50.

"Slave Songs of the United States," *Living Age,* XCVI (January 25, 1868), 230–242.

Smith, Reed. *Gullah (Bulletin of the University of South Carolina,* no. 190, November 1, 1926).

Smith, Robert Elmer. *Modern Messages from Great Hymns.* New York, [c. 1916].

"The Soul of a Race," *Music and Youth,* II (January, 1927), 105.

Spaeth, Sigmund. "Dixie, Harlem, and Tin Pan Alley: Who Writes Negro Music and How?" *Scribner's Magazine,* XCIX (January, 1936), 23–26.

Sperry, Willard L. *Religion in America.* Cambridge, [Eng.], 1946.

Thurman, Howard. *Deep River, An Interpretation of Negro Spirituals.* Mills College, Calif., 1945.

———. *The Negro Spiritual Speaks of Life and Death.* ("The Ingersoll Lecture, Harvard University, 1947.") New York, [1947].

Trux, H. J. "Negro Minstrelsy—Ancient and Modern," *Putnam's Monthly,* V (January, 1855), 73–79.

Vance, Lee J. "Folk-Lore Study in America," *Popular Science Monthly,* XLIII (September, 1893), 586–598.

Wallaschek, Richard. *Primitive Music: an Inquiry into the Origin and Development of Music, Songs, Instruments, Dances, and Pantomimes of Savage Races.* London, 1893.

"Wandering Negro Minstrels," *Leisure Hour,* XX (1871), 600.

White, Clarence Cameron. "The Musical Genius of the American Negro," *Etude Musical Magazine,* XLII (May, 1924), 305 f.

———. "Negro Music a Contribution to the National Music of America," *Musical Observer,* XIX (March, 1920), 13.

White, Newman I. *American Negro Folk-Songs.* Cambridge, 1928.

———. "Racial Feeling in Negro Poetry," *South Atlantic Quarterly,* XXI (January, 1922), 14–29.

Williams, Alberta. "A Race History Told in Song," *World Review,* IV (February 14, 1927), 30.

Wittke, Carl. *Tambo and Bones: A History of the American Minstrel Stage.* Durham, 1930.

"Worst Shadows," *Atlantic Monthly,* LXVII (January, 1891), 144.

BIBLIOGRAPHY

GENERAL WORKS

Abbott, John S. C. *South and North; or, Impressions Received during a Trip to Cuba and the South.* New York, 1860.

African Repository, vols. I–III (1825–1827).

Afro-American, November 23, 1940.

Alexander, Archibald. *A History of Colonization on the Western Coast of Africa.* Philadelphia, 1846.

Alexander, J. E. *Transatlantic Sketches.* London, 1835. Vol. II.

Allen, W. F. [Marcel]. "The Negro Dialect," *Nation,* I (December 14, 1865), 744.

American Baptist Year Book, 1871.

American Missionary Register, vol. VI (1825).

Among the Arabs: Adventures in the Desert, and Sketches of Life and Character in Tent and Town. London, 1875.

Andrews, Sidney. *The South since the War.* Boston, 1866.

Angelo, R. R. F. F. Michael, and De Carli, Dennis. "A Curious and Exact Account of a Voyage to Congo in the Years 1666 and 1667," in Pinkerton, John. *A General Collection of the Best and Most Interesting Voyages and Travels in All Parts of the World.* London, 1814. XVI, 148–194.

Aptheker, Herbert. *American Negro Slave Revolts.* ("Studies in History, Economics and Public Law," ed. by the Faculty of Political Science of Columbia University, no. 501.) New York, 1943.

Archives of Maryland. Baltimore, 1883–1938. Vols. I, VII, XXIV, XXXVII, XLI.

[Asbury, Francis]. *The Journal of the Rev. Francis Asbury, Bishop of the Methodist Episcopal Church.* 3 vols. New York, 1821.

Ashe, Thomas. *Travels in America, Performed in 1805.* Newburyport, 1808. Reprinted from London ed. of same year.

Aughey, John H. *Tupelo.* Lincoln, Neb., 1888.

Avary, Myrta Lockett. *Dixie after the War: An Exposition of Social Conditions Existing in the South, during the Twelve Years Succeeding the Fall of Richmond.* New York, 1906.

Bacon, Edward. *Among Cotton Thieves.* Detroit, 1867.

Baden-Powell, Major R. S. S. *The Downfall of Prempeh: A Diary of Life with the Native Levy in Ashanti 1895–96.* London, 1896.

Balm, Catherine Miller. *Fun and Festival from Africa.* New York, 1936.

Bancroft, Hubert Howe. *History of Central America.* New York, [n.d.]. Vol. II.

Barnes, Gilbert Hobbs. *The Anti-Slavery Impulse, 1830–1844.* ("The American Historical Association.") New York, [1933].

Bassett, John Spencer. *Slavery and Servitude in the Colony of North Carolina.* ("Johns Hopkins University Studies in Historical and Political Science," 14th ser., IV–V.) Baltimore, 1896.

———. *A Short History of the United States.* New York, 1921.

[Battell, Andrew]. *The Strange Adventures of Andrew Battell of Leigh, in Essex, Sent by the Portuguese Prisoner to Angola.* London, 1901.

———. "The Strange Adventures of Andrew Battell of Leigh, in Essex, Sent by the Portuguese Prisoner to Angola." In Pinkerton, John, *A General Collection of the Best and Most Interesting Voyages and Travels in All Parts of the World.* London, 1814. XVI, 317–336.

Batutah, Ibn, called Muhammad ibn 'abd Allah. *Travels in Asia and Africa 1325–1354,* trans. and selected by H. A. R. Gibb. ("The Broadway Travellers.") Ed. Sir E. Denison Ross and Eileen Power. London, [1929].

Bensom, Adolph (ed.). *America of the Fifties: Letters of Fredrika Bremer.* ("Scandinavian Classics," vol. XXIII.) New York, 1924.

[Berington, Simon]. *The Life and Adventures of Sig. Guadentio di Lucca.* 1st Am. ed. Norwich, 1796. (Copied from the original manuscript kept in St. Mark's Library at Venice.)

Bernhard, Karl, Duke of Saxe-Weimar-Eisenach. *Travels through North America.* Philadelphia, 1828. Vol. II.

Bickell, R. *The West Indies As They Are; or, A Real Picture of Slavery: but More Particularly As It Exists in the Island of Jamaica.* 3 parts. London, 1825.

[Bosman, William]. "A New and Accurate Description of the Coast of Guinea." In Pinkerton, John, *A General Collection of the Best and Most Interesting Voyages and Travels in All Parts of the World.* London, 1814. XVI, 337–547.

Botume, Elizabeth Huce. *First Days amongst the Contrabands.* Boston, 1893.·

Bremer, Fredrika. *The Homes of the New World.* Trans. Mary Howitt. 2 vols. New York, 1854.

Brinckerhoff, I. W. *Advice to Freedmen.* New York, [1864], 1867.

———. *The Freedman's Book of Christian Doctrine.* Philadelphia, 1864.

———. *Gambling and Lotteries.* New York, 1865.

Bristed, John. *America and Her Resources.* London, 1818.

Broun, Thomas L. "The Word 'Tote,'" *Publications of the Southern History Association,* VIII (July, 1904), 295 f.

Brown, William Wells. *My Southern Home: or, The South and Its People.* 3rd ed. Boston, 1882.

——. *The Negro in the American Rebellion, His Heroism and His Fidelity.* Boston, 1867.

Buckingham, J. S. *America, Historical, Statistic, and Descriptive.* London, [1841]. Vol. I.

——. *The Eastern and Western States of America.* London, [1842]. Vols. I, II.

——. *The Slave States of America.* London, [1842]. Vols. I, II.

Buckley, J. M. *A History of Methodists in the United States.* ("American Church History Series.") New York, 1896.

[Burwell, Letitia M.]. *Plantation Reminiscences,* by Page Thacker [*pseud.*]. N.p., 1878.

Butler, Benjamin F. *Autobiography and Personal Reminiscenses of Major-General Benj. F. Butler.* Boston, 1892.

Butt-Thompson, F. W. *West African Secret Societies, Their Organizations, Officials and Teaching.* London, 1929.

[Campbell, John Francis]. *A Short American Tramp in the Fall of 1864.* Edinburgh, 1865.

Candler, Allen D. *The Colonial Records of the State of Georgia.* Atlanta, 1904–1916. Vols. XXII, pt. 2, XXIII.

[Candler, Isaac]. *A Summary View of America.* London, 1824.

Carey, M[athew]. *Letters on the Colonization Society . . . to Which Is Prefixed the Important Information Collected by Joseph Jones, a Coloured Man, Lately Sent to Liberia, by the Kentucky Colonization Society, to Ascertain the True State of the Country—Its Production, Trade, and Commerce—and the Situation and Prospects of the Colonists.* 11th ed. Philadelphia, 1838.

Carroll, B. R. *Historical Collections of South Carolina.* New York, 1836. Vol. I.

Carroll, Joseph Cephas. *Slave Insurrections in the United States, 1800–1865.* Boston, [c. 1938].

Cartmell, T. K. *Shenandoah Valley Pioneers and Their Descendants.* Winchester, 1909.

Cate, Wirt Armistead (ed.). *Two Soldiers.* Chapel Hill, 1938.

Cathcart, William. *The Baptist Encyclopedia.* Philadelphia, 1881. Vol. I.

Chambers, W. *Things As They Are in America.* Philadelphia, 1854.

Charles, Father P. (ed.). *La Sorcellerie dans les pays de mission.* Paris, 1936.

Chesnut, Mary Boykin. *A Diary from Dixie.* Ed. Isabella D. Martin and Myrta Lockett Avary. New York, [1929].

Chreitzburg, Abel McKee. *Early Methodism in the Carolinas.* Nashville, 1897.

Christian Spectator, VII (August 1, 1825).

Clark, Walter. *The State Records of North Carolina.* Goldsboro, N.C., 1886–1907. Vols. XV, XVI, XIX–XXIII.

Clayton, Victoria V. *White and Black under the Old Regime.* Milwaukee, [c. 1899].

Cleveland, Catherine C. *The Great Awakening in the West, 1797–1805.* Chicago [1916].

Combe, George. *Notes on the United States of North America, during a Phrenological Visit in 1838–9–40.* Philadelphia, 1841. Vol. II.

Constitution, Government and Digest of the Laws of Liberia, as Confirmed and Established by the Board of Managers of the American Colonization Society, May 23, 1825. Washington, 1825.

Cooley, Rossa B. *School Acres.* New Haven, 1930.

Cooper, Thomas (ed.). *The Statutes at Large of South Carolina.* Columbia, 1836–1841. Vols. II, III, VII, VIII.

Creecy, James R. *Scenes in the South.* Washington, 1860.

[Creswell, Nicholas]. *Journal of Nicholas Cresswell, 1774–1777.* New York, 1924.

Crone, G. R. (ed. and tr.). *The Voyages of Cadamosto and Other Documents on Western Africa.* London, 1937.

Crooks, J. J. *A History of the Colony of Sierra Leone, Western Africa.* Dublin, 1903.

Crum, Mason. *Gullah.* Durham, 1940.

Cureau, Adolphe Louis. *Savage Man in Central Africa: A Study of Primitive Man in the French Congo.* Trans. E. Andrews. London, [1915].

Cuthbert, J. H. *Life of Richard Fuller.* New York, 1879.

Dallas, R. C. *The History of the Maroons, from Their Origin to the Establishment of Their Chief Tribes at Sierra Leone.* London, 1803. Vol. II.

Darwin, Charles. *Journal of Researches into the Natural History and Geology of Countries Visited during the Voyages of H. M. S. Beagle around the World.* New York, 1855. Vol. I.

Davenport, Frederick Morgan. *Primitive Traits in Religious Revivals.* New York, 1906.

Davis, John. *Travels of Four Years and a Half in the United States of America.* London, 1803.

Dawson, Sarah Morgan. *A Confederate Girl's Diary.* Boston, 1913.

Delafosse, Maurice. *The Negroes of Africa.* Trans. F. Fligelmann. Washington, [c. 1931].

De Leon, T. C. *Four Years in Rebel Capitals.* Mobile, Ala., 1892.

De Saussure, N. B. *Old Plantation Days.* New York, 1909.

Devereaux, Margaret. *Plantation Sketches*. Cambridge, 1906.

[Dobbins, H.]. *Life and Labor of Rev. Frank Dobbins, Pastor of Zion Baptist Church, Columbia, S.C*. Columbia, 1872.

Donnan, Elizabeth. *Documents Illustrative of the History of the Slave Trade to America*. Washington, 1930–1935. Vols. II–IV.

Douglass, Frederick. *Life and Times of Frederick Douglass*. Hartford, 1881.

——. *My Bondage and My Freedom*. New York, 1855.

[——]. *Narrative of the Life of Frederick Douglass*. Boston, 1845.

[Doyley, Edward]. *A Narrative of the Great Success God Hath Pleased to Give His Highness Forces in Jamaica, against the King of Spains Forces; together with a True Relation of the Spaniards Losing Their Plate-Fleet*. London, 1658. Photostat from the original in the John Carter Brown Library.)

Dresser, Amos. *Narrative of Amos Dresser*. New York, 1836.

Drewry, William Sidney. *The Southampton Insurrection*. Washington, 1900.

Du Bois, W. E. Burghardt. *The Negro Church*. Atlanta, 1903.

Duncan, John M. *Travels through Part of the United States and Canada in 1818 and 1819*. New York, 1823. Vol. II.

Edwards, Bryan. *The History, Civil and Commercial of the British Colonies in the West Indies*. 3rd ed. London, 1793–1801. Vols. I, II.

Ellis, A. B. *The Tshi-speaking Peoples of the Gold Coast of West Africa*. London, 1887.

Ellis, George W. *Negro Culture in West Africa*. New York, 1914.

"Emigrants from New Orleans," New Orleans *Picayune,* March 30, 1835.

Emilio, Luis F. *History of the Fifty-Fourth Regiment of Massachusetts Volunteer Infantry*. 2nd ed. Boston, 1894.

Ewbank, Thomas. *Life in Brazil*. New York, 1856.

"Extracts of the Journals of Mr. Commissary Von Reck." In Force, Peter. *Tracts and Other Papers to the Year 1776*. Washington, 1836–1846. Vol. IV.

"Extracts of Minutes of Twenty-fifth Anniversary of Providence Anti-Slavery Association of Ohio." In Christy, David, *Pulpit Politics: or, Ecclesiastical Legislation on Slavery*. 5th ed. Cincinnati, 1862.

Faux, W. *Memorable Days in America*. London, 1823.

Fearon, Henry Bradshaw. *Sketches of America*. 3rd ed. London, 1819.

Featherstonhaugh, G. W. *Excursion through the Slave States, from Washington on the Potomac, to the Frontier of Mexico*. New York, 1844.

"Fidelity of Slaves," *De Bow's Review,* XXIX (November, 1860), 579 ff.

[Finley, Robert]. *Thoughts on the Colonization of Free Blacks*. [Washington, 1816].

Fisher, Miles Mark. "Lott Cary, the Colonizing Missionary," *Journal of Negro History*, VII (October, 1922), 380–418, 427–448.

[Fitzroy, R.]. *Narrative of the Surveying Voyages of His Majesty's Ships Adventure and Beagle*. London, 1839. Vol. II.

Fleming, Walter L. *Documentary History of Reconstruction, Political, Military, Social, Religious, Educational & Industrial, 1865 to the Present Time*. Cleveland, 1906–1907. Vol. II.

Flint, Timothy. *Recollections of the Last Ten Years*. Boston, 1826.

Foote, Andrew Hull. *Africa and the American Flag*. New York, 1854.

Franklin, John Hope. *The Free Negro in North Carolina, 1790–1860*. Chapel Hill, 1943.

Frazier, E. Franklin. "The Negro Family in Bahia, Brazil," *American Sociological Review*, VII (August, 1942), 465 ff.

——. *The Negro Family in the United States*. Chicago, [1939].

French, M. *Address to Masters and Freedmen, with Marriage Code for Freedmen*. Macon, Ga., 1865.

Frobenius, Leo. *The Voice of Africa*. Tr. Rudolph Blind. London, 1913. Vol. I.

Fuller, Richard F. *Chaplain Fuller: Being a Life Sketch of a New England Clergyman and Army Chaplain*. Boston, 1863.

Gannett, H. "Are We to Become Africanized?" *Popular Science Monthly*, XXVII (June, 1885), 145–150.

Gay, Mary A. H. *Life in Dixie during the War, 1861–1862–1863–1864–1865*. 4th ed. Atlanta, [c. 1897].

Gillard, John Thomas. *The Catholic Church and the American Negro*. Baltimore, 1929.

Gilman, Caroline. *Recollections of a Southern Matron*. New York, 1838.

Godwin, Morgan. *The Negro's & Indians Advocate, Suing for Their Admission into the Church*. London, 1680.

Gorer, Geoffrey. *Africa Dances: A Book about West African Negroes*. New York, 1935.

Gorham, B. W. *Camp Meeting Manual*. Boston, 1854.

Grandfort, M. de. *The New World*. Trans. Edward C. Wharton. New Orleans, 1855.

Gratton, Thomas Colley. *Civilized America*. 2nd ed. London, 1859.

[Gray, Thomas R.]. *The Confessions of Nat Turner, Leader of the Late Insurrection, in Southampton, Va*. Baltimore, 1831.

Gregoire, H. *De la littérature des Nègres*. Paris, 1808.

Gurley, Ralph Randolph. *Life of Jehudi Ashmun, Late Colonial Agent in Liberia.* Washington, 1835.

Gurowski, Adam. *Diary.* Vol. I. Boston, 1862. Vol. II. New York, 1863.

Hakluyt, Richard. *The Principal Navigations, Voyages, Traffiques & Discoveries of the English Nation.* Glasgow, 1904. Vol. X.

Hall, Basil. *Travels in North America in the Years 1827 and 1828.* Edinburgh, 1829. Vol. III.

Hambly, Wilfrid D. *Culture Areas of Nigeria.* Frederick H. Rawson-Field Museum Ethnological Expedition to West Africa, 1929–30. ("Publication 346 Anthropological Series," vol. XXI, no. 8.) Chicago, 1935.

——. *Serpent Worship in Africa.* ("Publication 289 Anthropological Series," vol. XXI, no. 1.) Chicago, 1933.

Harper, William Rainey. *The Priestly Element in the Old Testament.* Chicago, 1905, citing William Robertson Smith, *Kinship and Marriage in Arabia.* Cambridge, 1885.

Harr, Wilber C. "A Christian Approach to a Pagan People in the Wurkum Hills of Northern Nigeria." Unpublished S.T.M. thesis, Union Theological Seminary, New York, 1940.

Haynes, Charles Henry. "Why Did Free Negroes Own Slaves?" M.A. thesis, Department of History, University of Chicago, 1928.

Hening, William Waller. *The Statutes at Large: Being a Collection of All Laws of Virginia, 1619–1792.* Richmond, etc., 1810–1823. Vols. I–IX, XI.

Henry, Howell Meadows. *The Police Patrol of the Slave in South Carolina.* Emory, Va., 1914.

[Henson, Josiah]. *The Life of Josiah Henson, Formerly a Slave Now an Inhabitant of Canada.* Boston, 1849.

Herskovits, Melville J. *Dahomey: An Ancient West African Kingdom.* 2 vols. New York, 1938.

——. *The Myth of the African Past.* New York, [c. 1947].

Herskovits, Melville J., and Herskovits, Frances S. *An Outline of Dahomean Religious Beliefs,* ("Memoirs of the American Anthropological Association," no. 41.) Menasha, [1933].

Higginson, Mary Potter (Thacker). *Thomas Wentworth Higginson.* Boston, 1914.

Higginson, Thomas Wentworth. "Denmark Vesey," *Atlantic Monthly,* VII (June, 1861), 728–739.

——. "Gabriel's Defeat," *Atlantic Monthly,* X (September, 1862), 337–345.

Higginson, Thomas Wentworth. *Travellers and Outlaws: Episodes in American History.* Boston, 1889.

History of the Baptist Denomination in Georgia. Atlanta, 1881.

Hoffman, Charles Fenno. *A Winter in the West.* 2nd ed. New York, 1835. Vol. I.

Holmes, Dwight Oliver Wendell. *The Evolution of the Negro College.* ("Teachers College, Columbia University, Contribution to Education," no. 609.) New York, 1934.

——. "Fifty Years of Howard University," *Journal of Negro History,* III (April, October, 1918), 128–138, 368–380.

[Hopley, Catherine Cooper]. *Life in the South.* London, 1863. Vol. I.

Humphreys, David. *An Historical Account of the Incorporated Society for the Propagation of the Gospel in Foreign Parts.* London, 1730.

Hutchinson, Paul. " 'Unconditional Surrender'—Again?" *Christian Century,* LXV (June 9, 1948), 567–568.

Jefferson, Thomas. *Notes on the State of Virginia.* 1st Am. ed. Philadelphia, 1788.

Jernegan, Marcus W. "Slavery and Conversion in the American Colonies," *American Historical Review,* XXI (April, 1916), 504–527.

Johnson, Guion Griffis. *Ante-bellum North Carolina; A Social History.* Chapel Hill, 1937.

Johnston, Harry Hamilton. *Liberia.* London, 1906. Vol. I.

Jones, Charles C. *Catechism of Scripture, Doctrine and Practice, for Families and Sabbath Schools.* 3rd ed. Savannah, 1844.

——. *The Religious Instruction of Negroes in the United States.* Savannah, 1842.

Jones, Bishop E. W. *Comprehensive Catechism of the A. M. E. Zion Church.* Charlotte, N.C., 1934.

Jones, J. William. *Christ in the Camp; or, Religion in Lee's Army.* Richmond, 1887.

Kemble, Frances A. *Journal of a Residence on a Georgian Plantation in 1838–1839.* New York, 1863.

Kingsley, Mary H. *Travels in West Africa, Congo Francais, Corisco and Cameroons.* London, 1897.

——. *West African Studies.* 2nd ed. London, 1901.

[Knight, Henry Cogswell] (*pseud.,* Singleton, Arthur). *Letters from the South and West.* Boston, 1824.

La Rochefoucauld-Liancourt, François Alexandre Frédéric, Duke of. *Travels through the United States of North America.* London, 1799. Vol. II.

Latham, Henry. *Black and White: A Journal of a Three Months' Tour in the United States*. London, 1867.

Latter Day Luminary, I, VI.

Leland, John. *The Virginia Chronicle*. Fredericksburg, Va., 1790.

[Lewis, George]. *Impressions of America and the American Churches*. Edinburgh, 1845.

Lewis, Matthew Gregory. *Journal of a West Indian Proprietor*. London, 1834.

Liberia, the Land of Promise to Free Colored Men. Washington, 1861.

Lieber, Francis. *The Stranger in America*. London, [n.d.]. Vol. II.

Lockwood, James D. *Life and Adventures of a Drummer Boy*. Albany, N.Y., 1898.

Loggins, Vernon. *The Negro Author*. ("Columbia University Studies in English and Comparative Literature.") New York, 1931.

Lowerey, I. E. *Life on the Old Plantation in Ante-bellum Days*. Columbia, S.C., 1911.

Lyell, Charles. *A Second Visit to the United States of North America*. New York, 1849. Vol. I.

——. *Travels in North America, in the Year 1841–2*. New York, 1846. Vol. I.

[McGuire, J. W. Brockenbrough]. *Diary of a Southern Refugee, during the War*. 2nd ed. New York, 1868.

Mackie, J. Milton. *From Cape Cod to Dixie and the Tropics*. New York, 1864.

McNemar, Richard. *The Kentucky Revival*. New York, 1846. Originally pub. in Cincinnati in 1807.

Madiou, Thomas. *Histoire d'Haiti: années 1492–1799*. 2nd ed. Port-au-Prince, 1922. Vol. I.

Marryat, Frederick. *A Diary in America*. London, 1839. Vols. II, III, 2nd pt.

Martineau, Harriet. *Society in America*. 4th ed. London, 1837. Vol. I.

Mathison, Gilbert Farquhar. *Narrative of a Visit to Brazil, Chile, Peru, and the Sandwich Islands*. London, 1825.

[Merolla, Girolamo]. "A Voyage to Congo, and Several Other Countries, Chiefly in Southern Africa," in Pinkerton, John, *A General Collection of the Best and Most Interesting Voyages and Travels in All Parts of the World*. London, 1814. XVI, 195–316.

Michaux, François A. *Travels to the Westward of the Alleghany Mountains*. Trans. from the French. London, 1805.

Minutes of the Virginia Portsmouth Baptist Association, 1832. (Virginia [Richmond] Baptist Historical Society).

Minutes of the Wood River Baptist Association, 1839. (Shurtleff College, Alton, Illinois).

Mode, Peter G. *Source Book and Bibliographical Guide for American Church History.* Menasha, [c. 1921].

Moister, William. *Memorials of Missionary Labours in Western Africa, the West Indies, and at the Cape of Good Hope.* 3rd ed. London, 1866.

Montule, Edouard de. *A Voyage to North America, and the West Indies, in 1817.* London, 1821.

Moore, Rachel Wilson. *Journal of Rachel Wilson Moore Kept during a Tour to the West Indies and South America in 1863–64, with Notes by George Truman.* Philadelphia, 1867.

Morrill, Kate Virginia. *My Confederate Girlhood.* Richmond, 1932.

Muir, C. Marshall. "How Surprising of God," *Christian Century Pulpit,* VII (October, 1936), 231–234.

Murat, Achille. *A Moral and Political Sketch of the United States of North America. With a Note on Negro Slavery, by Junius Redivivus* [*pseud.* of W. B. Adams]. London, 1833.

Murray, Charles Augustus. *Travels in North America during the Years 1834, 1835, & 1836.* New York, 1839. Vol. II.

Negro Plot. Boston, 1822.

Nichols, Roy F. "The Progress of the American Negro in Slavery," *Annals of the American Academy,* CXL (November, 1928), 116–121.

Nicolay, John E., and Hay, John. *Abraham Lincoln: A History.* New York, 1890. Vol. VI.

Nkrumah, [Francis] Kwia-Kofe. "The History of Religion in a Critique of West African Fetichism." Unpublished term paper, Lincoln University, Chester, Pennsylvania, 1940.

——. "Primitive Education in West Africa." Unpublished term paper, Lincoln University, Chester, Pennsylvania, 1940.

——. "The Significance of African Art." Unpublished term paper, Lincoln University, Chester, Pennsylvania, 1940.

Offenbach, Jacques. *America and the Americans.* London, [1877].

Olmsted, Frederick Law. *A Journey in the Back Country.* New York, 1860.

——. *A Journey in the Seaboard Slave States.* New York, 1856.

Owen, Nicholas. *Journal of a Slave Dealer:* "A View of Some Remarkable Axcedents in the Life of Nics. Owen on the Coast of Africa and America from the Year 1746 to the Year 1779." Ed., with Introduction, Eveline Martin. London, 1930.

Paine, Lewis W. *Six Years in a Georgia Prison.* New York, 1851.

Palmer, William Pitt. *Calendar of Virginia State Papers and Other Manuscripts.* Richmond, 1875. Vol. 1875.

Park, Mungo. *Travels in the Interior Districts of Africa: Performed under the Direction and Patronage of the African Association, in the Years 1795, 1796, and 1797.* New York, 1800.

——. "Travels." In Pinkerton, John, *A General Collection of the Best and Most Interesting Voyages and Travels in All Parts of the World.* London, 1814. XVI, 839–917.

Park, Robert. "The Conflict and Fusion of Culture," *Journal of Negro History,* IV (April, 1919), 111–133.

Parkhurst, Jessie W. "The Role of the Black Mammy in the Plantation Household," *Journal of Negro History,* XXIII (July, 1938), 349–369.

Parkinson, Richard. *A Tour in America, in 1798, 1799, and 1800.* London, 1805. Vol. II.

Paulding, J. K. *Slavery in the United States.* New York, 1836.

Payne, Daniel A. *History of the African Methodist Episcopal Church.* Nashville, 1891.

——. *Recollections of Seventy Years.* Nashville, 1888.

Pearson, Elizabeth Ware (ed.). *Letters from Port Royal Written at the Time of the Civil War.* Boston, 1906.

Pettingill, Ray W. (tr.). *Letters from America, 1776–1779.* Boston, 1924.

Pinckard, George. *Note on the West Indies, Including Observations Relative to the Creoles and Slaves of the Western Colonies, and the Indians of South America.* 2 vols. London, 1816.

Pleasants, Sally (McCarty). *Old Virginia Days and Ways.* Menasha, [c. 1916].

[Prince, Nancy]. *A Narrative of the Life and Travels of Mrs. Nancy Prince.* 2nd ed. Boston, 1853.

Ralph, Julian. *Dixie.* New York, 1896.

Ramseyer, Friedrick August. *Four Years in Ashantee.* London, 1875.

Rattray, R. S. *Akan-Ashanti Folk Tales.* Oxford, 1930.

——. *Ashanti.* Oxford, 1923.

——. *Ashanti Proverbs.* Oxford, 1916.

——. *Religion & Art in Ashanti.* Oxford, 1927.

Raumer, Frederick von. *America and the American People.* Trans. from the German by William W. Turner. New York, 1846.

Renny, Robert. *An History of Jamaica.* London, 1807.

Report of the American Colonization Society, vols. I–XI (1818–1828).

Ripley, Eliza. *Social Life in Old New Orleans.* New York, 1912.

Rippon, John. *The Baptist Annual Register for 1790–1800.* London, 1793–1802.

Royall, Anne. *Letters from Alabama on Various Subjects.* Washington, 1830.

Rush, Christopher. *A Short Account of the Rise and Progress of the African M. E. Church in America*. New York, 1843.

Russell, William Howard. *The Civil War in America*. ("Fuller's Modern Age," no. 1.) Boston, [1861].

——. *My Diary North and South*. Boston, 1863.

——. *Pictures of Southern Life, Social, Political and Military*. New York, 1861.

Scarlett, P. Campbell. *South America and the Pacific*. London, 1838. Vol. I.

Scherzer, Karl. *Travels in the Free States of Central America*. London, 1857. Vol. II.

Schwab, Jewel Huelster. *In the African Bush*. New York, [c. 1928].

Sherwood, H. N. "Paul Cuffee," *Journal of Negro History*, VIII (April, 1923), 184 ff.

A Short Journey in the West Indies. London, 1790. Vols. I, II.

Sibley, James L., and Westermann, D. *Liberia—Old and New*. New York, 1928.

Sierra Leone Company. *Substance of the Report Delivered by the Court of Directors of the Sierra Leone Company, to the General Court of Proprietors, on Thursday, March 27th, 1794*. Philadelphia, 1795.

Simmons, William J. *Men of Mark*. Cleveland, 1887.

Skinner, J. E. Hilary. *After the Storm*. London, 1866. Vol. I.

Smedes, Susan Dabney. *A Southern Planter*. 4th ed. New York, 1890.

Smith, Edwin W. *African Belief and Christian Faith*. London, 1936.

——. *The Secret of the African*. ("Long Lectures, 1927–1928") 2nd ed. London, 1930.

Stanbury, P. *A Pedestrian Tour of Two Thousand Three Hundred Miles, in North America*. New York, 1822.

Stirling, James. *Letters from the Slave States*. London, 1857.

Sutcliff, Robert. *Travels in Some Parts of North America, in the Years 1804, 1805, & 1806*. Philadelphia, 1812.

Swallow, S. C. *Camp-Meetings: Their Origin, History, and Utility*. New York, 1879.

Swaney, Charles Baumer. *Episcopal Methodism and Slavery, with Sidelights on Ecclesiastical Politics*. New York, [c. 1926].

Sweet, William Warren. *Revivalism in America: Its Origin, Growth and Decline*. New York, 1945.

——. *The Story of Religion in America*. New York, [c. 1939].

Tillman, Nathaniel. "A Possible Etymology of 'Tote'," reprinted from *American Speech*, XVII (April, 1942), 1289.

Tower, Philo. *Slavery Unmasked*. Rochester, 1856.

BIBLIOGRAPHY

Trollope, Frances. *Domestic Manners of the Americans.* New York, 1901. Vol. I. Originally published in March, 1832.

United States Bureau of Census. *Bulletin 8, Negroes in the United States.* Washington, 1914.

——. *Religious Bodies: 1936.* Part 1, vol. II. Washington, 1941.

——. *Third Census; 1810.* Microfilmed from the National Archives at Washington.

Walsh, Robert, Jr. *An Appeal from the Judgment of Great Britain Respecting the United States of America.* 2nd ed. Philadelphia, 1819.

Webster, Hutton. *Primitive Secret Societies.* New York, 1908.

Welby, Adlard. *A Visit to North America and the English Settlements in Illinois.* In *Early Western Travels, 1748–1846,* ed. Reuben Gold Thwaites. Cleveland, 1905. Vol. XII.

Wesley, Charles H. *Richard Allen, Apostle of Freedom.* Washington, [c. 1936].

Westermann, Diedrich. *Africa and Christianity.* ("Duff Lectures, 1935.") London, 1937.

——. *The African Today and Tomorrow.* London, 1939.

Whipple, Henry Benjamin. *Bishop Whipple's Southern Diary, 1843–1844.* Ed. with an Introduction by Lester B. Shippee. Minneapolis, [c. 1937].

Whitney, Annie Weston. "Negro American Dialects," *Independent,* LIII, pt. 1 (August 22–29, 1901), 1979–1981, 2039–2042.

Wightman, William May. *Life of William Capers, D.D.* Nashville, 1858.

Williams, George W. *A History of Negro Troops in the War of Rebellion, 1861–1865.* New York, 1888.

Williams, Wellington, *Appleton's Southern and Western Travellers' Guide.* New York, 1850.

Willis, N. Parker. *Health Trip to the Tropics.* New York, 1853.

Wilson, C. H. *The Wanderer in America, or, Truth at Home.* Thirsk, [Eng.], 1822.

Wilson, Joseph T. *The Black Phalanx.* Hartford, 1888.

Wise, John S. *The End of an Era.* Boston, 1899.

Woodson, Carter G. *A Century of Negro Migration.* Washington, 1918.

——. *The African Background Outlined.* Washington, [c. 1936].

——. *Free Negro Owners of Slaves in the United States in 1830.* Washington, [c. 1924].

——. *The History of the Negro Church.* Washington, [c. 1921].

[Woolman, John]. *The Journal of John Woolman.* With Introduction by J. Greenleaf Whittier. Boston, [c. 1871].

INDEX